THE ANARCHIST ROOTS OF GEOGRAPHY

The Anarchist Roots of Geography

TOWARD SPATIAL EMANCIPATION

Simon Springer

UNIVERSITY OF MINNESOTA PRESS
Minneapolis · London

An earlier version of chapter 1 was published as "Anarchism and Geography: A Brief Genealogy of Anarchist Geographies," *Geography Compass* 7, no. 1 (2012): 46–60. An earlier version of chapter 2 was published as "Anarchism! What Geography Still Ought to Be," *Antipode: A Radical Journal of Geography* 44, no. 5 (2012): 1605–24. Chapter 3 previously appeared as "Why a Radical Geography Must Be Anarchist," *Dialogues in Human Geography* 4, no. 3 (2014): 249–70; doi:10.1177/2043820614540851. Portions of chapter 4 were published as "Public Space as Emancipation: Meditations on Anarchism, Radical Democracy, Neoliberalism, and Violence," *Antipode: A Radical Journal of Geography* 43, no. 2 (2011): 525–62. Portions of chapter 5 were published as "War and Pieces," *Space and Polity* 18, no. 1 (2014): 85–96. An earlier version of chapter 6 was published as "Human Geography without Hierarchy," *Progress in Human Geography* 38, no. 3 (2014): 402–19; doi:10.1177/0309132513508208.

Copyright 2016 by the Regents of the University of Minnesota

All rights reserved. No part of this publication may be reproduced, stored in a retrieval system, or transmitted, in any form or by any means, electronic, mechanical, photocopying, recording, or otherwise, without the prior written permission of the publisher.

Published by the University of Minnesota Press
111 Third Avenue South, Suite 290
Minneapolis, MN 55401-2520
http://www.upress.umn.edu

Printed in the United States of America on acid-free paper

The University of Minnesota is an equal-opportunity educator and employer.

21 20 19 18 17 16   10 9 8 7 6 5 4 3 2 1

Library of Congress Cataloging-in-Publication Data
Names: Springer, Simon, author.
Title: The anarchist roots of geography : toward spatial emancipation / Simon Springer.
Description: Minneapolis : University of Minnesota Press, 2016. | Includes bibliographical references and index.
Identifiers: LCCN 2015036892 | ISBN 978-0-8166-9772-4 (hc) | ISBN 978-0-8166-9773-1 (pb)
Subjects: LCSH: Human geography—Political aspects. | Anarchism. | Globalization—Political aspects.
Classification: LCC GF50 .S67 2016 | DDC 304.2—dc23
LC record available at http://lccn.loc.gov/2015036892

For Marni
beauty came to me in the form of your love

The old order, supported by the police, the magistrates, the gendarmes and the soldiers, appeared unshakable, like the old fortress of the Bastille, which also appeared impregnable to the eyes of the unarmed people gathered beneath its high walls equipped with loaded cannon. But soon it became apparent that the established order has not the force one had supposed. One courageous act has sufficed to upset in a few days the entire governmental machinery, to make the colossus tremble.

—**Peter Kropotkin, *The Spirit of Revolt***

Contents

Introduction. Becoming Beautiful:
To Make the Colossus Tremble   1

1. A Brief Genealogy of Anarchist Geographies   25

2. What Geography Still Ought to Be   43

3. Returning to Geography's Radical Roots   65

4. Emancipatory Space   97

5. Integral Anarchism   131

6. The Anarchist Horizon   155

Acknowledgments   179

Notes   181

Bibliography   185

Index   219

INTRODUCTION

Becoming Beautiful

To Make the Colossus Tremble

Beauty must be defined as what we are, or else the concept itself is our enemy. Why languish in the shadow of a standard we cannot personify, an ideal we cannot live? To see beauty is to learn the private language of meaning which is another's life—to recognize and relish what *is*.
—**CrimethInc. Ex-Workers' Collective**

Let us become beautiful ourselves, and let our life be beautiful!
—**Élisée Reclus**

THE BEAUTIFUL GEOGRAPHIES OF ANARCHISM

A few years ago, Gerry Kearns (2009b, 58) wrote, "It must be admitted that anarchist studies in geography remain a hope rather than a reality." Plain and simple, this book aims to change that. For far too long, geographers have ignored anarchism and the beautiful praxis it implies. My intention with this book is to return anarchist studies to the center of geography's disciplinary map. Or, perhaps more accurately, I seek to remind readers that geography has never had, and nor should it desire, a single disciplinary plan or pivot. Instead, an anarchist approach to geography embraces partial, fragmented, and overlapping worlds, wherein empowerment and emancipation become possible as shifting islands of reflexivity between theory and practice. In this spirit of possibility, and long before the Marxist turn was initiated in the late 1960s and early 1970s, anarchist geographies were the primary form of radical geography, finding the bearings for a great deal of critical scholarship to follow, but without setting the compass to a single trajectory. While Marxists were a century away from making their mark on geography, anarchists Peter Kropotkin and Élisée Reclus were well-respected members of the academic community, where each played a crucial role in the development of geographical thought (Clark 2009; Kearns 2009b). Both men were brilliant and celebrated thinkers known for their scholarly achievements and scientific discoveries. Reclus was awarded the prestigious Gold Medal of the Paris Geographical Society in 1892 and was appointed chair of comparative geography at the University of Brussels two years later (Fleming 1988), whereas Kropotkin was invited to join the Imperial Russian Geographical Society and the British Association for the Advancement of Science and was even offered an endowed chair at the University of Cambridge in 1896. He ultimately declined Cambridge's offer, as it was contingent on him setting aside his politics (Morris 2003). Reclus was permanently banned from France in 1871 owing to his involvement in the Paris Commune, but his sentence was commuted to ten years, and he returned to France in 1879, benefiting from the general amnesty (Clark and Martin 2004). Meanwhile, in 1874, Kropotkin was arrested and imprisoned in St. Petersburg for subversive political activity but escaped in 1876 and fled his home country. French authorities arrested him again in 1882, this time for his involvement in the International Workers' Association, but he was released four years later and continued to be politically active (Morris 2003). The point is that neither man shied away from his political commitments. Both Kropotkin and Reclus refused to allow their appeals for anarchism to be silenced, and they equally resisted the disparagement of anarchism at every possible turn. The convictions of these two intrepid political thinkers left an indelible mark on the discipline of geography, and although they are arguably better known today for their anarchism than for their contributions to geographical thought, these two domains are actually inseparable. Neither Kropotkin nor Reclus treated his politics as distinct from his other work, and indeed it is fair to say that it was their commitment to anarchist ideals that invigorated their approaches to geography by infusing a unique and beautiful sense of creativity into their academic insights.

This book should accordingly not be read as an opening salvo for anarchist geographies but rather as an attempt to return to the radical roots of the discipline. Although there are all sorts of unsavory ideas in geography's disciplinary past, from the colonial impulses of Halford Mackinder's geopolitics (Kearns 2009a) to the social Darwinism of Friedrich

Ratzel's *Lebensraum* to the implicit racism of Ellen Churchill Semple's environmental determinism (Smith 1986; Keighren 2010), this is not the broken foundation on which I want to build. Instead, I want to appeal to the promise of spatial emancipation and to the idea that hope can be realized through the reinvigoration of an anarchist geography. This book accordingly sets the stage for a radical, rhizomatic politics of possibility and freedom through a discussion of the insurrectionary geographies that suffuse our daily experiences. By embracing anarchist geographies as kaleidoscopic spatialities that allow for nonhierarchical connections between autonomous entities, wherein solidarities are voluntarily assembled in opposition to sovereign violence, predetermined norms, and assigned categories of belonging, we configure a radical political imagination that is capable of demanding the impossible. Experimentation in and through space is the story of humanity's place on the planet, and the stasis and control that now supersede ongoing organizing experiments are an affront to our very survival. Singular ontological modes that favor one particular way of doing things disavow geography by failing to understand the spatial as an ongoing mutable assemblage that is intimately bound to temporality. Even worse, such stagnant ideas often align to the parochial interests of an elite minority and thereby threaten to be our collective undoing. What is needed is the development of new relationships with our world and, crucially, with each other. By infusing our geographies with anarchism, we unleash a spirit of rebellion that forgoes a politics of waiting for change to come at the behest of elected leaders and instead engages new possibilities of mutual aid through direct action in the *here* and *now*. Anarchism is accordingly framed as a perpetually evolving process of geographical prefiguration that seeks to refashion entrenched modes of understanding and being in the world vis-à-vis the authoritarian institutions, proprietary relations, and pugnacious geopolitics that dominate contemporary politics and their associated configurations of space. We can no longer accept the decaying, hideous, and archaic geographies of hierarchy that chain us to statism, capitalism, gender domination, heteronormativity, racial oppression, speciesism, and imperialism. Instead, geography must become beautiful, wherein the entirety of its embrace is aligned to emancipation.

FROM UNIVERSAL GEOGRAPHY TO RELATIONAL SPACE

In setting out to argue that geographical thinking should be reoriented toward the anarchist horizons of possibility, I draw heavily on both Kropotkin and Reclus. In particular, I've been inspired by Reclus's notion of a "universal geography," which has significant resonance with the contemporary "relational turn" we are witnessing in the discipline (Reclus 1894; Jones 2009). Similarly, Kropotkin's theory of "mutual aid" is a primary source of inspiration, an idea rooted in cooperation and reciprocity and thus corresponding very closely with current interest in the "commons." My argument throughout this book is that a reengagement with anarchism within geographical theory and practice brings us closer to the possibility of shaking off the chains that fetter us to statist, capitalist, racist, sexist, and imperialist ideas. If we are to make the Colossus tremble, as Kropotkin persuaded, then we must demonstrate to this force that we are awake and, critically, that we are aware of its geographical modes, which will not go unchallenged. Our greatest resource comes from our bonds to one another through the relational spaces of a universal geography and via the common interests of mutual aid. As Paul Routledge argues, "relational ethical positionalities need to be for dignity, self-determination, and empowerment, while acknowledging that any collaborative 'we' constitutes the performance of multiple lived worlds and an entangled web of power relationships. . . . It is about solidarity through the process of mutual discovery and knowing one another" (Routledge 2009a, 88–89). Recognizing such connection is an aesthetic realization that we *all* matter, that we are *all* part of the beauty of immanence. Within this recognition of our capacity for the beautiful come strength and the seed of something new, nourished by the possibilities of our desire for a better world.

In recent years, human geographers have begun actively thinking through how space, and the multitude of factors that comprise it, might be considered as a "relational assemblage" (Anderson and McFarlane 2011; Wood 2013). This emergent theory owes much to Doreen Massey's watershed book *For Space,* in which she argues that "conceptualising space as open, multiple and relational, unfinished and always becoming, is a prerequisite for history to be open and thus a prerequisite, too, for the possibility of politics" (Massey 2005, 59). What relational space refers to, then, is the idea that there are connections between and across spaces that comprise more than a single bond or immediately obvious linkage. Instead, relational space encourages us to think about space as a complex and iterative assemblage wherein ongoing and reciprocating exchanges between actors, events, and ideas continually play out through the process of life's evolving dance. As Ash Amin (2007) explains, relationality refers to how the "varied processes of spatial stretching, inter-dependence and flow, combine in situ trajectories of sociospatial evolution and change," where the result is

> no simple displacement of the local by the global, of place by space, of history by simultaneity and flow, of small by big scale, or of the proximate by the remote. Instead, it is a subtle folding together of the distant and the proximate, the virtual and the material, presence and absence, flow and stasis, into a single ontological plane. (103)

Thinking relationally is at once an insistence on the connection between space and time and a recognition that no place is isolated from the larger story of space (Massey 2005). Within this view, space is not simply an empty container waiting for something to fill it with content but is instead always and already filled with *matter* in the double sense of *physical substance* as a noun and in terms of *having significance* as a verb. Relational space also attempts to attend to the question of what "relations" mean, their nature, and crucially how they relate to questions of power (Massey 2004). A relational geography is, in short, a way to try to make sense of a world that is infinitely complex and in an ever-changing process of becoming. Yet relational space is also indicative of a politics, one with great possibility for expanding our circle of empathy and reorganizing the landscapes of power though strengthened bonds of solidarity. So rather than simply *becoming,* space, in its idealized political form, is about *becoming beautiful.* It is precisely in such beauty that we can envisage a connection to Reclus's much older theory of a universal geography.

With his expansive *The Earth and Its Inhabitants: The Universal Geography,* Reclus went to extraordinary lengths to advance the idea that all people should share the Earth as siblings and collectively refuse any claim to the superiority of one culture over another. Surely this is an optimistic idea, and from the vantage point of the postcolonial, poststructuralist present, the very language of "universal" may leave a bad taste in one's mouth. Reclus's thinking was undoubtedly set within the limits of a nineteenth-century European philosophy, but as Federico Ferretti argues, his universalism was "not the affirmation of a necessary assimilation or a fixed evolutionary process: it is more an affirmation of his hope in the planetary diffusion of the principles of 'cooperation' and 'free federation'" (Ferretti 2013, 1352). Accordingly, it is important to view his work as an attempt to advance an alternative to the colonialist and racist discourses that dominated European experience at the time. So with Reclus we can see an early iteration of a politics of possibility that looks to connection, or relationality, as its impetus. The language was different and far less nuanced than we can see within the current relational turn in geography, but the sentiment of drawing linkages across space to foster a broader empathetic horizon is largely the same. There are other parallels to be found with relational thinking, for Reclus was not just concerned with humans but had an expanded view that emphasized our integral relationship with the environment that specifically sought to restore balance and equality between humans and the biosphere. Kropotkin endorsed similar ideas in his masterwork, *Mutual Aid: A Factor in Evolution,* where he looked to the symbiotic relations between peoples, plants, and animals as the enmeshment of humanity within the web of life (Dugatkin 2011). Both men therefore stood in stark contrast to a long history of Western thought that positioned humans at the apex of some imagined hierarchy, a position that has deep resonance with the connectivity arguments coming out of geography's relational turn and with other contemporary offshoots within the discipline, such as theories of emotion and affect, hybrid geographies, and nonrepresentational theory (Anderson 2006; Pile 2009; Whatmore 2002; Thrift 2007).

Reclus's geography was of course an anarchist one, and so he sought to spread awareness for the significance and viability of anarchist ideas, wherein his relational thinking was also manifest. He advocated for a decentralized version of power, wherein decision making was to be guided by voluntary association and radical democracy rather than as a coercive preserve of the elite or a vacuous and apolitical process of voting (Reclus, n.d.). Extending beyond the local frame, he saw much virtue in the notion of free federation among communities, which demonstrates a relational connection between the situatedness of direct access to power and a broader sense of belonging in the world (Clark and Martin 2004). To Reclus, anarchists should work to free themselves from imposed or preconceived ideas by gradually surrounding themselves with those who choose to live and act in a similar fashion. He thus also hinted at what are today referred to in anarchist studies as *prefigurative politics,* a term coined by Carl Boggs to denote the forms of social relations and modes of organization that are being enacted in the present as a reflection of the future society being sought (Boggs 1977). In short, prefiguration is a collapsing of the means and ends that attempts to give form to our ideals by building "a new society in the shell of the old" right *here* and *now* (Ince 2012). For Reclus, such a politics became possible "through small, loving and intelligent societies," which would eventually translate into the "great fraternal society" of the universal geography he so desired (Fleming 1988). Reclus was thus also advancing the notion that personal and social transformations were intimately linked, which has been taken up in anarchist practice and theory through the notion of *affinity groups,* which come together out of shared interests and common goals (Clark 2013). In other words, Reclus advanced a relational notion of the commons by employing a decidedly geographical imagination that envisioned a connection between the immediate context and the wider social frame.

RECLAIMING THE COMMONS AS MUTUAL AID

The idea of the commons refers to a communal sense of resources and land use, whereby communities and individuals share that which they collect, cultivate, and create. Put differently, resources and land are simply held in common. Prior to recorded human history, it is thought that the world existed in a state of universal commons that lasted for tens of thousands of years. Indeed, the transformation of the symbiotic equilibrium of the commons into the uneven capitalist relations we see today was only made possible by human claims to private property, a process known as enclosure or primitive accumulation (Marx [1867] 1976). Processes of agrarian change have repeatedly seen people lose their self-sufficiency by being pushed off their commonly held land and into wage labor. The entire structure of our relation to each other and our world has been dramatically transformed from cooperation to competition in the pursuit of capital, a process facilitated by the state, which evolved in concert with capitalism as a means to entrench class privilege though the monopolization of violence (Bakunin [1882] 2010; Kropotkin 1897). As Leo Tolstoy ([1900] 2004, 30, 32) explained,

> history shows that property in land did not arise from any wish to make the cultivator's tenure more secure but resulted from the seizure of communal lands by conquerors and its distribution to those who served the conqueror.... The fruit of their toil is unjustly and violently taken from the workers, and then the law steps in, and these very articles which have been taken from the workmen unjustly and by violence are declared to be the absolute property of those who have taken them.

Part of Kropotkin's project with *Mutual Aid,* and indeed the origin of the book, was to offer a rebuttal to the supposedly Darwinian ideas of "survival of the fittest" and "all against all" that underpinned the very idea of capital accumulation. Kropotkin understood such arguments as a mischaracterization of Darwin's actual project, and so he wanted to explicitly point out that evolution was as much characterized by cooperation between organisms and their environments as it was a direct struggle among individuals for limited resources, a contention that he maintained was as true for biology as it was for politics (Kropotkin [1902] 2008; Dugatkin 2011).

For Kropotkin, mutual aid was a form of organizing drawn from time immemorial, wherein voluntary reciprocal exchange was the norm. Mutual aid was thought to provide strong community bonds and foster a sense of deep affinity and empathy for other human begins as well as for nonhuman animals and the wider biosphere. It was meant as recognition for our irreducible entanglement in the web of life and as a refusal of the hierarchy that pervaded our thinking about the world we live in and our connections to others. The relationship to the commons should be immediately evident, as a sense of something being "held in common" is only made possible via an appreciation for reciprocity and cooperation. In short, any given commons is a geographical manifestation of mutual aid. What this suggests is that the so-called tragedy of the commons—a rallying point for defenders of capitalism and neoliberal economists everywhere—is little more than a myth (Angus 2008). The refusal of this fabrication has gained significant traction in recent years thanks in no small part to the work of Elinor Ostrom, who won the 2009 Nobel Prize in Economics. Her work validates long-held anarchist principles by challenging the conventional wisdom that common property is poorly managed and should be either privatized or regulated by the state (Ostrom 1990). The tragedy of the commons, which was first articulated by Garrett Hardin, is often treated as an irrefutable justification for private property and the privatization of land, yet there is no empirical basis to his argument, nor was it informed by historical or current practice. Hardin, who used a hypothetical example of cattle grazing, utterly failed to reflect the reality of the commons as a social institution and instead demonstrated that private ownership represents the heart of the actual problem (Hardin 1968; McKay 2008). He failed to realize that his argument never considered cattle as potentially being a commonly held resource in addition to land, and instead he showed just how limited his own imagination was as he positioned them as being already privately owned and grazing indiscriminately in a supposedly common field. What he actually demonstrated, then, was the "tragedy of capitalism" that arises through individual utility-maximizing behavior. The commons where *never* a free-for-all of the type that Hardin describes; instead, they were well managed by common agreements, reciprocal arrangements, and shared interests between those who actually used them (Harvey 2011).

Part of the reason why Hardin's myth became so prevalent stems from the ongoing confusion over what property actually means and how it has become a taken-for-granted concept in contemporary political discourse. At the heart of anarchist thought is a distinction between *property* and *possession*, which was outlined by Pierre-Joseph Proudhon ([1865] 2011). Proudhon traced property to the patriarchal Roman law concept of sovereign right, whereby a proprietor could "use and abuse" *his* property as *he* wished, so long as *he* retained state-sanctioned title. Property in Proudhon's reading was a juridico-institutional means for exploitation, and he viewed it as an insult to the liberty, equality, and security of the community. In short, property was considered a categorical threat to the commons. Proudhon contrasted the supposedly God-given, sovereign right of property with possession, which he understood as a practice of actual use that therefore could not be mobilized for exploitation. Thus a house that one lives in is regarded as a possession, whereas a house that is rented becomes a means for exploiting others and can be considered property. The commons is likewise rooted in actual use rather than sovereign right and is similarly a possession, where the only difference is that it is communally rather than individually used. So while property attempts to mobilize the means of production as a natural, sovereign right of an individual or "proprietor," Proudhon ([1840] 2008) argued that this was an illegitimate form of use, and he considered it a form of theft from the commons. This is not to say that a means of production should not exist, which is of course impossible, but rather that such means should not belong to a sovereign proprietor as a so-called natural right. Instead, everyone connected to the said means of production should share in the bounty and surpluses it produces as a *commons*. Property is fundamentally at odds with the notion of the commons insofar as it relies on coercion, exclusion, hierarchy, and, most notably, enforcement (or law) to maintain its viability. The commons has no such mobilization of force and is instead a reciprocal exchange of common interest and shared benefit, in other words, *mutual aid*. So whereas property is inextricable from the apparatus of the state, the commons is in contrast the domain of anarchism.

Property is a relation of domination, and as I have argued at length elsewhere, it should be understood as a distinctive form of violence (Springer 2015). So when one hears of anarchists supposedly committing "violence" against property, a deep sense of cynicism should be reserved, as this can hardly be considered violence at all. Instead, it actually represents a pushback *against* violence. Likewise, I do not consider self-defense a form of violence, as there is no impetus for coercion or domination but rather a desire for self-preservation. Throughout this book, I advocate a peaceful stance for anarchism, and in an effort to be clear from the outset, I want to indicate what I mean by this commitment to nonviolence. When I refer to "violence," I am calling into question an unequal power relation that involves some element of coercion and/or domination over others, which can be either direct and immediately visible or indirect and spatially and temporally diffuse (Springer 2012a). So although I consider my arguments as pacifist in their orientation, I do not assume this to mean that people should simply kneel at the foot of their oppressor when the weight of violence comes crashing down upon their backs. There is often a distinct need to rise and defend oneself, which should similarly not be confused with "violence." At the same time, I cannot lend my support to premeditated or preemptive attacks against life and limb that intend to maim or kill, regardless of the social position from which such strikes are organized. Violence begets violence, and in keeping with a relational understanding of space, any path toward emancipation that includes violence as part of its practice will only and inevitably result in further bloodshed (Springer 2011). Because the prefigurative politics of anarchism interpret means and ends as inseparable, and because anarchism is a desire for a more equitable and peaceful world, one should expect that violence *cannot* form part of its content. I advocate a peaceful stance for anarchism in these terms, wherein we require a more precise theorization that recognizes the rebellion of the oppressed as something other than "violence," because violence is always a mechanism in the service of subjugation.

In the final analysis, it is the case that the notions of relationality and the commons are not mutually exclusive or diametrically opposed. Indeed, when we think about their connections as part of the pillars of anarchism, the relational and the commons come together as the two most fundamental components of procuring a universal geography and of rehearsing mutual aid. The anarchist notion of voluntary association further speaks to the relational connections across space and between various actors with shared interests. Such affinities, which are built through *relational* connections, are manifested as direct action in the hope of claiming spaces as *common*. As the Collective Autonomy Research Group (2014, 887) argues, "ideas and practices spread within anarchist spaces, communities and outward through non-hierarchical processes of 'cross-pollination' (sharing principles and practices through face-to-face discussions as people move between various collectives and meeting spaces) that grow out of a commitment to principles of mutual aid and co-production of knowledge. Anarchists set up and self-manage spaces that allow for expressions and practices of collective autonomy in the here and now." We are able to (re)claim the commons, not through violence, but rather through our connections to each other and the idea that we are all imbued within a relational assemblage of the shared goal of a better life. This is precisely how the commons becomes common. Similarly, we are able to recognize our affinities, bonds, and solidarities only when we have a functioning sense of the commons, as it enables us to understand our relations to others as meaningful. This synergy is why the struggle over space is so vitally important to convening a new and beautiful politics in our world, and it goes some way toward explaining why anarchism and geography make such good bedfellows. The idea of the commons and the theory of relational space work in tune with one another, functioning as an iterative process of empowerment and collectivity. In short, much like the anarchist idea that theory and practice are two sides to the same coin known as *praxis,* you cannot separate a claim to the commons from the relational connections that exist between individuals acting in the interest of mutual aid.

DO WE SPEAK A DEAD LANGUAGE?

Language is a difficult proposition. We often have trouble actually saying what we mean, and the flip side of this is that sometimes we don't even mean what we say. Language fails us in a multitude of ways precisely because it dwells in representation rather than being an "authentic" experience of the world, if such a thing can even be said to exist. Language mediates how we think, informs how we act, and conditions how we relate to one another. When, for example, contemporary discourses position capitalism as an inevitability of our current moment of postmodernity, as a society we invest a whole lot of time and energy into allowing this notion to become "true." A vast archive of ideas, expressions, and axioms compels us to believe that a "rising tide lifts all boats" and that "there is no alternative" to the neoliberal conjuncture. We speak the language of capitalism, a listless form of communication that we have been instilling in our children for many generations now. Our self-worth is invested in its ideals, our morality is centered on its vices, and our daily routines are structured around its demands. Yet there is no fundamental truth to the idea that capitalism is an inevitable condition of the present moment. The world can be reimagined in ways that break with capitalist modalities, and simply because we have become content to speak with the forked tongue of consumerism, individualism, and materialism does not mean this is the only language we can learn. The epigraph that opens this chapter suggests that we can learn the private language of affording meaning to the lives of others, a break with the aesthetics of capitalism in favor of the immanence of our collective beauty. One approach in realizing this disruption from the doldrums of life as it is currently lived under capitalism is, as the CrimethInc. Writers' Bloc (2013, 6) so passionately persuades, to "*Write barbarously!* Build your arguments on the slopes of Vesuvius! Send your prose into uncharted seas! Break with common sense and convention in such a way that *everyone else joins in*! When in Rome, do as the Vandals do: *sack it*. Axe clichés and replace them with a coinage of your own mint. Topple the Tower of Babel, the imperial project of imposing a unitary logic on language and thought." This seems like an excellent start in shaking things up, but how do we begin to construct an alternative to capitalism? It is a question of practice as much as it is a question of language. Fortunately, these are questions that cannot be cleaved off from one another. Emancipation as a process of living into a new geographical reality cannot focus on singular trajectories and isolated points of contestation. Here too is the importance of a relational approach, for it allows us to construct a broader sense of affinity and thus a more powerful version of solidarity, wherein language and practice are pivotal. But again, how do we get *there* from *here*?

Anarchists insist on prefiguration, and so the insurrection begins anywhere and everywhere, in *this moment,* in *this place.* There is no abstracted outside location where our resistance to capitalism might begin, and we should all know that tomorrow never comes, so a politics of waiting for the revolution can never liberate us from anything. We always and unavoidably live our lives in the ever-flowing present, where each instant of experience is actually *today.* But we still have to understand each other in the moments that we share, and in setting our minds free from the shackles of domination, anarchists have never shied away from education as a principal means of convincing people to act in more ethical and egalitarian ways (Sussia 2010; Haworth 2012). For Kropotkin, "the education we all receive from the State, at school and after, has so warped our minds that the very notion of freedom ends up by being lost, and disguised in servitude," and so he looked to a more complete notion of education, beyond the rule of the classroom, that viewed manual labor and intellectual pursuits as integral (Kropotkin 1897; [1912] 1994). This view of education is a precursor to the well-loved idea that geography is learned "through the soles of our feet" and corresponds closely with the desire of contemporary anarchists to see theory and action merged (Amster et al. 2009; Ward [1973] 2001). How can we hope for freedom when we think with minds caged in the fog of subjugation, when we still speak the dead language of our oppressors? As the preceding discussion of the commons should evoke, we need a point of contact where our understandings converge so that we might be able to live together, share our ideas, and engage in the practices of mutual aid. What is missing from this discussion is an indication of how the very notion of what we hold in "common" has been distorted, captured, assimilated, and eviscerated by the hierarchies that currently dominate our lives. Most notably, we can look to capitalism and the state and to how these categories have produced new forms of rationality or transformed our sense of belonging through nationalism, but we can also recognize how sexist, racist, abilist, speciesist, heteronormative, and cisnormative discourses have done much the same. Each of these registers of domination constrains and conditions how we think about the world by using language as a weapon that we unknowingly turn upon ourselves. This suicidal impulse, reflected in the apocalyptic conditions of endless war and a planet on the threshold of environmental collapse, is not just about territorial conflict and the treachery of industry; it is about a lack of understanding our integral bonds with each other and with Gaia itself, where the meaning and beauty of our lives have been silenced by the destructive language we speak.

Writing is not separate from language, and how we write about the world constitutes a deeply political choice. Part of the reason I hope to restore an anarchist current in geographical practice and thought is because I want to see a freer version of geography emerge. I view disciplining others into a singular way of knowing, being, and doing geography as an offense to the possibilities of space (Massey 2005). Within this restrictive disciplinary rationale, jargon and neologisms are generally viewed in a pejorative light, which often simply serves to conceal a lack of understanding that confines us to a preestablished pattern of thought. Yet specialized language, which is all jargon actually is, pervades in all of geography's nooks and crannies (Cresswell 2013). Small hills are called "drumlins," coordinates become "geodetic data," and the repetition and rehearsal of identity is streamlined as "performativity." Poststructuralism has repeatedly demonstrated how the very notion of truth is necessarily and unavoidably constructed, whereby comprehension emerges from incomplete, subjective, and disputed positions. Yet when I suggest that theory and action, or language and practice, are inseparable, there is no direct translation between an epistemology of understanding and a shift in our material conditions toward emancipation. The struggle for freedom and social justice is difficult work that requires direct action, but anarchists refuse to establish a set program that concretizes this process, as though there is a single recipe we can follow. What those who advocate for exclusively realist, scientific, or empirical frames for geographical scholarship often forget is that these too are discursive fields laden with their own jargon, technobabble, and gobbledygook. For better or for worse, each one of us—academic and nonacademic alike—is immersed in a specific epistemic field. To the extent possible, shaped by the societal context in which we find ourselves, and certainly limited by existing hierarchies, we each choose with whom to converse. At times this takes more formal patterns, which is often an unconscious move that should signal the degree to which hierarchies have conditioned our thought and action. At other times, such as when we speak to our friends, we do so in unique and creative ways, developing inside jokes, shared expressions, and nicknames that demonstrate our affinity for one another. As academics, we do much the same, penning our words with a particular audience in mind in the hope that our message will be appreciated and thus potentially travel further.

Both writing and language are powerful tools when aimed at dismantling hegemonic ways of seeing and disrupting existing power constellations. The articulation of theory, to which this book hopes to contribute, accordingly allows antiauthoritarian and nonhierarchical discourses to permeate the seemingly impenetrable bedrock of a broad spectrum of material interventions (Jiwani 2011). Because theory is integrally linked to action in the anarchist imagination, direct action similarly revitalizes our systems of thought and the expression of philosophy. There is an ongoing circuit of exchange, affirmation, progression, revision, and modification. As a consequence of acknowledging this reciprocating relationship of praxis, I want to reject the idea that an original contribution to geographical scholarship must only arise from empirical interpretations of actual experience. This book is accordingly not a detailed analysis of particular geographical expressions of anarchism in practice; rather, it advances an anarchist geography by insisting that anarchism is so intimately tied to the everyday that once we begin to theorize the mundanity of anarchism, we will be able to see its expression very clearly in so many of the routine things we do (Scott 2012). Colin Ward ([1973] 2001, 18) pointed to this exact idea when he wrote that anarchist society "is always in existence, like a seed beneath the snow . . . rooted in the experience of everyday life, which operates side by side with, and in spite of, the dominant authoritarian trends of our society." And so a view of geography as empiricism alone is never enough. We need geographical theory, and accordingly, I make no apologies for the theoretical content found within these pages. At times this theory may be difficult for some readers, and it may even feel unfamiliar and peculiar, but for anarchists to have any chance of success, we need to fill our lungs with the fresh air of creativity and be willing to wrestle with difficult questions. In doing so, we can invigorate our practice of anarchism. By approaching the merger of theory and practice, or *praxis,* with an open mind, we allow a material space for radical transformation to follow. To keep the horizons of possibility open and alive, we must be prepared to engage a new imagination, an imagination that actually requires that we add new words to our vocabulary and be ready to experiment with language. So while notions of "prefiguration," "affinity," "relationality," and "rhizomatic politics" might seem challenging at first, they are crucially important components in the lexicon of emancipation and provide fertile ground for us to think through what an anarchist geography might actually look like.

THE COMING ANARCHY

Peter Kropotkin (1887, 153) once intuitively wrote that, "by taking for our watchword anarchy, in its sense of no-government, we intend to express a pronounced tendency of human society. In history we see that precisely those epochs when small parts of humanity broke down the power of their rulers and reassumed their freedom were epochs of the greatest progress, economical and intellectual." So I begin this exploration of anarchist geographies by looking to the past in an effort to better understand the present and future potential trajectories of anarchism. There is a long and disjointed history between anarchism and geography, characterized by towering peaks of intensive intellectual engagement and low valleys of ambivalence and disregard. While recognizing and appreciating a deeper connection to time immemorial, chapter 1 traces a genealogy of anarchist geographies back to the modern development of anarchism into a distinct political philosophy following the Enlightenment. The initial rise of geographers' engagement with anarchism occurred at the end of the nineteenth century, owing to Reclus and Kropotkin, who developed an emancipatory vision for geography despite the discipline's enchantment with imperialism at that time. The realpolitik of the war years in the first half of the twentieth century and the subsequent quantitative revolution in geography represent a nadir for anarchist geographies. Yet anarchism was never entirely abandoned by geographical thought, and the counterculture movement of the 1970s gave rise to radical geography, which included significant interest in anarchist ideas. Unfortunately, another low occurred during the surge of neoliberal politics in the 1980s and early 1990s, but hope springs eternal, and from the late 1990s onward, the antiglobalization movement and DIY culture have pushed anarchist geographies into more widespread currency. In surveying the literature, I hope to alert readers to the ongoing and manifold potential for anarchist geographies to inform geographical theory and, importantly, to give rise to more practice-based imperatives where building solidarities, embracing reciprocity, and engaging in mutual aid with actors and communities beyond the academy speak to the "freedom of geography" and its latent capacity to shatter its own disciplinary circumscriptions.

Chapter 2 picks up the emancipatory thread by establishing a manifesto for anarchist geographies that refuses sovereign violence, preordained rules, and regulated identities in favor of nonhierarchical relations, voluntary association, mutual aid, solidarity, direct action, autonomy, and self-management. In its rejection of the multivariate apparatuses of domination, this chapter represents a proverbial call to nonviolent arms for all those who seek to put an end to the seemingly endless series of tragedies, misfortunes, and catastrophes that characterize the miasma and malevolence of the current neoliberal moment. But this is not simply a demand for the end of neoliberalism and its replacement with a more moderate and humane version of capitalism, nor does it merely insist on a more egalitarian version of the state. It is instead the resurrection of a prosecution within geography that dates back to the discipline's earliest days. It is a call for anarchy! In promoting an anarchist agenda, I set out to trace how statism and colonialism are two sides of the same coin and outline some sketches of the possibilities of anarchist geographies in imagining alternatives to the current system.

Chapter 3 questions how and why radical geographers have been preoccupied with Marxism for four decades, largely ignoring an earlier anarchist tradition that thrived a century before radical geography was claimed as Marxist in the 1970s. When anarchism has been considered, it has often been misused as a synonym for violence or derided as a utopian project. Yet it is incorrect to assume anarchism as a "project," which instead reflects Marxian thought. Anarchism is more appropriately considered a protean process that perpetually unfolds through the insurrectionary geographies of the everyday and the prefigurative politics of direct action, mutual aid, and voluntary association. Unlike Marxism's stages of history and revolutionary imperative, which imply an end state, anarchism appreciates the dynamism of the social world. In staking a renewed anarchist claim for radical geography, this chapter attends to the divisions between Marxism and anarchism as two alternative socialisms, wherein the former positions equality alongside an ongoing flirtation with authoritarianism, while the latter maximizes egalitarianism and individual liberty by considering them as mutually reinforcing. I contend that radical geographers would do well to reengage anarchism precisely because there is a sense of vitality to this philosophy that is missing from Marxian analyses and their continuing reliance on outmoded ideas such as vanguardism and the dictatorship of the proletariat.

In establishing an anarchic framework for understanding public space as a vision for radical democracy, chapter 4 proceeds as a theoretical inquiry into how an agonistic public space might become the basis of emancipation. Public space, when liberated from an authoritarian ethos, is presented as an opportunity to move beyond the technocratic elitism that so often characterizes both civil societies and the neoliberal approach to development. The spaces of the public are further recognized as the battlefield on which the conflicting interests of the world's rich and poor are set. Contributing to the growing recognition that geographies of re-sistance are relational, where the "global" and the "local" are understood as co-constitutive, a radical democratic ideal grounded in material public space is presented as paramount to repealing "archic" power in general and neoliberalism's exclusionary logic in particular. Public space itself then becomes a basis through which anarchism evolves as an actual practice of lived experience.

There is increasing recognition among geographers that conceptual-izing the spatiality of peace is a vital component of our collective praxis. Situated within this emergent literature, chapter 5 seeks to position anar-chism as an ethical philosophy of nonviolence and the absolute rejection of war. Such an interpretation does not attempt to align nonviolence to any particular organized religious teaching. Instead, I argue that the current practices of religion undermine the geographies of peace by frag-menting our affinities into discrete pieces. Advancing a view of anarchism as nonviolence, I go beyond religion to conceptualize peace as both the unqualified refusal of the manifold-cum-interlocking processes of domi-nation and a precognitive, prenormative, and presupposed category rooted in our inextricable entanglement with each other and all that exists. Yet far from proposing an essentialist view of humanity or engaging a natu-ralized argument that reconvenes the "noble savage," I contextualize my arguments within the processual frameworks of radical democracy and agonism that were set out in the previous chapter. In doing so, I seek to redress the ageographical and ahistorical notions of politics that compose the contemporary postpolitical zeitgeist.

Chapter 6 questions how contemporary geographical thought has been constrained by a political economic imagination rooted in binarism, which is exemplified in debates surrounding neoliberalism. Neoliberal proponents call for decentralization and increased capital flows, while Marxists respond by pairing centralization with the eventual revocation of capitalism. The latter view considers hierarchy necessary, a position that promotes authority and problematically regards horizontal politics as favorable to neoliberalism. Anarchism's coupling of decentralization with anticapitalism is dismissed because Marxism cannot understand or accommodate the unfolding nature of prefigurative politics. Marxism demands a revolution with a *master* plan and considers horizontality a future objective. Such a temporal reading of emancipation ignores the insurrectionary possibilities of the present and implies a politics of waiting. The spatial implications of centralized hierarchy are also questionable, and I challenge this vertical ontology of Marxism. A flat ontology has significant resonance with anarchism, imparting that politics should operate horizontally through a rhizomatic politics rather than vertically. This ontological shift suggests that we need not wait for the emergence of a "greater" class consciousness, as one can immediately disengage capitalism by reorienting economic landscapes in alternative ways. Consequently, this final chapter argues that a nonhierarchical vision of geography gains significant traction when we reject scale. By welcoming the anarchist horizon as a metaphor for a new kind of politics, hope becomes more than a distant ideal. It is repositioned as the strength and beauty we each hold right *here* in our hands.

HOPE BEYOND HOPE

"So it came first—a gleam of hope to the proletaire, a summons to rise and shake off his material bondage," Voltairine de Cleyre (1901, 28) wrote of the innate potential for societal transformation. "Steadily, steadily, the light has grown," she continues, "as year by year the scientist, the literary genius, the artist, and the moral teacher, have brought to it the tribute of their best work, their unpaid work, the work they did for love. Today it means not only material emancipation, too; it comes as the summing up of all those lines of thought and action which for three hundred years have been making towards freedom; it means fullness of being, the free life." Hope is the daylight in our eyes, the song from the sun that sets our passions alight. It allows us to dream of something better, something more. Yet anarchism is not about breaking away from society and fleeing from the systems and structures that dominate our lives. It is about refusing them *here* in this space, and *now* in this moment, by converting thoughts into action through prefiguration. As Reclus (1884, 637) proclaimed, "never will we separate ourselves from the world to build a little church, hidden in some vast wilderness. Here is the fighting ground, and we remain in the ranks, ready to give our help wherever it may be most needed. We do not cherish premature hopes, but we know that our efforts will not be lost." In other words, anarchism takes hold of hope by refusing to let it linger as an ideal never realized, a promise unfulfilled, or a dream not lived. It is not enough to yearn for something more, something different, and something new. We must be willing to embrace our fear of the unknown and realize that the familiar landscapes of hierarchy are little more than a debilitating crutch, crippling our creative capacities by beguiling us with their unyielding series of false promises. For centuries now, we have been conditioned to believe that their "old order," supported by police, magistrates, gendarmes, and soldiers, is the first and last chance for humanity to thrive. Yet, "instead of order they bring forth chaos; instead of prosperity, poverty and insecurity; instead of reconciled interests, war; a perpetual war of the exploiter against the worker" (Kropotkin [1880] 2005, 36).

This is an "order" that has brought the world to the precipice of environmental catastrophe, and now, as we choke on the ashes of complacency through blackened lungs, it threatens to jump headlong into the abyss. It is an "order" that has flirted openly with nuclear annihilation, asking us to trust its supposed fidelity to our well-being while it conspires against us, surging ever onward toward the apotheosis of war. It is an "order" that has repeatedly demonstrated its willingness to abuse, indoctrinate, exploit, punish, ridicule, harass, fleece, regulate, curse, imprison, tax, vilify, mock, judge, monopolize, fine, repress, and condemn us as part of its moral faculty (Proudhon [1851] 2007). It is a vile abomination, a parasitic void, a Colossus emboldened by artifice, animated by greed, and swallowed by the flagrancy of its own ego. Yet we willingly feed this revolting beast a steady diet of our own flesh. Our young are consumed as its soldiers, our old become its sages, and the sick are celebrated as our commanders, clergy, and kings. Weary of the circular ruins that have been piled high at the hearth of humanity, anarchists seek new forms of organization. We ask how it is that *words*, so often left to hang empty and breathless in the wind like the echoes of distant bells, might be given life by being changed into *actions*. For Kropotkin the answer was easy, even if he recognized that it meant a great deal of hard work. He looked to an endless commitment to transformation as the key, wherein courage, care, and the spirit of community become just as contagious as cowardice, compliance, and the politics of command and control.

To renew ourselves and thrive, we need to start seeing each other. I mean more than simply opening our eyes beyond myopic self-interests and instead really taking the time to look deeply and carefully at the meaning of each other's lives. The fact that there is consciousness in the universe is an amazing revelation. It is a gift beyond all measure. Yet life is tragically fragile, and for now, we can only confirm that it clings defiantly to a speck of dust somewhere at the edge of the Milky Way. This sentiment alone should give us moment for pause. If anything, the minutia of our differences should inspire wonder as opposed to doubt, solidarity instead of hostility, and empathy in lieu of apathy. Our strength against the fragility of life is derived, as Kropotkin ([1902] 2008) argued, from our ability to engage in mutual aid. If we are to make a lasting stand against the forces of the cosmos, which positions us as an infinitesimally small blip in its grand and glorious dance, then we must relish the collective strength we share with each other and the entirety of Gaia that nurtures and supports us. The death grip that we have administered on the Earth over the past few centuries—primarily through the institutions of capital and the state—suggests that the value we place on life has been eclipsed by the avarice of human arrogance. If life is to continue to flourish on this planet, it is by now commonplace and even trite to suggest that it is high time that we tried a radically different approach. Yet hope for a better future cannot bloom when fear cripples our willingness to experiment.

We can no longer be content to dwell in the dream of possibility, to trust the proclamations of academics or follow the commands of a president. Deep down we know that what is really required to change the shape and course of our world is a single act of courage, kindness, or community that originates from within ourselves. In the singular, any such act may appear meaningless against the oppressive deluge of the status quo. Multiplied by our numbers, and committed in solidarity with others, the Colossus into which we have all breathed life begins to shake with fear and gasp for air. How can we make plans for the future on something as frail as hope when we have not spent the time cultivating our desires into the strength of actual lived experience? This question reveals the importance of anarchism: it is a beautiful enabler. Without embracing our capacity for living *now* and doing for ourselves *in this moment* what we would otherwise leave to the protocols of authority, we kneel exposed at the foot of the giant with his cruel and ugly shadow drawn upon our backs. Those of us who embrace anarchism don't simply yearn for the light. We stand and walk toward it, claiming that strength is to be found not in what is dreamed possible but as an illumination of the powerful beauty we collectively represent. So let us reject the darkness that threatens to devour us all. Let us convene a new language of aesthetics that places each and every one of us at the center of its conversation. Let us become beautiful by recognizing the meaning of each other's lives in concert with our own. But most of all, let us awaken to the fact that *beautiful is something we already are.* This sentiment forms the heart of an anarchist geography. It is our path to spatial emancipation.

1

A Brief Genealogy of Anarchist Geographies

Anarchy, a society without government, has existed since time
immemorial. Anarchism, the doctrine that such a society is
desirable, is a much more recent development.
—**Robert Graham**

Anarchist theory is a geographical theory.
—**Richard Peet**

Anarchism and geography have had a long courtship. Like in any extended romance, there have been periods of deep engagement and connection and times when ambivalence and even separation have occurred.
Yet if we are to accept anarchism as the dismantling of unequal power
relations and the pursuit of reorganizing the way we live in the world
along more egalitarian, voluntary, altruistic, and cooperative lines, then it
becomes necessary to appreciate anarchism as a geographical endeavor.
Similarly, if geography is to be progressively understood as "a means of
dissipating...prejudices and of creating other feelings more worthy of
humanity" (Kropotkin 1885, 943), then it seems that anarchism has a
great deal to contribute to such an agenda. The late nineteenth century
accordingly saw a flourishing of geographical writings from influential
anarchist philosophers such as Peter Kropotkin and Élisée Reclus, who
were both very well respected geographers in the times and spaces in
which they lived their lives, having contributed much to the intellectual
climate (Morris 2003; Fleming 1988). Although explicit engagement
with their work faded following their deaths in the early twentieth century, the impact of these two visionary thinkers continues to reverberate
within contemporary geographical theory, influencing everything from
the way that geographers think about ethnicity and "race" to questions
of social organization and capital accumulation to conceptualizations of

urban and regional planning, as well as within discussions surrounding environmentalism.

The antiauthoritarian vision and critical concern for social justice that Reclus and Kropotkin advanced in their work sadly skipped a few generations as the war years of the early twentieth century shifted concerns to realpolitik and the quantitative revolution took hold of geography soon thereafter. In concert with the rise of the New Left and the counterculture movements of the 1970s, anarchism was once again back on the agenda and was afforded serious consideration by academic geographers, who utilized Marxian, feminist, poststructuralist, and anarchist theories to set the tone for what is now known as radical geography (Chouinard 1994; Peet 1977). Unfortunately, the 1980s and 1990s represented another dry spell, even though some important work that employed both geographical and anarchist concerns was still being done during these years. More recently, as the current conjuncture of intensifying neoliberalization, deepening financial crisis, and ensuing revolt—as witnessed in the Occupy Movement and the Arab Springs—has begun to push anarchist theory and practice back into widespread currency, a new generation of geographers has been stretching the boundaries of radical geography by placing anarchism at the center of its practices, theories, pedagogies, and methodologies. As the house of cards that capitalism has built slowly collapses under its own weight, the result has been a lot of renewed interest in anarchism both outside and inside the academy. Given geography's position as a scholarly enterprise that takes some measure of pride in straddling various disciplinary lines, it is critically important for geographers to be involved in this conversation.

This chapter is intended as a review of the existing literature on anarchist geographies. I trace the origins, developments, flourishings, declines, and renewals of anarchist thought within geography. Readers should note from the outset that this chapter is not intended to offer an overview and appraisal of the various geographies of anarchism that have been employed in different locations or the spatial tactics that anarchists have used in resisting various forms of domination. In this sense, I take anarchist geographies to be the theoretical terrain in which anarchism has been established as a political philosophy, as opposed to the geographies of anarchism that represent anarchism in its actually existing practice. I recognize that this sets up somewhat of a false dichotomy, particularly because direct action is about as close to a tenet as one might expect to find within the anarchist tradition, meaning that thought *(anarchist geographies)* is never separable from practice *(geographies of anarchism)*. However, by adopting this specific approach, charting a path through the existing literature seemed like a useful exercise.

My decision to focus primarily on anarchist thought was also made for historical reasons. Early engagements with anarchism were primarily rooted in thought, representing a low point for organized anarchist activity (Ince 2010a). As Blunt and Wills (2000, 2) lament, "it is frustrating that Kropotkin and Reclus were not able to combine their anarchist ideas with their geographical scholarship as they might do today." So the reduction in direct engagements with anarchism within academic geography since the time of Reclus and Kropotkin did not necessarily signal the decline of anarchism as a relevant political idea; rather, it is perhaps indicative of how anarchism left the academy for the greener pastures of practice on the streets as direct action, civil disobedience, and Black Bloc tactics; in the communes and intentional communities of the cooperative movement; amid DIY activists and a range of small-scale mutual aid groups, networks, and initiatives; as tenants' associations, trade unions, and credit unions; online through peer-to-peer file sharing, open source software, and wikis; among neighborhoods as autonomous migrant support networks and radical social centers; and more generally within the here and now of everyday life. The closer we come to the present moment, the more the literature begins to take a turn toward an appreciation for praxis as a number of geographers have begun identifying with anarchism, where the result has been a burgeoning consideration of both sides of the theory–practice divide. Readers should accordingly take the cited literature on anarchist geographies as a cue for exploring in more depth the geographies of anarchism that have been productively established in various contexts (Maxwell and Craib, 2015), and better still, as a point of departure in putting anarchism into practice within their own daily lives. Similarly, I hope that this book will be useful in encouraging other geographers to explore anarchist thought and practice. Anarchism offers a rich and fertile ground for those working from a geographical perspective, where all that is required for it to bloom is more individuals willing to till its bountiful soils.

THE ORIGINS OF ANARCHIST GEOGRAPHIES

The anthropological record confirms that before recorded history, human organization was established without formal authority, where only the rise of hierarchical societies necessitated the formulation of a critical political philosophy called "anarchism" that rejected coercive political institutions (Barclay 1982). Some have traced the origins of anarchist thinking to Taoism in ancient China, whereas others have noted that the first use of the word *anarchos*, meaning "lack of a ruler" and from which the contemporary word *anarchy* arises, arose in Europe and can be traced back to Homer's *Iliad* (Graham 2005; Marshall 1992; Verter 2010). Although these developments should be recognized as important historical antecedents, it is more difficult to contend that they are part of anarchism's actual genealogy. Anarchism—as opposed to anarchy—is a modern political philosophy, born of Enlightenment thinking, where William Godwin was "the first to formulate the political and economical conceptions of anarchism, even though he did not give that name to the ideas developed in his work" (Kropotkin 1910). His book *Enquiry Concerning Political Justice and Its Influence on Modern Morals and Manners* (Godwin [1793] 1976) laid a foundation of critique against government and its related institutions of property, monarchy, and law as impediments to the ostensibly natural and inevitable "progress" of humanity.

Godwin's focus on the state gave an implicit geography to anarchist thought, so that by the time Pierre-Joseph Proudhon ([1840] 2008) picked up on this line of criticism with his monumental *What Is Property? or, An Inquiry into the Right and Principle of Government,* as the first person to ever explicitly call himself an "anarchist," Proudhon already had a philosophical edifice that was deeply concerned with the ways in which human beings had come to arrange, order, and codify their relations in and across space as a result of the Industrial Revolution. Proudhon railed against property, considering it an institution that sanctioned theft from the commons. By aligning the proprietor with the sovereign, he conceptualized a relational geography between property and the state. Yet his ire was not limited to these two institutions, as Proudhon also attacked notions of profit, wage labor, worker exploitation, capitalism, and the theological idea of the Church, all of which had a profound influence on a then young Karl Marx, which confirms anarchism and Marxism as sharing a lineage within socialist thought. Proudhon applied the term *mutualism* to his version of anarchism, envisioning the workers as being directly involved in and controlling the means of production, which he considered the only legitimate incarnation of "property."

Writing at the same time as Proudhon, Mikhail Bakunin contributed much to anarchist theory but remains something of an enigma who inspired great controversy in his lifetime and even to this day (Marshall 1992). What is clear in Bakunin's vision is that he possessed a profound hatred for the sociopolitical conditions in which he lived, and much like it did for Proudhon, this manifested as complete distrust for the state. Bakunin's view of the state was directly related to his beliefs about humanity, as he saw people as more or less equal, naturally social, and therefore desiring solidarity, and he held that people intrinsically want to be free (Guérin 2005). Consequently, Bakunin's anarchism is focused on the problem of establishing a free society within a context of egalitarianism and mutual interaction. The arrangement of existing societies into states was to Bakunin completely artificial and unacceptable. He argued that the territorializing institution of the state was necessarily violent and antisocial, which actively denied alternative forms of nonhierarchical organization that would enable the fulfillment of humanity (Bakunin [1873] 2002). His pessimistic view of the state led to a rivalry with Marx, where in the long march of history, Bakunin's concern that worker's governments and the dictatorship of the proletariat would evolve into bureaucratic police states has been proven true. It is this very question—rooted in the structuring of sociospatial organization—that continues to animate the concerns of many contemporary anarchists.

Bakunin and Proudhon were not just anarchists, as each man also considered himself a proponent of socialism. Their ideas were very influential in late-nineteenth-century Europe, contributing much to the First International in 1864 and the subsequent Paris Commune of 1871, when workers overthrew the municipal government in revolt against authoritarianism (Archer 1997). These events demonstrate the alignment of anarchist and socialist practice from a very early stage, as both Proudhon and Bakunin faced off with Marx at various times throughout the libertarian movement, attempting to make a case for the more emancipatory version of socialism, which they firmly believed to be anarchism. In making a liberal critique of socialism, and a socialist critique of liberalism, anarchism was envisioned, and is still intended, as a thoroughgoing alternative to capitalism. Current efforts by the libertarian right to appropriate anarchism for their so-called version of "free market anarchism" or "anarchocapitalism" have no connection to the intellectual tradition and history of anarchist political thought and action. Although it calls for eliminating the state, the political system they propose is rooted, not in the collective, egalitarian, and democratic self-management of everyday life, but in a distorted sense of neosocial Darwinism that promotes individual sovereignty and a "survival of the fittest" mentality through the free market. *Anarchocapitalism* is accordingly an oxymoron, as it is entrenched in the very system of capitalist domination that anarchists have long sought to abolish.

THE RISE OF ANARCHIST GEOGRAPHIES

Given the tacit geographical framework that Proudhon and Bakunin laid alongside the foundations for anarchist thought, it is perhaps somewhat unsurprising that Élisée Reclus and Peter Kropotkin, two of anarchism's most renowned philosophers, were also geographers. Reclus's primary contribution, other than giving "social geography" its name (Dunbar 1978), was his liberationist ideals, which he charted in meticulous detail in *The Earth and Its Inhabitants: The Universal Geography* (Reclus 1894). Reclus envisaged a coalescence between humanity and the Earth itself, regarding the former as "nature becoming self-conscious." Although the universalism of his thought has perhaps become unfashionable as a result of poststructuralism's influence on the academy, one cannot ignore the profound influence that his social and ecological ethics have had in the development of radical thought, which stretches far beyond what many would consider anarchism. "Above all else," John Clark (2009, 109) explains, "Reclus placed what he called 'the social question'—the historical problematic of liberatory social transformation—at the center of his geographical project. By integrating this 'social question' into geography he expanded the scope of the discipline far beyond the limits generally observed in his era, incorporating into it issues of economic class, race, gender, power, and social domination, organizational forms and scale, urbanization, technology, and ecology." Reclus was dedicated to extending compassion, altruism, and the capacity for love beyond our immediate families, our nations, or even our species—a process he believed would simultaneously disavow and diminish all forms of domination. On humanity's path toward a greater planetary consciousness, Reclus bravely imagined that such a trajectory of reciprocal empathy, generosity, and respect would help the world to collectively discover a more profound emotional meaning in our shared experiences as earthlings (Clark and Martin 2004). Long before the affective turn put emotional implications at the forefront of critical geography, Reclus was already establishing a 'caring geography' of the sort Vicky Lawson (2009) advocates. In line with his holistic view of an integral planetary system united in affinity and affection, Reclus advocated for the conservation of nature, opposed animal cruelty, and practiced vegetarianism, thereby anticipating contemporary social ecology and the animal rights movement (Fleming 1988; Marshall 1992), while also foreshadowing veganarchism (Dominick 1995).[1]

Although greatly influenced by the mentorship of Reclus (Ward 2010), Kropotkin's work has received more attention as of late; influential works such as *The Conquest of Bread* (Kropotkin [1892] 2011), *Mutual Aid: A Factor in Evolution* (Kropotkin [1902] 2008), and *Fields, Factories, and Workshops* (Kropotkin [1912] 1994) are now regarded as groundbreaking texts that have been instrumental to anarchist philosophy. Kropotkin developed his views at least partially in response to the social Darwinism of his time, where he took exception to the notion of fierce competition as the primary tenet of evolution and, in particular, to its use as a rationalization for the dominance of capitalism. He believed a more harmonious way of life rooted in cooperation was possible, and he sought to offer a scientific basis to the idea that mutual aid was in fact the natural order of things. Kropotkin accordingly viewed capitalism as an affront to human freedom because it promoted privilege, scarcity, and poverty. Several years spent in Siberia as a young man made a huge impression on Kropotkin, allowing him to directly observe cooperation among both nonhuman animals and prefeudal societies, from which he concluded that mutual aid and voluntary cooperation are the most important factors in the evolution of many species, including humans, by enabling their ability to survive. His time in Siberia instilled in him a very different geographical imagination than that of the Marxists, where he emphasized not the centrality of the industrial worker but the agriculture, local production, and decentralized organization of rural life, allowing him to envision a place for self-sufficiency and question the supposed need for centralized government (Galois 1976). Through his experiences, observations, and travels, Kropotkin also viewed teaching geography, particularly to children, as an exercise in intellectual emancipation insofar as it afforded a means not only to awaken people to "the harmonies of nature" but also to dissipate their nationalist and racist prejudices, a promise that geography still holds (Kropotkin 1885).

Though the intersections between anarchism and geography became less overt as the twentieth century dawned, anarchist ideas remained vital to the philosophical milieu of radical ideas. One of the best examples of such vibrancy is the influence of Emma Goldman, who brought anarchism into direct conversation with feminism and, in doing so, turned a new page for anarchist geographies. Although not a geographer by training, and never directly engaging with geographical thought, other than her deep appreciation of Kropotkin, her focus on those institutional structures of domination that exist beyond the state instilled a heightened focus on the body as a space for radical politics. She was an outspoken opponent to marriage, railed against homophobia, and promoted free love, wherein the question of sexualities, and specifically the freedom to choose, became a primer on liberation (Goldman [1917] 1969). Her concern for the corporeal well-being of the individual extended into a commitment to atheism as a bulwark against "the perpetuation of a slave society" and the false promises of heaven, a view of free speech as an essential component of social change, and a understanding of prisons as the extension of an economic system committed, not to justice, but to penalizing the poor (Goldman [1923] 1996, 233). Near the end of her life, Goldman traveled to Spain to support the anarchist revolution, where, between 1936 and 1939, a peasant and worker's movement took control of Barcelona and large areas of rural Spain, collectivizing the land and implementing anarchist organizing principles (Goldman 2006). These events demonstrated to the world that anarchism could work in practice, and the Spanish case is still invoked by anarchists as one of the movement's most successful moments (Ealham 2010).

Two decades after Goldman's death in 1940, Murray Bookchin resurrected the environmental focus of Reclus, developing his anarchist critiques into what he dubbed "social ecology," which views ecological problems as inextricably bound to and often as the result of social problems. In 1962 Bookchin published an impassioned critique of various environmental ills with *Our Synthetic Environment*. Although it received little attention because of its radicalism, the book predated Rachel Carson's ([1962] 2002) watershed *Silent Spring* by several months. Strongly influenced by the ethical naturalism of Reclus and Kropotkin, throughout the 1960s, Bookchin promoted his libertarian and ecological ideas among the counterculture movements of the time through a series of pioneering essays later compiled in *Post-scarcity Anarchism* (Bookchin [1971] 2004). Colin Ward also published a number of influential works around this time, including *Anarchy in Action* (Ward [1973] 2001), *Housing: An Anarchist Approach* (Ward 1976), and his most well known book, *Child in the City* (Ward [1978] 1990), which once again demonstrated the importance of geography to anarchist practice and thought. The majority of Ward's writings concentrated on issues of housing and planning laws, which he critiqued as circumscribing people's ability to care and provide for themselves. Proudhon and Kropotkin had a clear influence on the solutions Ward proposed, with recommendations philosophically rooted in autonomous, nonhierarchical forms of solidarity that overturned authoritarian methods of sociospatial organization (White and Wilbert 2011).

THE ROLE OF ANARCHISM IN RADICAL GEOGRAPHY

In the wake of the quantitative revolution, some geographers had begun to notice the anarchist currents happening outside and on the margins of the discipline. The publication of the first issue of *Antipode: A Radical Journal of Geography* announced the arrival of a new ethic in human geography, concerned not with Stochastic models, inferential statistics, and econometrics but rather with qualitative approaches that placed the actual lived experiences of human beings at the center of its methodological focus. Positivist geographies were critiqued on the basis of their being but one single version in a multitude of other possible ways of knowing and being in the world, limited in their own narrow outlook by methods of inquiry that predetermined what questions were even worthwhile asking (Galois

1976). Within this atmosphere, Marxist and feminist critiques quickly found a place within an emerging radical geography. Yet anarchism also played a key role in its foundations, as the epistemological critique that radical geography offered in many ways mirrored anarchist evaluations of the state, which was interpreted as but one possible form of organization within an infinite number of alternative spatial arrangements. It is perhaps unsurprising, then, that Richard Peet (1975), founding editor of *Antipode*, was so inspired by Kropotkin that he argued radical geography should adopt his anarchocommunism as its point of departure. Kropotkin's work was similarly embraced by Myrna Breitbart (1975), who argued against the privation of the majority through a reading of the organization of human landscapes, which were said to unfairly advantage a privileged minority rather than being established through principles that benefit everyone.

A few years later, Breitbart (1978a) organized a special issue on anarchism and the environment for *Antipode*, explicitly placing anarchist ideas at the center of radical geography. The issue demonstrated the ongoing influence of anarchist thought and practice on geography as well as geography's influence on anarchism. Included in the issue were explorations of worker collectivization and spatial practices during the Spanish Revolution, including how such alternative organizational impulses influenced a new generation of left-libertarianism within contemporary Spanish politics (Amsden 1978; Breitbart 1978b; Garcia-Ramon 1978; Golden 1978). The inner workings of an anarchist community within Paterson, New Jersey, around 1900 were also unpacked in detail, which enabled readers to draw some comparisons with the Spanish case (Carey 1978). Reclus and Kropotkin received accolades in the issue, as Gary Dunbar conveyed the importance of Reclus's geographical vision for freedom, while G. M. Horner teased out the implications of Kropotkin's anarchogeography on the spatial organization of cities and Richard Peet explored the ethics of Kropotkin's work in relation to the sociospatiality of decentralization as a means to achieve a geography of human liberation. Kropotkin's essay "What Geography Ought to Be" was also reprinted in this special issue, along with Bookchin's "Ecology and Revolutionary Thought," which signaled the enduring value of anarchist writings and their relevance to the radical geographical thought that was emerging at the time (Dunbar 1978; Horner 1978; Peet 1978; Kropotkin 1885; Bookchin [1965] 1978).

The newsletter of the Union of Socialist Geographers also published a short themed section on anarchist geographies in 1978, arising from an informal ten-week reading–discussion group comprising students and faculty members that took place at the University of Minnesota in 1976. This included an opening essay that reviewed and critiqued key works by Kropotkin, Ward, and Bookchin, among others, which were read by the Minnesota group (Lauria 1978); a paper that sought to remind readers "how ignorant and fearful our colleagues and friends are to [anarchist] ideas" and delineate some possible future directions to the study of anarchism from a geographical perspective (Pissaria 1978, 6); and an article that considered the degree to which anarchist organization might be (im)possible given the scale and complexity of contemporary social relations and political economic forms (Porter 1978). Although the themed issue had a limited audience and life-span given its newsletter status, it demonstrates the keen interest in anarchism that was brewing among radical geographers working at that time. The Minnesota group and the efforts of *Antipode* were important moments of reflection and indicated a sense of optimism toward the potential of anarchist ideas to reinvigorate a collective geographical practice that was increasingly turning its attention toward social justice. Unfortunately, these progressive encounters between early radical geographers and anarchism were short-lived, quickly eclipsed by the voluminous efforts of those working within the Marxist and feminist schools of critique. So while Kropotkin offered "a radical vision more ecological and less state-centric than the Marxism that drove the countercultural agenda in Anglo-American geography," Gerry Kearns (2009b, 58) notes that "the anarchist critique of Marxism was never developed with either the theoretical or empirical force of its radical rival and thus these dimensions are still underdeveloped in modern radical geography."

The 1980s saw significantly fewer anarchist writings within geography. If one were to speculate on the reasons for this, the muted optimism and decline of the New Left that coincided with the rise of Thatcherism in the United Kingdom and Reaganomics in the United States stand out as likely explanations. Nonetheless, the decade when neoliberalism really began to rear its ugly head did see the publication of Bookchin's ([1982] 2005) magisterial *The Ecology of Freedom,* in which he sought to unite what he viewed as the domination of nature with social hierarchy, weaving political, anthropological, psychological, scientific, and geographical themes into a single narrative. With globalization making its way into vernacular to arguably become the buzzword of the decade, the political happenings of the 1980s gave rise to some introspective reflection within geography. Important geographers from the past, such as Halford Mackinder, Ellen Churchill Semple, Ellsworth Huntington, Isaiah Bowman, and Thomas Holdich, were not spared by Jim MacLaughlin (1986), who argued that their work had contributed to a persistent ethnocentrism and state centricity within geography, wherein Kropotkin and Reclus were once again invoked in exhorting geographers to abandon the inherited prejudices of the discipline and begin exploring alternatives to the state. The 1990s fared little better in terms of the number of geographers actively exploring the potential of anarchist geographies. Cook and Pepper offered a notable exception, having organized a special issue of the short-lived journal *Contemporary Issues in Geography and Education,* in which the legacy of Kropotkin was once again uncovered (Cook and Pepper 1990; Cook 1990; Pepper 1990). But so too was Goldman's relevance treated to a geographical reading, while the spatialities of anarchist communes and community experiences were explored, and even Ward and Breitbart contributed papers on the potentialities of anarchism within urban life (Newman 1990; Hardy 1990; Rigby 1990; Ward 1990a; Breitbart 1990). Elsewhere, Paul Routledge's (1998, 2003a) concept of antigeopolitics started to fill in the anarchist gap in the geographical literature in the late 1990s; although he never explicitly connected this concept to anarchism, a focus on counterhegemonic struggle and the "assertion of permanent independence from the state" (245) resonated strongly with anarchist ideas.

THE NEW ANARCHIST GEOGRAPHIES

Richard White and Colin Williams (2012, 1639) have persuasively argued that "a core element of geography must (at all levels) turn towards its anarchist roots once more, dedicate resources not only to de-mystifying the anarchist tradition, but where relevant and possible, engaging directly with the (new) challenges and critiques that anarchism extols as a political and social ideology." It is in this spirit of seeking new forms of organization and greater clarity on anarchism's potential that anarchist geographies have been revitalized as of late, emphasizing a DIY ethos of autonomy, direct action, radical democracy, and noncommodification. Attending to the radical possibilities of DIY culture in particular, Keith Halfacree (1999) argued that such an outlook serves as an important case in thinking through how theory and practice should be considered complementary, wherein he uses the occupation of derelict land to illustrate these connections. The Trapese Collective (2007) has similarly argued from an anarchistic perspective on the importance of a DIY approach to everyday geographies in transforming our lives. Elsewhere, Paul Chatterton (2002) has argued in favor of squatting as a legitimate spatial practice of taking control of one's own life. Within these accounts is a decidedly autonomous focus that clearly draws inspiration from anarchist thought, particularly Hakim Bey's (1991b) account of "temporary autonomous zones," which are impermanent spaces that arise in response to sociopolitical action that eludes formal structures of hierarchical control. Jenny Pickerill and Paul Chatterton (2004) adopted a similar approach when they advanced what they dubbed "autonomous geographies" in attempting to think through how spectacular protest and everyday life might be productively combined to enable alternatives to capitalism. Autonomous geographies were conceived in a decidedly anarchistic sense, insofar as they are considered as spaces in which a desire to constitute collectivist, noncapitalist, and antinormative forms of solidarity and affinity come to the fore. The resonance with Routledge's (2003b, 2009b) work should not go unnoticed, as his notion of convergence space as a conceptual aid in appreciating how grassroots networks and activists come together through multiscalar political action to produce a relational ethics of struggle is also inspired by a broadly anarchistic outlook.

Within these accounts, the explicitly anarchist tactic of direct action is either explicitly advocated or implied. Other geographers have similarly attended to direct action, appreciating the overtly geographical implications of this form of political activism, while anthropologist David Graeber's recent ethnography of direct action has many resonances with contemporary geographical theory and its increasing tendency to liberate epistemological and ontological views from the illusion of disinterested objectivity (Anderson 2004; Heynen 2010; Graeber 2009b). Direct action as method involves an impassioned political commitment to our area of study, an affective embrace of those actors who are struggling against domination, and a willingness to resist alongside them (Autonomous Geographies Collective 2010). The geography of direct action itself typically plays itself out in public space, where an anarchist approach that calls for a more comprehensive radicalization of democracy in critiquing the punitive and technocratic circumscriptions that neoliberal policy reforms place on nonhierarchical and noninstitutional forms of political engagement can be seen as particularly productive. Such concerns for public space are highlighted in the works of anarchists such as Jeff Ferrell and Randal Amster, who both embrace nonviolent activism in their respective accounts of resisting the revanchism of urban order and the ongoing criminalization of the homeless (Ferrell 2001; Amster 2008). An appeal to nonmonetization frames much of this recent work, which is openly adopted by Chris Carlsson through the concept of "Nowtopia," which signifies the potential utopia of the present moment that comes when people abandon capitalism in their everyday lives (Carlsson 2008; Carlsson and Manning 2010). Though such radical critiques are novel in the current conjuncture where capitalism represents a powerful conceptual prison that attempts to lock in a singular way of being in the world, some of my own recent work demonstrates historical and contemporary precedents in drawing parallels between anarchist views on noncommodification and the traditional landholding practices of rural and indigenous peoples, particularly Cambodians (Springer 2013). In critiquing forced evictions as a particularly malevolent form of ongoing primitive accumulation in Cambodia, I employ a Proudhon-inspired reading of property that positions anarchism as the only meaningful form of postcolonialism insofar as it recognizes the authority, hierarchies, and violence of the modern state as tantamount to the colonial state (Springer 2015).

Inspired by the ongoing analytic power and transformative potential of anarchist theories and practices, two new special issues on anarchist geographies have recently emerged in *Antipode* and *ACME: An International E-Journal for Critical Geographies* (Springer et al. 2012b; Clough and Blumberg 2012). The issues bring together a diverse range of anarchist perspectives, theoretical concerns, and practical approaches, while the latter also includes attempts to bridge anarchist and autonomist Marxist geographies (Mudu 2012). Other themes that emerge in the issues are territoriality and how an anarchist perspective offers a more emancipatory conceptualization through reimagining space via a prefigurative politics (Ince 2012); a critique of the oppositional practice of dumpster diving and the ways in which it remains at least partially entangled with capitalism (Crane 2012); and a reinterpretation of existing economic landscapes, where mutual aid can be read as integral to our current modes of organization, demonstrating how anarchist geographies actually inform everyday patterns of human activity (White and Williams 2012). Jeff Ferrell (2012) develops a geographical theory of "drift," wherein those groups set adrift by neoliberalism in a sea of alienation, political expulsion, forced removal, and marginalization might use anarchist tactics to drift closer together and therein undo the prescribed spatiopolitical order. Heynen and Rhodes (2012) address the influence of civil rights–era organizing on the formation of Black Anarchism and how both contributed to antiauthoritarian politics and possibilities. Considering indigenous and anarchist geographies as both harmonizing and dissonant, Barker and Pickerill (2012) encourage activists to complement rather than attempt to replicate indigenous relationships to place, therein allowing for stronger alliances. Nathan Clough (2012) focuses on the actual practice of anarchist organizing, examining "affective structures" of the radical politics wherein social struggle is engaged through both direct action and the emotional organizing principle of affinity, a field of interaction that itself becomes the focus of contestation. Farhang Rouhani (2012a; 2012b) has papers in both issues, where he outlines how pedagogical approaches within geography could potentially engage with anarchist ideas in reimagining the educational landscape and offers a mapping of the connections between anarchist and queer geographies. Mark Purcell (2012) critiques Richard Day's contention that anarchism has not been taken seriously enough in radical scholarship by arguing that, at least as far as radical geography is concerned, the influence of Foucault, Deleuze, and Guattari has fostered a strong "anarchistic" sensibility, even if it is not immediately recognized as anarchist. The *Antipode* issue also includes Uri Gordon's (2012, 1742) reflections on anarchist geographies, where he urges scholars operating within the "anarchademic enterprise" to think through their revolutionary strategies and question whether adopting a postanarchist lens requires us to abandon strategy as a valid category for our struggles. The obvious implication of these two special issues is that anarchist geographies are once again on the upswing.

THE FREEDOM OF GEOGRAPHY

As a testament to the lasting legacy of Élisée Reclus and Peter Kropotkin, both men received entries in the *International Encyclopedia of Human Geography* (Clark 2009; Kearns 2009b), while their visions of freedom continue to be raised by contemporary geographers. For example, in employing Kropotkin's theory of mutual aid, Shaun Huston (1997) used an explicitly geographical approach to bring the importance of a spatial focus to the attention of anarchists in the journal *Anarchist Studies*. Kenneth Hewitt (2001) brought some much-needed mainstream recognition to the work of Kropotkin, delivering a keynote address to the Canadian Association of Geographers that explored the salience of Kropotkin's commitment to the vulnerable in the context of ongoing state violence and human rights violations. Gerry Kearns (2004, 337) examines how the progressive geographical imagination of Kropotkin contrasted sharply with the colonial vision of Halford Mackinder, suggesting that anarchism and imperialism "were the political pivot around which contesting geographies were organized" at the end of the nineteenth century. Even more recently, Federico Ferretti (2011) alerted us to the enormous collection of correspondence between Reclus and Kropotkin that is held by the State Archive of the Russian Federation and to the significance of these letters in aiding contemporary historical geographers in better understanding the relationships between geography, politics, and public education and the role of heterodox geographers in the construction of geographical knowledge. Such renewed attention to these historical figures is, of course, to be welcomed, as the implications of their work continue to resonate within geography more than a century after their deaths. Yet what is needed now is not simply a view toward the past but a view toward the future, wherein a sustained focus on developing theory in relation to anarchist geographies and ongoing investigations of actually existing geographies of anarchism in practice may breathe new life into the profound contributions anarchism might yet make to geography, and vice versa. As Myrna Breitbat (2009, 115) argues, the contemporary challenge "is the same as that posed by Kropotkin a century ago: the need for geography to reinvigorate active exploration of local environments as a means of fostering more critical social analysis, developing more effective networks of resistance, and spurring the creative incubation of alternative social and work environments to meet real needs and unmet desires." Though this work is already under way, and the recent special issues on anarchist geographies in *Antipode* and *ACME* are welcome indications that anarchism is still a relevant political theory and a viable approach to thinking about and practicing geography (Clough and Blumberg 2012; Springer et al. 2012b), there is much more work yet to be done.

A range of contemporary issues—from the overt uprisings of the Arab Spring and the Occupy Wall Street movement; to the spectacle of street theater, Critical Mass bicycle rides, radical samba, and Reclaim the Streets parties; to the subversive resistance of monkeywrenching, tree sitting, rooftop occupations, and culture jamming; to lifestyle choices of dumpster diving, unschooling, and squatting; to the mutual aid activities of child-minding co-ops, community kitchens and gardens, building coalitions, and freecycling; to the organizing capabilities of microradio, infoshops, book fairs, and Indymedia—all have decidedly spatial implications, and each would accordingly stand to benefit from analyses that employ an explicitly anarchogeographical perspective. Similarly, on the more theoretical side of things, anarchism has much to contribute to enhancing geographical knowledge, where themes such as state theory and sovereignty; capital accumulation, land rights, and property relations; gentrification, homelessness, and housing; environmental justice and sustainability; industrial restructuring and labor geographies; policing, fear of crime, and critical legal geographies; agrarian transformation and landlessness; urban design and aesthetics; critical geopolitics and antigeopolitics; more-than-human geographies and nonrepresentational theory; activism and social justice; geographies of debt and economic crisis; community, belonging, and the politics of place; geographies of war and peace; community planning and participation; informal economies, livelihoods, and vulnerability; cultural imperialism and identity politics; biopolitics and governmentality; postcolonial and postdevelopment geographies; situated knowledges and alternative epistemologies; and the manifold implications of society–space relations all seem particularly well suited to a more overt infusion of anarchist ideas, and where new research insights and agendas might productively arise. Notwithstanding, and in reflection upon Gordon's (2012) valuable critique, one of the potentially most fruitful directions for a reinvigoration of anarchism within geographical theory would be for geographers to begin working with some of the progressive developments that have been occurring in what has been called "postanarchism" (May 1994; Newman 2010; Rousselle and Evren 2011) and its attempted merger of poststructuralist and anarchist thought. This is an area of inquiry that I've begun exploring from a geographical perspective within my own work (Springer 2015), but there is significant scope for more geographers to weigh in.

The sheer diversity of the topics that geographers could potentially engage from an anarchist perspective speaks to the notion that the discipline of geography is highly undisciplined. Historically, this has been a reason for much second-guessing and an inferior sense of self among some geographers, spawning movements like the quantitative revolution, which was an attempt to "rein geography in" so that it would conform more to the prevalent scientific order of things (Barnes 2009). Yet, in the current moment, as Marxist, feminist, and poststructuralist critiques have gained a firm foothold in contemporary geographical theory, many geographers increasingly recognize that such openness and variation should be embraced as one of geography's great strengths. As an undergraduate, it was the unrestricted versatility of the discipline that first attracted me to geography. Employing a geographical approach to me always meant that I was free to explore whatever my interests were, without having to conform to a particular way of doing things. My experiences as a student left me with a real sense that geography was not so much about reinscribing borders, reinforcing territories, and reifying demarcations as it was about critically interrogating the limits of our geographical imaginations so that we might be liberated from the spatial circumscriptions of our own collective making. So while the geography of freedom was at the center of anarchist theory in the past (Fleming 1988), in the present, it is the freedom of geography that positions the discipline as an ideal location from which to explore the ongoing relevance and potential of anarchist thought and practice.

2
What Geography Still Ought to Be

We, "frightful Anarchists" as we are, know only one way of
establishing peace and goodwill among women and men—
the suppression of privilege and the recognition of right.... It
pleases us not to live if the enjoyments of life are to be for us
alone.... It is sweeter for us to wander with the wretched and
the outcasts than to sit, crowned with roses, at the banquets
of the rich. We are weary of these inequalities which make us
the enemies of each other; we would put an end to the furies
which are ever bringing people into hostile collision, and all of
which arise from the bondage of the weak to the strong under
the form of slavery, serfage and service. After so much hatred
we long to love each other, and for this reason are we enemies
of private property and despisers of the law.
—**Élisée Reclus**

Anarchism is a maligned political philosophy; of this there can be no
doubt. Typically anarchism is portrayed as a chaotic expression of violence
perpetrated against the supposedly peaceable "order" of the state. Yet such
depictions misrepresent the core of anarchist thought, which is properly
understood as the rejection of all forms of domination, exploitation, and
"archy" (systems of rule), hence the word *an-archy* (against systems of
rule). Anarchism is a theory and practice that seeks to produce a society
wherein individuals may freely cooperate as equals in every respect, not
before a law or sovereign guarantee—which enters new forms of authority,
imposed criteria of belonging, and rigid territorial bindings—but before
themselves in solidarity and mutual respect. Consequently, anarchism
opposes all systems of rule or forms of archy (i.e., hierarchy, patriarchy,
monarchy, adultarchy, oligarchy, anthroparchy, etc.) and is instead premised upon cooperative and egalitarian forms of social, political, and
economic organization, where ever-evolving and autonomous spatialities

may flourish. Although it has often been said that there are as many anarchisms as there are anarchists, my contention is that anarchism should embrace an ethic of nonviolence precisely because violence is recognized as both an act and process of domination.

Violence has formed the basis of many historical anarchist movements, and it would be disingenuous simply to wish away this constituent as somehow "nonanarchist." Yet before anarchists such as Paul Brousse, Johann Most, Errico Malatesta, and Alexander Berkman popularized revolutionary violence and propaganda of the deed, earlier anarchists (or proto-anarchists) such as William Godwin, Pierre-Joseph Proudhon, Henry David Thoreau, and Leo Tolstoy rejected violence as a justifiable means to overthrow the tyranny of the state. From its outset, anarchism accordingly sympathized with nonviolence, which was reflected in the *Peaceful Revolutionist,* a weekly paper edited by Josiah Warren in 1833 and the first anarchist periodical ever produced (Bailie 1906). That anarchism has since become derided as a *direct* synonym for violence—rather than acknowledged as an ideology that has at times engaged both violence *and* nonviolence—speaks to the discursive buttressing of the status quo against alternative sociospatial and political economic formations and to the limited geopolitical imagination or ideological indoctrination of those who either cannot or simply refuse to conceive of a world without states. Yet the originary critique of anarchism is that the state is tantamount to violence, or as Godwin ([1793] 1976, 380) put it, "above all we should not forget, that government is an evil, an usurpation upon the private judgment and individual conscience of [hu]mankind." Kropotkin ([1898] 2002, 144) expressed similar ideas when he argued that "if you wish, like us, that the entire liberty of the individual and, consequently, his [or her] life be respected, you are necessarily brought to repudiate the government of man by man, whatever shape it assumes; you are forced to accept the principles of Anarchy that you have spurned so long. You must then search with us the forms of society that can best realize that ideal and put an end to all the violence that rouses your indignation."

Given the postcolonial view that contemporary human geography now espouses, radical geographers would do well to think more critically about how acceptance of the state actually recapitulates the violence of colonial modes of thought and practice. In reinvigorating the potential of anarchist geographies and in realizing the critical praxis anarchism demands, my feeling is that nonviolence should be understood as an ideal for anarchists to live into (Baldelli 1971). This is the story of anarcho-feminist Emma Goldman, who, in her younger years, flirted with violence but eventually came to reject it (Goldman [1923] 1966, 253):

> The one thing I am convinced of as I have never been in my life is that the gun decides nothing at all. Even if it accomplishes what it sets out to do—which it rarely does—it brings so many evils in its wake as to defeat its original aim.

Thus if anarchism is positioned against the state, and in particular the monopolization, institutionalization, and codification of violence that such a spatial organization represents, then it should follow that anarchism offers an alternative geographical imagination that refuses violent means. Again, as established in the introduction, a nonviolent position does not forego resistance and self-defense.

I begin this chapter by exploring how geographers have taken up anarchist thought. Specifically, I argue that although anarchism factored heavily into the radicalization of human geography in the 1970s, this early promise was quickly eclipsed by Marxism, which has (along with feminism) since become a cornerstone of contemporary radical geography. The following section problematizes the utilitarianism—or means to an end character—of Marxian thought, which is argued to reiterate the colonial precepts Marxism ostensibly seeks to disrupt. Anarchism is presented as a preferable alternative insofar as it disavows nationalism and recognizes that there is no fundamental difference between colonization and state making other than the scale upon which these parallel projects operate, meaning that any substantively "postcolonial" positionality must also be "poststatist" or anarchic. Next I seek to provide a partial answer to the question of alternatives to the state and how new forms of voluntary human organization might be enabled to blossom. Rather than advancing a revolutionary imperative, I encourage an embrace of the immediacy of the *here* and *now* as the most emancipatory spatiotemporal dimension, precisely because it is the location and moment in which we actually live our lives. I also take neoliberalism's illusion of state dissolution head-on at this stage and remind readers that "small government" is still government, so although the rationalities, strategies, technologies, and techniques of neoliberal governance are new, the disciplinary logic of the state remains unchanged. In concluding the chapter, I offer some thoughts on the future of radical geography and in particular where I think anarchist geographies can provoke a more liberationist framework that potentially breaks from both the discursive formations of neoliberalism and the limitations of Marxism vis-à-vis contemporary oppositional struggles.

To reiterate, anarchist geographies are understood here as kaleidoscopic spatialities that accomodate multiple, nonhierarchical, and protean connections between autonomous entities. Solidarities, bonds, and affinities that are volunatarily assembled are anarchist geographies insofar as they are positioned in opposition to and free from the presence of sovereign violence, predetermined norms, and assigned categories of belonging. Through such rejection of the multivariate apparatuses of domination, this chapter, and indeed this book, can be read as a proverbial call to nonviolent arms for those geographers and nongeographers alike who seek to put an end to the seemingly endless series of tragedies, misfortunes, and catastrophes that characterize the miasma and malevolence of the current neoliberal moment. But this is not simply a demand for the end of neoliberalism and its replacement with a more moderate and humane version of capitalism, nor does it merely insist upon a more egalitarian version of the state. It is instead a condemnation of capitalism and the state in whatever guise they might adopt; an indictment of all manner of exploitation, manipulation, and domination of humanity; a disavowal of the privations of the majority and the privileges of the minority that have hitherto and by common consent been called "order"; and the resurrection of a prosecution within geography that dates back to the discipline's earliest days. This is nothing more and nothing less than a renewed call for anarchism.

FOR ANARCHIST GEOGRAPHIES

"Many critical scholars probably take some aspects of anarchist thought for granted, but there has been very little development of the tradition within geography in the last 100 years," write Blunt and Wills (2000, 38). "Yet as many people have questioned the basis of so-called 'grand theory' and any claims to universal explanatory ideas," they continue, "we might expect anarchism to come into its own." In light of Kropotkin's and Reclus's foundational contributions to the discipline of geography

(Breitbart 1981; Dunbar 1978; Horner 1978), and anarchism's important role in the emergence of a more radical geographical praxis (Breitbart 1978b; Peet 1978), it is indeed surprising that this vibrant intellectual tradition has, until recently, been largely ignored by geographers since the late 1970s. Writing at the height of geography's infatuation with co-lonialism during the late nineteenth and early twentieth centuries, and in stark contrast to contemporaries such as David Livingstone, Halford Mackinder, and Friedrich Ratzel, who spent their days advancing an imperialist vision for the discipline (Godlewska and Smith 1994; Kearns 2009a), Kropotkin and Reclus each possessed a resolute antiauthoritar-ian imagination. Kropotkin's theory of the voluntary reciprocal exchange of resources for common benefit, or "mutual aid," was a direct challenge to the social Darwinism found in the writings of Mackinder, Ratzel, and, in particular, biologist Thomas Henry Huxley (1888) in his essay "The Struggle for Existence" (Kinna 1992). "They came to conceive of the animal world as a world of perpetual struggle among half-starved individuals, thirsting for one another's blood," Kropotkin ([1902] 2008, 3) writes in his magnum opus, *Mutual Aid*.

> They made modern literature resound with the war cry of woe to the vanquished, as if it were the last word of modern biology. They raised the "pitiless" struggle for personal advantages to the height of a biological principle which [hu]man[s] must submit to as well, under the menace of otherwise succumbing in a world based upon mutual extermination.

In arguing that the reality of mutual aid among nonhuman animals un-dermined the naturalistic arguments for capitalism, war, and imperialism that dominated geographical thought at the time, like the social Dar-winists, but in precisely the opposite way, Kropotkin sought to find in nature the social form he wanted to legitimate in society (Kearns 2004). Geography was accordingly to be conceived not as a program for imperial hubris but as a means of dissipating prejudice and realizing cooperation between communities (Kropotkin 1885).

Like his friend and ally Kropotkin, the anarchist vision of Reclus was similarly rooted in geography. Reclus advanced an integral approach wherein every phenomenon, including humanity, was conceived as insepa-rable from other living beings and geographical features of the land itself

(Clark 1997). Earth was accordingly interpreted as a unified whole, where any coherent account of the world required a simultaneous recognition of all the multiple interconnecting factors. For Reclus (1905; qtd. in quoted in Clark and Martin 2004, 5), "it is only through an act of pure abstraction that one can contrive to present a particular aspect of the environment as if it had a distinct existence, and strive to isolate it from all the others, in order to study its essential influence." Although the focus here was the "natural" system, the holism of Reclus's work actually demanded that social phenomena be considered as imbued within and co-constitutive of the natural "universal geography" he envisioned (see Reclus 1894). For Reclus, the preceding quote had as much relevance to the prevailing ideas of human organization, whether Marxian or neoclassical, as it did to nature, which hints at the limitations of these two economic theories. Yet, while Reclus's ideas of integrality inspired the social ecology of Murray Bookchin (1990a) and other strands of the radical environmentalist movement, the political implications of his work with respect to human organization have been essentially overlooked by geographers for more than a century. His continuing political significance, Clark and Martin (2004) argue, comes in large part from his egalitarian vision of a "globalization from below" based on the integrality he revealed and promoted, which offers a theoretical alternative to the dominant corporate and statist versions of globalization. In contrast to our present moment of a world divided into "haves" and "have-nots," wherein the geography of access to capital largely adheres to the peaks and valleys of the Westphalian system, Reclus (1905) envisioned a free and stateless world with "its center everywhere, its periphery nowhere" (qtd. in Clark and Martin 2004, 4).

While contemporary human geography has appropriately moved on from appeals to science as the *sine qua non* of "truth," retaining Reclus's and Kropotkin's skepticism for and challenges to the dominant ideologies of the day has much to offer contemporary geographical scholarship and its largely unreflexive acceptance of the civilizational, legal, and capitalist discourses that converge around the state. The perpetuation of the idea that human spatiality necessitates the formation of states is writ large in a discipline that has derided the "territorial trap," on one hand (see Agnew 1994; Brenner 1999), yet, on the other hand, has confoundingly refused to take the state-centricity critique in the direction of state dissolution.

Contemporary geographers have accordingly failed to engage the emancipatory potential of anarchist praxis, largely overlooking contributions from Hakim Bey (1991b), Murray Bookchin (1990a), and Pierre Clastres ([1989] 2007) on the importance of alternative configurations *to* the state, favoring instead discussions surrounding alternative configurations *of* the state, particularly by way of Marxian theory. In its present form, such concern focuses on explaining how neoliberalizing processes facilitate state transformation and endurance (see Agnew 2009; Harvey 2005; Peck 2001), offering a counterpoint to popular commentaries that globalization is eroding the state and producing a borderless world that signifies the end of both history and geography (see Fukuyama 1992; O'Brien 1992). In other words, while neoclassical-cum-neoliberal ideas have been vigorously debated and discredited by geographers working from broadly Marxian perspectives, contemporary geography has not seen anarchist critiques of Marxism develop with the same theoretical and empirical force of its radical rival, an endeavor long overdue.

Although still very much underrepresented in the geographical literature, recent contributions from Paul Chatterton (2002), Keith Halfacree (1999), Nik Heynen (2010), and Anthony Ince (2010b) offer welcome interventions that point toward the continuing promise of anarchist ideas in both theory and practice. As welcome as these engagements are, there is still a great deal of theoretical terrain yet to be explored by geographers. In particular, I am thinking of the profound contributions being made by scholars working outside of geography, such as Lewis Call (2002), Todd May (1994), Saul Newman (2010), and Rousselle and Evren (2011) on the possibilities and potential of postanarchism. While poststructuralist ideas are now commonplace in the discipline, human geographers have—with few exceptions (see Brown 2007; Springer 2015)—failed to explore the potential of postanarchist thought.[1] Postanarchism is not a movement beyond anarchism but a renewal of anarchist ideas through the infusion of poststructuralist theory, thus allowing us to retain an emancipatory spirit, while abandoning appeals to science and the essentializing epistemologies and ontologies that characterize "classical" anarchist thought. It is incumbent upon radical geographers to begin examining the contemporary importance of anarchist action and postanarchist theories in resisting capitalism rather than simply recapitulating those state-centric, road-to-nowhere arguments that call for more equitable distributions of power *within* the state. The state, after all, in the classic anarchist critique, is a hierarchical institution premised on deference to authority. As ostensibly "nonanarchist" thinkers like Giorgio Agamben (1998) and Walter Benjamin ([1921] 1986) have recognized, it is precisely because of the state's juridico-sovereign character that it can never actually be egalitarian. And so geographers should be keen to ask, where do supposedly liberationist arguments that continue to embrace the state leave us, except with the structures of hierarchy and domination firmly in place?

While not the sole concern of anarchists, the state nonetheless forms the primary locus of anarchist thought. Although Marxists have increasingly questioned the logic of state power, it is beyond the scope of this chapter to develop a taxonomy that situates precisely where the multiple variants of Marxian thought sit with respect to the state. At the risk of oversimplifying the complexity of the intersections between the two principal alternatives of socialist thought, it is nonetheless fair to say that the question of the state is the originary differentiation between Marxism and anarchism. Indeed, the main division between anarchism and Marxism emerged from differences in opinion over the degree of autonomy afforded to the workers in the postrevolutionary conjuncture and the closely related question of the monopoly of violence. Anarchists rejected any such monopoly on the premise that violence is first and foremost the primary dimension of state power and, accordingly, any state, whether controlled by the bourgeoisie or captured by the workers, will inevitably come to function as an instrument of class domination. In contrast, Marxists believed that because a minority class rules most societies prior to socialism, the achievement of a classless society requires the previously disadvantaged class to seize the state and acquire a monopoly over violence. Yet the desire to overturn the state and create a liberated socialist system via despotic power is a contradiction that anarchists disavowed. The related Marxian notion of withering away the state was similarly seen as a contradiction. As Mikhail Bakunin ([1873] 1953, 288) observed,

> if their State is going to be a genuine people's State, why should it then dissolve itself? ... [Marxists] say that this State yoke—the dictatorship—is

a necessary transitional means in order to attain the emancipation of the people: Anarchism or freedom, is the goal, the State or dictatorship is the means. Thus, to free the working masses, it is first necessary to enslave them.

Such noticeable inconsistency appalled anarchists, and during the First International, this discrepancy became the fundamental divide between socialists. Whereas Marxism traditionally represented the statist edge of the socialist political spectrum, or at the very least accepted the state in utilitarian terms as a means to an end through a provisional dictatorship of the proletariat, anarchism has always been the domain of libertarian socialism, rejecting the idea that a realigned state will ever wither and lead to an emancipated condition.

COLONIALISM IS DEAD, LONG LIVE COLONIALISM?

I am not enthusiastic about Marx's own enthusiasm for capitalism. Marx and the classical political economists saw capitalism through a similar celebratory lens; only Marx tempered his view by suggesting that it was a necessary phase to pass through on the way to communism and not a glorious end state, as with the liberal project of Adam Smith. Writing a century later, Bill Warren—arguably one of the most controversial writers within the Marxist tradition—picked up on this tenor of Marx's work. Warren (1980, 136) argued that "imperialism was the means through which the techniques, culture and institutions that had evolved in Western Europe over several centuries—the culture of the Renaissance, the Reformation, the Enlightenment and the Industrial Revolution—sowed their revolutionary seeds in the rest of the world." He correctly interpreted the integral relationship between capitalism and imperialism but painted imperialism as a "necessary evil" on the path toward some greater good. The banality of Warren's depiction of imperialism ensured that his detractors were many, but he was really revisiting the Marxism expressed in *The Communist Manifesto* (Marx and Engels [1848] 2002), in which, although Marx condemned the violence of primitive accumulation, he nonetheless retained a "view of this violent expropriation as necessary for the furthering of human possibilities" (Glassman 2006, 610). Despite finding capitalism morally repugnant, when compared with the feudal mode of production that preceded it, Karl Marx ([1867] 1976) recognized capitalism as having a number of virtues, acknowledging it as amazingly productive, sparking human creativity, igniting awesome technological change, and ushering in potentially democratic forms of government. It is this optimistic side of Marx that Warren (1980) followed in arguing that, at an early stage, capitalism's exploration and inhabitation of new territories were carried out through the guise of colonialism and imperialism and that, though this form of capitalism had drawbacks for those territories that were occupied, it had important benefits as well. Education levels were said to have improved, life expectancy was thought to have increased, and the form of political control was considered more democratic than that which existed before colonialism.

If all of this sounds familiar, it is essentially the same set of discursive principles that presently guide neoliberalization, which David Harvey (2003) has appropriately recognized as a "new imperialism." The refrain is that people have been made better off, and although imperfect in its execution—which is largely blamed on the continuing "interference" of the state in markets—eventually the "trickle-down effect" will bear fruit and the promised utopia will materialize. Rather than wait for the market to sort things out on its own schedule, the difference with Marx is that he wanted to quicken the pace at which an egalitarian social contract is arrived upon through revolution. To be clear, I am not suggesting ideological consonance between Marxism and neoliberalism here but instead seek to illuminate how both rest upon the notion that the state can be used as a means to achieve a "liberated" end. In contrast, an anarchist position rejects the interlocking violence of the state, imperialism, and capitalism outright and is unimpressed with this utilitarian strain of Marxian thought. The means of capitalism and its violences do not justify the eventual end state of communism, nor does this end justify such means. This particular resonance of Marxist thought resembles neoliberalism, where although the utopian end state is conceptualized differently, the penultimate means to achieving the "final product" is virtually the same. Whereas post-Marxists appropriately foreground gender, sex, ethnicity, race, and other ostensibly "noncapitalist" categories as equally important lines of differentiation that mark the hierarchies, inequalities, and violences of our world under neoliberalism (Wright 2006), anarchism goes further by rejecting the substantive violence that is imbricated within and implicitly accepted by Marx's linear approach to history based on "stages of development." As Emma Goldman ([1923] 2003, 260–61) once argued, "there is no greater fallacy than the belief that aims and purposes are one thing, while methods and tactics are another. . . . The means employed become, through individual habit and social practice, part and parcel of the final purpose; they influence it, modify it, and presently the aims and means become identical." Although "Red Emma" was of course an anarchist, such unease with the utilitarianism and essentialism of Marxian thought can similarly be regarded as the genesis of poststructuralism (Peters 2001), which instead focuses on the complexity and heterogeneity of our present condition and refuses totalizing theories through a rejection of absolute "truths."

Although poststructuralist critique has quickly become one of the most vibrant philosophical variants within the discipline, and Foucault, Deleuze, and Lacan have all cultivated critiques within the fertile ground of antistate thinking (May 1994; Newman 2001), contemporary human geography has been slow to engage ideas that call for Leviathan's end. I can only speculate on the reasons for this lacuna, but it seems that the predominance of Marxist ideas has some role to play. Traditional Marxism, and its espousal of statist ideology, is well traversed in the geographical literature, where the influence of Harvey (1973; 1982; 2005; 2009) looms large. Although occasionally lamented by political geographers critical of the limited geopolitical vision state centricity affords (see Johnston 2001; Taylor 1996), statist forms of organization have nonetheless taken on a certain platitude within the discipline. The state is typically either implicitly accepted or not subjected to the type of examination that penetrates its fundamental precepts, even if feminist geographers have helped to redefine the parameters upon which the state is actually conceived (see England 2003; Gibson-Graham 1996; Sharp 2007). Nonetheless, a significant swath of contemporary human geography has raised the question of the state only insofar as to determine how neoliberalism has reconfigured its orientation, with Marxist geographers calling for renewed and reimagined versions of social welfare (Harvey 2005; Peck 2001) and poststructuralist geographers arguing that governmentality renders the state nearly invisible through self-regulating, autocorrecting subjects (Barry, Osborne, and Rose 1996; Larner 2000). The potentiality of the latter to reveal the ongoing force of statist logics and the violence this engenders through altered disciplinary rationalities and mutated techniques of biopolitical control is scarcely realized, to say nothing of poststructuralism's coincidence with anarchist thought (see Newman 2010).

That radical geography retains a decidedly statist focus perhaps also betrays the colonial origins of the discipline itself and a hesitation in breaking from old disciplining habits. Yet the contemporary nation-state, following Benedict Anderson (1991) and Michael Billig (1995), must be understood as a smaller-scale replica of the colonial state. Although differing in their diffusion and distribution across space, both national and colonial state powers express the same violent principles of a privileged few wielding influence over others and imposing a singular identity upon antecedent ways of imagining belonging. Marx was not oblivious to this critique, yet here again he advanced a utilitarian ideal. As capitalism spread around the globe, it gave rise to powerful resistance movements by oppressed workers and peasants—led by vanguards—which Marx believed would eventually engender the transcendence of capitalism. In particular instances, Marx supported nationalist struggles, viewing nationalism as another "stage in development" toward a future workers' internationalism (Lewis 2000). Yet from an anarchist perspective, it is hard to see the emancipatory end when the means are shot through with violence. What "national liberation" actually represents is the trading of one set of elites for another, and thus one form of colonialism for another. Though the territorial expression has been scaled down, the underlying logic remains unchanged. Just as the colonial state sought and was frequently able to impose a monopoly on violence, the struggle to create the nation-state is likewise a struggle for the monopoly of violence (Harris 2004). What is created in both instances—a colonial or national state—is itself a means of violence. In recognizing this congruency—notwithstanding Gillian Hart's (2008, 680) "properly postcolonial frame of understanding" that continues to privilege the state—to be "postcolonial" in any meaningful sense is to also be "poststatist" or anarchic, wherein the hierarchies, order, authority, and violence upon which these parallel state projects have been built are rejected outright. Moreover, internationalism by definition can never actually transcend the state; instead, it continues to presuppose and assume nations. By calling for transgeographical cooperation between nations, Marx's internationalism fails to move beyond the notion of the nation-state as the foundational unit of belonging.

Why, then, has contemporary radical geography not developed an "anticolonial imagination" that rises to the poststatist challenge that Anderson (2005) argues such a vision actually demands? Reclus and Kropotkin demonstrated long ago that geography lends itself well to emancipatory ideas, and "it was no accident that two of the major anarchists of the late Nineteenth Century were also geographers" (Ward 2010, 209). There exists an extraordinary latent potential within contemporary radical geography to become even more radical in its critiques, and thus more liberationist in its focus, by embracing an anarchist ethos. Anarchism is able to recognize capitalism, imperialism, colonialism, neoliberalism, militarism, nationalism, classism, racism, ethnocentrism, Orientalism, sexism, genderism, ageism, childism, ableism, speciesism, homophobia, transphobia, sovereignty, *and* the state as interwoven facets of domination. The mutually reinforcing composition of these various dimensions of "archy" consequently means that to uncritically exempt one from interrogation is to perpetuate this omnicidal conglomeration as a whole. Unlike the circumscriptions of Marxian geography, the promise of anarchist geographies rests precisely in their ability to think integrally and therein refuse to assign priority to any one of the multiple dominating apparatuses, as none is reducible to another (Brown 1996). This means that no one struggle can wait on any other. It's all or nothing, and the a priori privilege of the workers, the vanguards, or any other class over others is to be rejected on the basis of its incipient hierarchy.

IMAGINING ALTERNATIVES

The question of alternatives to the state is foremost in the minds of those skeptical of anarchism. In this vein, David Harvey (2009, 200) asks, "How will the reifications of this anarchist ideal actually work on the ground in absolute space and time?" Although anarchists have theorized multiple possibilities, ranging from collectivist to individualist, syndicalist to mutualist, voluntaryist to communist, I advocate a nondoctrinaire, postanarchist approach, and accordingly, my response is to begin by refusing to offer a prescriptive overview of what forms of social organization I think should be developed. The answer to this question is not to be determined by a single individual but rather collectively through continuous dialogue and ongoing adaptive innovation. In this sense, Harvey's critique of anarchism is problematic on two counts. First, when have space and time ever been "absolute," other than in the reductionist lens of positivism? This assessment belies Harvey's own recognition of the dialectical influence of space and time, expressed as "space-time." Second, he attempts to apply the tenets of Marxian thought and its "stage-based" thinking to a philosophical position that eschews such predetermined linearity. Harvey conceptualizes place making as an end-state politics, which incorrectly positions anarchism as an ostensibly completable *project*—the shared ideal of both Marxism and neoliberalism—rather than appreciating it as a living, breathing, and forever protean *process*. Some may view my restrained position as a copout, but I want to remind readers that any attempt to prescribe a fixed model in isolation from the larger social body recapitulates both the neoliberal project and an authoritarian disposition, as each argues in favor of one way of doing things. It also reinforces the arrogance or ignorance of the so-called expert by presuming to know what is best, without appreciating one's limitations (Mitchell 2002). Even Donna Haraway, as brilliant a thinker as she is, once exposed her own limitations in revealing, "I have almost lost the imagination of what a world that isn't capitalist could look like. And that scares me" (Harvey and Haraway 1995, 519). The same nascent fear should be similarly evoked when one critically reflects upon the state and its seemingly all-consuming pervasiveness. We treat this particular form of hierarchical organization and territorialized dominance as though it is unavoidable, and in doing so, we actively forget that the bulk of the time that humans have existed on planet Earth has been characterized by nonstatist organization. The state is thus no more inevitable than it is needed.

Neoliberalism is particularly virulent inasmuch as it contributes to a new element of our collective forgetting by reconfiguring the state in such a way that facilitates a failure to notice its ongoing deleterious effects (Springer 2010b). The discourse behind this illusion of dissolution attempts to convince us that neoliberalism represents our liberation as individuals, emancipating us from the chains of what it calls "big government." Yet the literature has amply demonstrated that the state continues to matter to neoliberal modalities (see England and Ward 2007; Peck 2001). Likewise, the monopoly of violence the state claims for itself remains just as forceful and oppressive under the disciplinary logic of a neoliberal state as it does under any other state configuration—feel-good moments of ostensible democracy (read "electoral authoritarianism") notwithstanding. What *is* actually lost through neoliberalism's supposed "streamlining" of the state is most obviously the shared social provisions previously afforded to citizens. This "rollback" results in the collapse of social trust, actively anticipating the Hobbesian-cum-Darwinian myth of all against all, where only the strong survive. People are encouraged not to look to each other for support in their everyday transactions or even when the going gets tough but simply to stop being "lazy" and get to work. Neoliberal discourse positions the system itself as being beyond reproach, so any existent "anomalies," such as impoverishment or unemployment, are dismissed as distinctive personal failures. Those who do not "succeed" at this perverse game are easily resolved by the punitive neoliberal state through their criminalization. Incarceration is seen as a more viable solution than addressing the mounting inequalities and ongoing poverty of the majority (Peck 2003). This disciplinary stratagem is particularly debilitating because, for popular power to be realized, the conditions for social cooperation must be present, meaning quite simply that people have to trust each other.

Neoliberalism in particular, and capitalism more generally, works to destroy trust by making us compete with one another and profit from each other's vulnerability. Similarly, the state destroys trust by warning us that *homo homini lupus* will become the rule in the absence of sovereign power (Cohn 2010). To reestablish trust, it would seem that smashing capitalism alone is not enough. In convening a postneoliberal reality— that is, the realization of a context that completely breaks from the current zeitgeist—sovereignty and the state itself must also be dismantled. Doing so, at first glance, appears to raise the problematic of getting from *here* to *there* and from *now* to *then*. Although positioning the idea of revolution as having fallen from view, Neil Smith (2010) instead exemplifies the ongoing infatuation on the Left by suggesting that the recent financial crisis should be the basis upon which the "revolutionary imperative" is renewed. But wanting a global revolution to emerge from the recent economic crisis affords an instrumental role to a single global economic system, which oddly resurrects the neoliberalism-as-monolithism argument (for a critique, see Springer 2010c). This criticism hints at Smith's implicit embrace of the utilitarian role Marx afforded capitalism and colonialism, a position that anarchists find objectionable. While pitying the victims of colonialism, Marx consoled himself with the thought that its far-reaching abuses would only hasten the day when the entire world would be consumed by a single crisis, thus inaugurating the revolutionary swell he so desired. This is an overly passive approach, because if revolution is to result from a capitalist crisis, then this implies a politics of waiting for the day when "all that is solid melts into air" (Marx and Engels [1848] 2002, 223). There is something to be said for Anselme Bellegarrigue's (1848) insistence that "there are, in truth, no worse counter-revolutionaries than revolutionaries; because there are no worse citizens than the envious."

The question of lost trust becomes particularly acute at the moment of "melting," because, as Pierre-Joseph Proudhon ([1864] 2005, 108) warned, there is "danger in waiting until moments of crisis, when passions become unduly inflamed by widespread distress." In the time that has passed since the latest crisis first hit in late 2008, sadly, it has become increasingly obvious just how possible it is—in the absence of trust—for people to accept racist, nationalist, and fundamentalist alternatives. Rather than biding our time in waiting for the levee to break, geographers could instead anarchically embrace the *here* and *now* as the space-time within which our lives are actually lived (see Vaneigem [1967] 2012). Acknowledging the enabling power of this immediacy is emancipatory in itself, as it awakens us to the possibility that we can instantaneously refuse participating in the consumerist patterns, nationalist practices, and hierarchical positionings that confer legitimacy on the existing order and instead engage a DIY culture centered on direct action, noncommodification, and mutual aid (Graeber 2009b; Halfacree 2004; Trapese Collective 2007). In aligning to J. K. Gibson-Graham's (2008) contention that "other worlds" are possible, and to Sara Koopman's (2011) concern for the nonviolent counter-hegemonic struggle of what she calls "alter-geopolitics," the power of *here* and *now* further allows us the freedom to imagine and begin prefiguring the alternative free institutions and voluntary associations that will smooth the transition toward a truly postcolonial–postneoliberal future. Yet the significance of imagining alternatives to the current order is not to establish a fixed program for all time but instead to provide a point of alterity or exteriority as a way of questioning the limits of this order (Newman 2010). As Roger Baldwin (2005, 114) affirms, "these are not dreams for a distant future, nor a stage to be reached when other stages are gone through, but processes of life about us everywhere which we may either advance or hold back." It is only in the precise space and moment of refusal, which is the *here* and *now*, that individuals are self-empowered to chart their own paths, free from the coercive guidance of a sovereign authority or the cajoling influence of a patronizing academic. Where geographers are actually well positioned to contribute, as feminists thinkers have demonstrated (see Lawson 2009; Nolin 2010), is toward the issue of building trust by shattering prejudices and intervening with creative new energies rooted in the nurturing capacity of emotion and everyday life as the actual terrains of human interaction. By engaging the "affective turn" (Thien 2005) in understanding emotional connectivity and the politics of affinity as the fundamental basis upon which any lasting transformation might take place, it is to such intimacy and immediacy that the possibilities of anarchist geographies could be productively dedicated. Rather than prioritizing the particularisms of class, as is the Marxian imperative, or surrendering to the politics of racism, as neoliberalism would have us do (Goldberg 2009), anarchism demands that any process of emancipation be infused with nonuniversalizing, nonhierarchical, and noncoercive relationships based on mutual aid and shared ethical commitments (Day 2005).

Ultimately, what anarchism has to offer is precisely the opposite of neoliberalism. While rescinding the inherent elitism and authoritarianism of the state, anarchism wants to align the collective goods produced through human cooperation according to need, a process that does not require an administrative framework but instead pivots around an ethics of reciprocity. An anarchist perspective further recognizes that the latent new forms of organization that might evolve beyond the territorial logic of the state must exist in a continual process of reflexivity and revision by those practicing them so as to quell any and all potential hierarchies before they can be allowed to germinate. Anarchist geographies of cooperation are to be born from outside the existing *order*, from sites that the state has failed to enclose, and from the infinite possibilities that statist logics ignore, repel, plunder, and deny. As Kropotkin (1887, 153) eloquently explained,

> while all agree that harmony is always desirable, there is no such unanimity about order, and still less about the "order" which is supposed to reign on our modern societies; so that we have no objection whatever to the use of the word "anarchy" as a negation of what has been often described as order.

Anarchist geographies are those potential forces that perpetually haunt the state with the fact that it is merely one sociospatial possibility among an unlimited number of others. Yet alternatives to the state do not arise from the order that they refuse, even if this order is contradictory and oppressive, but from the anarchic profusion of forces that are alien to this order and from those very possibilities that this order seeks to dominate and distort (Colson 2001). Radical geographers accordingly have much to learn from developing deeper connections with those peoples—like the indigenous tribes of Zomia—who have continually outwitted the state and mastered what James C. Scott (2009) calls the "art of not being governed." What is at stake here is neither the end of the state, nor the realization of an end-state politics, but an "infinitely demanding" struggle of perpetual evasion, contestation, and solidarity (Critchley 2007). We are not required to view the state as the exclusive site of sociopolitical change or as the lone focus of a revolutionary paradigm, as have all too often been the historical precedents (Holloway 2002). In the spirit of the epigraph that opens this chapter, we can instead focus our anger and sadness inward, where sustained indignation for our own good fortune can lead to a realignment of our ethical compass, compelling us to stand and refuse alongside others less fortunate than ourselves. Empathy is the death of apathy, and it begins not when the state is streamlined, withered away, or dismembered, but *here* and *now*.

THE RADICAL FUTURE

The etymology of *radical* is from the Latin *radix*, meaning "root." Contemporary radical geographers would do well to explore this originary dimension by (re)engaging with the contributions of Kropotkin and Reclus, who fearlessly critiqued colonial domination at a time when mainstream geography marched hand in hand with the imperialist project. But radical geography today needs more than the insights of the past; it also requires a future, an injection of new ideas that encompass the intellectual strides made by poststructuralist and feminist thought to move beyond what is already "known." Within anarchist studies, the critical edge of this philosophical endeavor is postanarchism, which does not seek to move "past" anarchism but instead rejects the epistemological foundations of "classical" anarchist theories and their adherence to the essentialisms of the scientific method. Postanarchist thought accordingly seeks to reinvigorate anarchist critique by expanding its conception of domination from the state and capitalism to encompass the circuitous, overdetermined, and multivariate networks that characterize contemporary power and by removing its normative and "naturalist" frames in embracing situated and empathetic knowledges. Applying this philosophical critique to radical geography today requires one to make a conscious ethical and emotional choice, "whether to be allied with the stability of the victors and rulers, or—the more difficult path—to consider that stability as a state of emergency threatening the less fortunate with the danger of complete extinction" (Said 1993, 26). To choose the latter requires a sustained effort to shatter the "commonsense" spell of neoliberal governmentality, as government is not merely the political structures or management protocols of the state but the government of the conduct of individuals and groups; it is "to structure the possible field of action of others," their *direction* and their *location* (Foucault 1982, 790).

This is a process many geographers are already engaging through attention to the entanglements of power (Crampton and Elden 2007; Sharp et al. 2000) and participatory action research (Kindon, Pain, and Kesby 2007), and through nonrepresentational theory (Thrift 2007), but without explicitly connecting them back to the anarchist critique. Yet if the mercurial horizons of space-time ensure that our lived experiences are continual performances that defy the theoretical divisions of predetermined identities and codified subjectivities, then what is more "realistic" than acknowledging the perpetually unfolding means of anarchism? Anarchist geographies would thus ideally seek to question the spatiality upon which governance is premised and argue for an unstructured "field of action," where individuals may voluntarily and/or collectively decide their own *direction*, free from the presence and pressures of any higher or ultimate authority. The *location* of such liberation from all variants of sovereign power is not rooted in ideas of fixity, as in the "territorial trap" of the state, but in the inexorable assertion of freedom through processual associations of affinity that may be entirely transient or slightly more permanent (Day 2005). The key potentiality, though, is that any affiliation is free to coagulate or dissolve under conditions of free will and individual choice, where no presence—such as the monopoly of force or independent control of the means of production—enforces either subjugation or communal continuity. "Freedom as a means breeds more freedom," said Vernon Richards (1995, 214) on the anarchist position. "To those who say this condemns one to political sterility and the Ivory Tower our reply is that 'realism' and their 'circumstantialism' invariably lead to disaster. We believe … that it is more realistic to … influence minds by discussion than to mould them by coercion."

The political geographies of boundaries and borders would become infinitely messier, overlapping, and variable under anarchism, to the point where attempting to map them into a rigid ordering or grid, as is the epistemological notion behind modern cartography, would be an exercise in futility. Such mapping, either literally, as in an actual map, or through techniques such as the census and the museum is constitutive of state logic to begin with (Anderson 1991), and the purpose of anarchist geographies should be to dissolve any such categorization and classification schemas that promote spatiotemporal permanence. This is not to suggest that anarchism is reduced to chaos, but any geographical organization would proceed as an ethics of empathy as opposed to a politics of difference, as the latter is always carved out through oppression. Anarchism, spatially arranged in these terms, would allow us to recognize whole people rather than attempting to make them as subjects or citizens that conform to particularized spaces and segmented political goals. Peter Kropotkin (1885, 943) articulated a similar vision when he wrote,

> In our time of wars, of national self-conceit, of national jealousies and hatreds ably nourished by people who pursue their own egotistic, personal or class interests, geography must be … a means of dissipating these prejudices and of creating other feelings more worthy of humanity.

Anarchist geographies might accordingly be productively characterized by their integrality, where all attempts to construct false dichotomies of separation are rejected and instead humanity is recognized as intimately intertwined within all the processes and flows of the entire planet (Massey 2005). Such a radical reconceptualization of the discipline would, in realizing Élisée Reclus's (1894) vision, render it conceptually akin to both the Jewel Net of Indra from Buddhist philosophy and the Gaia hypothesis, inasmuch as attempts at separating political, economic, social, cultural, environmental, and any other "subdisciplinary" variant would be viewed as fabrications that attempt to tame, order, restrain, partition, and contain the irreducible whole.

New forms of affinity are already emerging as a "relational ethics of struggle" (Routledge 2009a), wherein it is no longer the worker who is conceived as the agent of historical change but anticapitalist protesters who compose a heterogeneous group that defies universal subjectivation to the proletariat identity (Notes from Nowhere 2003). Such recognition could form a point of departure in unsettling the orthodox position Marxism holds within radical geography today. This emergent form of struggle is clearly not interested in formulating strategies that replicate traditional representative structures, signifying a paradigm shift away from effecting change from within the state by realigning its character toward autonomous movements positioned in opposition to the state (Pickerill and Chatterton 2006). In this context, Saul Newman (2010, 182) identifies a series of new political questions and challenges: "freedom beyond securities, democracy beyond the state, politics beyond the party, economic organization beyond capitalism, globalization beyond borders, [and] life beyond biopolitics." Yet these are not just political questions; each is also profoundly geographical. Although geographers are already examining these very issues, there has been little attention to the ways in which anarchism might foster a more rigorous investigation of these emergent geographies. Consequently, conceptualizing a "way forward"—beyond the dominating strictures of neoliberalism and the enduring animosities of colonialism—requires a deeper engagement with anarchist philosophies. Committing radical geography to an anarchist agenda would necessitate a negation of the false dichotomy the discipline maintains between the academy as a space of knowledge production, on one hand, and wider society as the domain of social struggle, on the other (Autonomous Geographies Collective 2010). Accordingly, intensified networks of solidarity with those involved in direct action on the streets may well be the future of radical geography. From here, ideas that allow for new geographical imaginations and materializations that transcend state-based politics may blossom; more "glocalized," ephemeral, and voluntary forms of noninstitutional organization may bloom; and Kropotkin's ([1902] 2008) theory of mutual aid, along with Reclus's (1894; also see Fleming 1988) contributions to the ideals of human freedom, may be treated to the same contemplation that Marx has hitherto received from radical geographers. Anarchism, as Kropotkin (1885) recognized more than a century ago, is "what geography ought to be."

3
Returning to Geography's Radical Roots

Anarchist society, a society which organizes itself without authority, is always in existence, like a seed beneath the snow, buried under the weight of the state and its bureaucracy, capitalism and its waste, privilege and its injustices, nationalism and its suicidal loyalties, religious differences and their superstitious separatism.... Far from being a speculative vision of a future society, [anarchism] is a description of a mode of human organization, rooted in the experience of everyday life, which operates side by side with, and in spite of, the dominant authoritarian trends of our society.
—Colin Ward

It is often said that Anarchists live in a world of dreams to come, and do not see the things which happen today. We do see them only too well, and in their true colors, and that is what makes us carry the hatchet into the forest of prejudice that besets us.
—Peter Kropotkin

Responding to David Harvey's (1972) influential essay on revolutionary and counterrevolutionary theory in geography, which in hindsight effectively inaugurated a "radical turn" for the discipline, Steen Folke (1972) outlined an argument as to "why a radical geography must be Marxist." The upper-middle-class background of most academics and the realization that geography had up to that point largely developed in a way that expressed dominant social forces troubled both scholars. These were welcome and long overdue criticisms, but the problem with both of these accounts is that anarchist ideas were nowhere to be found, which is troubling precisely because an earlier tradition of radical geography existed, and indeed thrived, a century before Folke claimed radical geography as exclusively Marxist. Harvey's profound influence and prolific output

65

since that time merely solidified what Folke had considered obligatory. Radical geography—at least until the late 1980s and early 1990s, when feminist critique began to demand our collective attention—had become essentially synonymous with Marxian analysis. Yet how could a "radical" geography truly be radical without digging down into the foundations that had been laid by the anarchist geographies of Élisée Reclus and Peter Kropotkin? The pair were extremely influential in their time: each had written a surfeit of radical geographical literature from an anarchist perspective as the sun was setting on the nineteenth century. Did Folke not consider it important to explore these roots? Indeed, the contemporary usage of the word *radical* comes from the Middle English sense of "forming the root" and earlier still from the Latin *radix*, meaning quite literally "root." How can geography claim itself as "radical," then, without engaging with this earlier tradition of anticapitalist geographical thought? In what has evolved into a long career of critical geographical scholarship, Harvey's work has only very minimally touched on Kropotkin and Reclus, and when he has addressed their work, it has been with a certain sense of ambivalence.[1]

To the credit of other radical geographers emerging in the 1970s, scholars like Richard Peet (1975; 1978), Myrna Breitbart (1975), Bob Galois (1976), and Gary Dunbar (1978) did in fact engage with Kropotkin and Reclus in their attempts to inaugurate a new critical trajectory for the discipline. Anarchism also received wider attention through special issues of the *Union of Socialist Geographers Newsletter* (Lauria 1978) and the journal *Antipode* (Breitbart 1978b). As demonstrated in the first chapter, although interest in anarchism by geographers has waxed and waned over the last century, it has continued to crop up through periodic bursts of interest, with Cook and Pepper's (1990) special issue of *Contemporary Issues in Geography and Education* representing another high point of engagement. Yet the irregularity of these initiatives meant that they were essentially eclipsed by the sustained attention that Marxist perspectives received, where Harvey's work in particular has subsequently become the touchstone for the vast majority of radical geographers who have followed. That Marxian geographers have chosen to largely ignore anarchism is actually nothing new. Marxists have long demonstrated a tendency to define anarchism as nothing more than opposition to the state, while also dismissing—or at least affording little consideration to—anarchism's shared rejection of capitalism and its refusal of the institution of private property. But as John Clark (1984, 128) contends, the essence of anarchism is not simply opposition to the state itself but the practical and theoretical struggle against domination in all its grotesque plurality, where

> sophisticated and developed anarchist theory does not stop with a criticism of political organization, but goes on to investigate the authoritarian nature of economic inequality and private property, hierarchical economic structures, traditional education, the patriarchal family, class and racial discrimination, and rigid sex and age-roles, to mention just a few of the more important topics.

Thus to diminish anarchism to nothing more than a political tendency against the state is to willfully exclude anarchism from its place in the wider socialist movement. This makes sense from a Marxian perspective, as it allows Marxists to present their ideology as the only serious anticapitalist option.

The current moment of neoliberalism, and its emphasis on minimal states and individual responsibility, does little to persuade Marxists that they should reevaluate their neglect of anarchist ideas and its emphasis on the abolition of government. Neoliberalism has had precisely the opposite effect, where its unequivocal destruction of social provisions, its apparent reconstitution of class power, and its increasingly obvious exacerbation of inequality have all breathed new life into Marxian analysis. Yet, while the antistate rhetorics of neoliberalism and the oxymoronic notions of "anarchocapitalism" and "free market anarchism" in particular would appear to add fuel to the fire of Marxian critiques of anarchism, the only thing burning here is a straw person. As the great anarchist and adversary of Karl Marx Mikhail Bakunin (qtd. in Leier 2006, 190) once warned, "liberty without socialism is privilege and injustice. Socialism without liberty is slavery and brutality." Thus the appropriation of the word *anarchism* by the extreme political right takes the most simplistic and reductionist terms, ignoring the actual philosophy behind anarchism and its commitment to anticapitalism. "We are communists," Kropotkin ([1887] 2002, 152) proclaimed. "But our communism is not that of the authoritarian school: it is anarchist communism, communism without government, free communism. It is a synthesis of the two chief aims

prosecuted by humanity since the dawn of its history—economical freedom and political freedom."

Inspired by Kropotkin's visionary thought, as well as Reclus's passion for social justice, this chapter stakes a renewed claim for radical
geography, a claim that is more in tune with the etymology of *radical*
and that focuses on the roots of anarchism that these two great thinkers
brought to bear on geographical praxis. I position this chapter alongside recent interest in such a radical revival that has emerged in the
form of special issues on anarchist geographies in the journals *Antipode*
(Springer et al. 2012b) and *ACME* (Clough and Blumberg 2012) and hope
to open a dialogue that assesses the resurgent importance of anarchism
in geographical praxis. In particular, I demonstrate how anarchism goes
beyond a simplistic interpretation of being a philosophy that exclusively
positions itself against the state and outline the problematics of this notion being perpetuated. I then focus on the division between anarchist
and Marxian thought by raising the question of monopoly, highlighting how anarchism rejects this logic, while Marxism maintains certain
contradictions in this respect, particularly in terms of its class-centric
view of the proletariat and its role vis-à-vis the transition to socialism.
Next I turn my attention to the question of revolution, which has been
foremost in the minds of radical geographers, including a recent call
from Neil Smith (2010) for a revival of the revolutionary imperative. I
question the wisdom of such a demand by drawing a distinction between
insurrection and revolution, where the former enables an embrace of
process and prefigurative politics, whereas the later is critiqued on the
basis of its implicit politics of waiting, its totalizing logic, and its ageographical tendencies. The primary motivation here is to suggest that a
radical geography would do well to begin a process of reengaging with
anarchist thought and practice, as a certain vitality to this philosophical
position is missing from contemporary Marxian analyses that continue
to rehash particular ideas—such as vanguardism and a dictatorship of the
proletariat—long past their expiration date. So let us carry the hatchet
and make room for the seeds beneath the snow by debunking some of
the myths that have been perpetuated about anarchism—spring is upon
us, and a forest of prejudice awaits!

BEYOND STATE CENTRICITY

Political geographer Peter Taylor (1991a, 214–15) once declared that he was "broadly sympathetic to the anarchist 'political' position" and sought "to locate anarchism within a broader radical critique." Taylor's account is useful insofar as he traces the evolution of anarchist ideas back to a single socialist movement of the early 1800s, where distinctions are blurred, while also attending to the eventual splinters that arose during the First International in 1864 and their magnification through the Bakunin–Marx rift that played out during the 1870s. Yet his account also drew a particular caricature of anarchist thought by positioning it as an isolated and singular vision concerned almost exclusively with the state. Taylor (1994; 1996) had much to say about state centricity throughout the 1990s, so it is peculiar to see him project this notion onto anarchist thought. His argument draws a series of false dichotomies that paint socialist, nationalist, feminist, and anarchist approaches into their own distinct boxes whereby exclusive priority is given to challenging capitalism, imperialism, patriarchy, and the authority of the state, respectively. This rigid coding allowed Taylor (1991a, 225) to conclude, "We do not need a 'new anarchism' based on the new material circumstances of the late twentieth century but a combined movement where all four forms of grievance are mutually respected." Oddly enough, Taylor (1991b, 660) explicitly contradicted himself in a book review published that same year, where he argued that there was indeed an "urgency and justification for a new anarchism." Either way, Taylor's reading of anarchism is problematic.

Clark and Martin (2004, 95) note that critics sometimes contend that anarchist thought "has emphasized opposition to the state to the point of neglecting the real hegemony of economic power. This interpretation arises, perhaps, from a simplistic and overdrawn distinction between the anarchist focus on political domination and the Marxist focus on economic exploitation." Had Taylor given a more generous reading to anarchist thought through the whole of its historical trajectory, he would have recognized that, although the question of the state is certainly at the forefront of anarchist critique, it is not the sole domain of concern. In fact anarchism has just as much at stake in undermining class power, balancing cross-cultural exchanges, and reforming gender relations as it does in subverting the dominance of the state. As anarchists such as Bakunin ([1873] 2002), Kropotkin ([1912] 1994), Reclus (Fleming 1988), and Goldman ([1917] 1969) demonstrated many years ago, these elements are hardly "new" to anarchism, as each was just as concerned with the disastrous effects of capitalism as he or she was with the tyranny of the state. Indeed, given that Proudhon was the first person ever to declare himself an anarchist, it seems genuinely odd to suggest that the state was ever the sole concern of anarchism. *What Is Property? or, An Inquiry into the Principle of Right and of Government* was Proudhon's ([1840] 2008) magnum opus, where his answer, "property is theft," became a rallying cry against capitalism and an early defining feature of the anarchist movement. More recently, a new crop of anarchist geographers has advanced a composite understanding of anarchism. In particular, Anthony Ince (2010b, 294) contends that "anarchism's holism—its recognition of the many different factors that influence and feed off each other as interrelated and inseparable in capitalist systems—means that it is ideally suited to an analysis of capitalism's contested geographical terrain." So although Taylor shows a measured degree of support for anarchism, unfortunately, in presenting anarchism as a single-minded concern for the state—rather than appreciating it as an enduring, manifold, and protean critique of all forms domination—he actually contributes to the confusions of ideology that inform the so-called anarchocapitalists as well as to the crude rhetoric that detractors have employed to discredit anarchism.

The likening of anarchism to nothing more than a rejection of the state works in unison with the idea that anarchist ideals are rooted in a lack of organization that embraces chaos. Yet anarchism is not synonymous with chaos and collapse, nor is it opposed to organization. It is about actively reinventing the everyday through a desire to create new forms of organization and "enacting horizontal networks instead of top-down structures like states, parties, or corporations; networks based on principles of decentralized, non-hierarchical consensus democracy" (Graeber 2002, 70). Organization can not only facilitate solidarity and mutual aid, it is an inescapable condition of social life, and as Errico Malatesta ([1897] 1977, 84) once pointed out, "the agelong oppression of the masses by a small privileged group has always been the result of the inability of the oppressed to agree among themselves to organize with others for production, for enjoyment and for the possible needs of defense against whoever might wish to exploit and oppress them. Anarchism exists to remedy this state of affairs." In other words, when conceived as a social process, we begin to recognize that anarchism is deeply woven into the fabric of humanity, which demands a historical treatment that goes beyond simplistic tropes (Bookchin 1996). It is in the spirit of seeking new forms of organization that anarchist geographies have been revitalized as of late, emphasizing a DIY ethos of autonomy, direct action, radical democracy, and noncommodification (see Springer et al. 2012b; Clough and Blumberg 2012), all of which extends beyond mere opposition to the state.

If not through a centralized state, how anarchism might be organized and what forms of action this will take are two of the most common questions asked of anarchists. Many anarchists, myself included, are often hesitant to describe an anarchist society in any detail, and although this is frequently misinterpreted as a dodge, there is good reason for such evasiveness. Anarchism is not about drafting sociopolitical blueprints for the future; instead, anarchists have been more concerned with identifying social tendencies, wherein the focus is resolutely on the possibilities of the *here* and *now*. Accordingly, the examples of viable anarchist alternatives are nearly infinite. Anarchist organizing is limited only by our imagination, where the only existent criteria are that they proceed nonhierarchically and free from external authority (Graeber 2004). This could include almost any form of organization, from a volunteer fire brigade for safety to community gardens for food to cooperatives for housing to knitting collectives for clothes. Rather than a central political body, anarchists conceive of social organization as local voluntary groupings that maintain autonomy through a decentralized system of self-governed communes of all sizes and degrees that coordinate activities and networks for all possible purposes through free federation. The coercive pyramid of state dynamics is replaced with a web of free association wherein each locality is free to pursue its own social, cultural, and economic arrangements. The global postal system provides some hints as to how this might work, as local associations can syndicate to deliver complex functions without uniformity or overarching bureaucracy. Postal services function not through a central world authority but through voluntary agreements between different post offices, in different countries (Ward 2004).

Humans have always lived in societies, and although the formalized rule of the state is quite a recent phenomenon in the long march of history, we nonetheless need reminding that it is "but one of the forms of social life" (Kropotkin [1898] 2002, 131). We must radically flip our mind-sets, as anarchist organization does not replace top-down state mechanisms in the sense of standing in for them. They abolish them by people instead building what they need for themselves, free from coercion or imposed authority. Throughout human history, people have organized themselves collectively to satisfy their own needs. Organization under anarchism is no different in this regard. As Colin Ward ([1973] 2001, 28) contends, "given a common need, a collection of people will, by trial and error, by improvisation and experiment, evolve order out of the situation—this order being more durable and more closely related to their needs than any kind of order external authority could provide." This insight is derived from Kropotkin's ([1902] 2008) observations of the history of human society, where he documented the centrality of cooperation linked to everyday life and described it as mutual aid. Although differentiated across space and time, mutual aid was and still is continuously present in human societies, even if its development is not uniform and the forms it takes are contextually specific. At certain times, in particular places, mutual aid has been central to social life, while at other times, the geographies of mutual aid have been all but hidden beneath domination, violence, and competition. Yet irrespective of adversarial conditions, mutual aid is always present, and "the moment we stop insisting on viewing all forms of action only by their function in reproducing larger, total, forms of inequality of power, we will also be able to see that anarchist social relations and non-alienated forms of action are all around us" (Graeber 2004, 76). The provision of social welfare did not originate with the state; it "evolved from the vast network of friendly societies and mutual aid organizations that had sprung up through working-class self-help in the 19th century" (Ward 1994, 27). Thus mutual aid is not a hypothetical model for how society might be shaped; it is already happening, providing ongoing opportunities for togetherness and emancipation.

Unlike Marxists, who view history in utilitarian terms, anarchists recognize that means and ends cannot be separated (Baldelli 1971). The anarchist project, then, is one that aligns with feminism insofar as it is an attempt to promote the feminization of society through extending cooperation, equality, compassion, and sharing, which constitute mutual aid relations and contrast with the aggression, racism, exploitation, misogyny, homophobia, classism, and rivalry of our male-dominated, modern society (Goldman [1917] 1969). Anarchism does not trace a line or provide a model but instead points to a strategy of breaking the bonds of coercion and the chains of exploitation by encompassing an infinite number of everyday acts of resistance and cooperation. Childcare co-ops, street parties, gardening clinics, learning networks, flash mobs, community kitchens, unschooling groups, independent media collectives, rooftop occupations, freecycling activities, direct action organizations, radical samba, peer-to-peer file sharing, sewing workshops, tree sitting, monkey wrenching, spontaneous disaster relief, culture jamming, book fairs, microradio, building coalitions, collective hacking, dumpster diving, wildcat strikes, neighborhood tool sharing, tenants' associations, workplace organizing, and squatting are all anarchism in action, each with decidedly spatial implications, and this is just the tip of the proverbial iceberg. So what forms of action does anarchism take? "All forms," Kropotkin ([1880] 2005, 39) answered,

> indeed, the most varied forms, dictated by circumstances, temperament, and the means at disposal. Sometimes tragic, sometimes humorous, but always daring; sometimes collective, sometimes purely individual, this policy of action will neglect none of the means at hand, no event of public life, in order to keep the spirit alive, to propagate and find expression for dissatisfaction, to excite hatred against exploiters, to ridicule the government and expose its weakness, and above all and always, by actual example, to awaken courage and fan the spirit of revolt.

It should be clear, then, that the practice of mutual aid, which rests at the very core of anarchism, is as much a critique of capitalism, imperialism, and patriarchy as it is of the authority claimed by the state.

The problematic alignment of anarchism to nothing more than anti-state modes of thought and practice serves to marginalize this particular trajectory of socialist thought, making it seem less viable or desirable among those who might otherwise be sympathetic to anarchist leanings.

This is a strategy that attempts to infuse Marxism with a certain critical purchase over leftist thinking that anarchism supposedly lacks, when in reality—as we will see in the following section—both anarchism and Marxism sprung from the same roots of socialist critique but eventually splintered in different directions stemming from differences in opinion over the role of the state. Yet this divergence does not mean that anarchism dropped all of its other substantive content to become purely an antistate ideology, as some Marxists seem to assume. "All in all, Marxist claims that anarchists view the state as the 'chief evil' or see the destruction of the state as the 'main idea' of anarchism are simply talking nonsense," Iain McKay rightly argues. "In fact, rather than anarchists having a narrow view of social liberation, it is, in fact, Marxists who do so. By concentrating almost exclusively on the (economic) class source of exploitation, they blind themselves to other forms of exploitation and domination that can exist independently of (economic) class relationships" (McKay 2008, 112). Unfortunately, anarchism's historical alignment with socialism has not stopped Marxists from suggesting that anarchist ideas grease the rails toward a neoliberal future (see Dean 2012a; 2012b; Harvey 2012b), a delusion that has been exacerbated by conservatives, particularly within the United States, and their inane misappropriation of the term *anarchism* to signify their own demonization of the state so that capital may become completely unfettered. Such readings are profound misrepresentations of anarchism as a political philosophy, willfully engaging in caricature by dismissing anarchism's anticapitalist roots. And yet Marxists, beginning with Engels, have repeatedly trotted out the myth that anarchists consider the state as the main or only enemy:

> In Bakunin's view, the struggle against the main concentration of power in society, the state, was *no less necessary* than the struggle against capital. Engels, however, puts the matter somewhat differently, arguing that for Bakunin the state was the main enemy, as if Bakunin had not held that capital, too, was an enemy and that its expropriation was a necessary even if not sufficient condition for the social revolution.... [Engels's account] distorts Bakunin's argument, which also held capital to be an evil necessary to abolish. (Gouldner 1982, 863–64, emphasis original)

In short, anarchism has just as much of a critical bite against capitalism as Marxism could ever claim for itself, where the primary difference has been that Marxism continues to want to work with particular forms of monopoly, whereas anarchism refuses to involve itself in such an exclusionary practice. Indeed, to anarchists, "the State...and capitalism are facts and conceptions which we cannot separate from each other. In the course of history these institutions have developed, supporting and reinforcing each other. They are connected with each other—not as mere accidental coincidences. They are linked together by the links of cause and effect" (Kropotkin [1908] 1995, 94).

OF MONOPOLIES

That anarchism is firmly embedded in socialist practice and thought has been true since its inception as a political philosophy, when Pierre-Joseph Proudhon ([1840] 2008, 241) became the first person in history to declare, "I am an anarchist." Alongside Pierre Leroux, Marie Roch, Louis Reybaud, and Robert Owen, Proudhon is rightfully considered a preeminent godparent of socialism. His ideas were so influential in late-nineteenth-century France that it is impossible to disentangle his critique of property from the libertarian movement that resulted in the Paris Commune of 1871 (Archer 1997). Like Marx ([1867] 1976), but nearly three decades before him, Proudhon ([1840] 2008, 116, emphasis original) devised that capitalists cheat their workers because they produce more value than wage labor affords them, and it is accordingly the workers who are ethically entitled to control the means of production:

> Whoever labors becomes a proprietor....And when I say proprietor, I do not mean simply (as do our hypocritical economists) proprietor of his allowance, his salary, his wages—I mean proprietor of the value he creates, and by which the master alone profits. As all this relates to wages and the distribution of products...many persons talk of admitting working people to share in the products and profits; but in their minds this is pure benevolence: they have never shown—perhaps never suspected—that it was a natural right, inherent in labor, and inseparable from the function of producer....This is my proposition: *The laborer retains, even after he has received his wages, a natural right of property in the thing which he has produced.*

Proudhon located the power to produce without working at the heart of capitalism's exploitation, an idea that "anticipat[ed] what Marx and

Engels were later to call the appropriation of surplus value" (Enrenberg 1996, 55). Similarly, Proudhon opposed all non-labor-based income, including rent, dividends, interest, and profit. In fact, anyone familiar with both would recognize that Marx's ([1867] 1976) first volume of *Capital* recapitulated many of the ideas first presented in Proudhon's *What Is Property?*, but without proper acknowledgment. Unlike Marxists, who have paid little attention to Proudhon largely owing to Marx's own "highly distorted" accounts that were "almost always charged with scorn" (McKay 2008, 65), anarchists continue to engage with Proudhon's work and have long been aware that we find "the theory of surplus value, that grand 'scientific discovery' of which our Marxists are so proud of," in his writings (Rocker 1981, 77).

Few Marxists are aware of this history, but it is hard to argue with the evidence, as "Marx's discussions of Proudhon's ideas ... span almost the entirety of his career" (Thomas 1980, 193). Marx, like Proudhon before him, argued that abolishing interest-bearing capital was destructive of capitalism. Marx, like Proudhon before him, differentiated between possession and private property and argued that cooperatives should replace capitalist firms. Marx, like Proudhon before him, argued that the working classes must emancipate themselves. Marx, like Proudhon before him, regarded property as the subjugation of the labor of others by means of appropriation. Marx, like Proudhon before him, saw the cooperative movement as a necessity of transitioning away from capitalism and thus recognized the need for communal land and workplaces. Marx, like Proudhon before him, proclaimed the need for "scientific socialism." Marx, like Proudhon before him, argued that the state was an instrument of class rule, although they differed in terms of whether a temporary proletariat dictatorship was necessary to see it properly undone.[2] "It was at this point—the necessity of striking down monopoly—that came the parting of their ways. Here the road forked. They found that they must turn either to the right or to the left—follow either the path of Authority or the path of Liberty. Marx went one way ... and Proudhon the other. Thus were born State Socialism and Anarchism" (Tucker 1883, 7). In this light, it is utterly peculiar that so few geographers have actually engaged with Proudhon, until we recall that Marx first made a name for himself by ridiculing the then well-known socialist through "the perpetuation of a spiteful distortion of his thought," using his fame "to get people to read the work of a then unknown radical thinker" (Vincent 1984, 230). Clearly annoyed by Marx's antics, Benjamin Tucker (1883, 2) argued that Proudhon "demonstrated to the world" both the "historical persistence of class struggles in successive manifestations" and "the tendency and consequences of capitalistic production . . . time and time again during the twenty years preceding the publication of *Das Kapital*." But then again, as Iain McKay (2011, 70) argues with tongue in cheek, "all this could be just a coincidence and just a case of great minds thinking alike—with one coming to the same conclusions a few years after the other expressed them in print." And so we find only fleeting references to Proudhon in Harvey's entire body of work, until his book on Paris, where the French socialist can finally and hardly be avoided (Harvey 2013).[3]

This omission, which stems from the "persistent misconceptions concerning Proudhon's thought result[ing] from the continued reverence shown to Marx and, as a result, his assessment of Proudhon" (Vincent 1984, 230) set a tone for radical geography that is clearly visible in the number of articles we find making reference to early proponents of socialism in human geography journals since the publication of Harvey's (1973) first major Marxist work four decades ago. Marx has clearly monopolized the discipline's collective attention (see Table 1). As Edward Hyams (1979, 92) writes, "no good Marxists have had to think about Proudhon. They have what is mother's milk to them, an *ex cathedra* judgement. For the essence of Marxism . . . is authority." Awkward as it may be, the written record proves that Proudhon first suggested many key aspects of Marxism. McKay (2011, 70–71) is completely unforgiving in his assessment of the historical record:

> *The Poverty of Philosophy* was written in reply to *Proudhon's System of Economic Contradictions* [aka *The Philosophy of Poverty*]. What to make of it? First, it must be remembered that this work is not really about Proudhon but Marx. Proudhon's fame is used to get people to read the work of a [then] unknown radical thinker and for that thinker to expound his ideas on various subjects. Second, it is a hatchet-job of epic proportions—although as few Marxists bother to read Proudhon as Marx has pronounced judgment on him, they would not know that and so they contribute to . . . Marx's "desire to denigrate" his "strongest competitors." While, undoubtedly, Marx makes some valid criticisms of Proudhon, the book is full of distortions. His

aim was to dismiss Proudhon as being the ideologist of the petit-bourgeois and he obviously thought all means were applicable to achieve that goal. So we find Marx arbitrarily arranging quotations from Proudhon's book, often out of context and even tampered with, to confirm his own views. This allows him to impute to Proudhon ideas the Frenchman did not hold (often explicitly rejects!) in order to attack him. Marx even suggests that his own opinion is the opposite of Proudhon's when, in fact, he is simply repeating the Frenchman's thoughts. He takes the Frenchman's sarcastic comments at face value, his metaphors and abstractions literally. And, above all else, Marx seeks to ridicule him.

Proudhon, the anarchist, accordingly played a pivotal role in the development of Marxian thought. His work was Marx's first point of departure in establishing a name for himself. Although today Marxists tend to claim the Paris Commune for themselves, as it is widely regarded as the first assumption of power by the working class during the Industrial Revolution, Proudhon's influence on a young Marx, whether for better or for worse, is undeniable (Hyams 1979).

While McKay certainly doesn't hold back in his assessment of the origins of Marxian thought, and some may feel uncomfortable about the implications, my intention with the preceding discussion is not to smear Marx and establish Proudhon as the rightful intellectual ancestor of socialism; rather, I hope to shed some light on the history of anarchism's relationship with Marxism and, in doing so, offer a more honest appraisal of the intellectual milieu of the time, which emerged from "endless conversations and arguments in cafes, classrooms, bedrooms, barber shops involving thousands of people inside and outside the academy (or Party)" (Graeber 2007, 304). Any "Great Man" theory is a fiction of the academic game, where winning means other scholars turn your name into an adjective. It is very telling, then, that we now have anarchism, named for an idea, and Marxism, named for a man, as the two main variants of socialist thought. Although Proudhon was evidently frustrated by Marx, referring to *The Poverty of Philosophy* (Marx [1847] 2013) as "a tissue of vulgarity, of calumny, of falsification and of plagiarism" (Thomas 1980, 211), much like Kropotkin, Bakunin, Reclus, and the other anarchists of the nineteenth century, Proudhon didn't think of himself as having invented anything particularly new. After all, anarchism's basic principles

TABLE 1. Number of articles referring to early proponents of socialism in human geography journals since 1973.

Journal	Engels	Kropotkin	Marx	Proudhon	Reclus
Annals of the Association of American Geographers	45	19	180	5	20
Antipode	173	41	560	24	18
Economic Geography	16	1	101	0	0
Environment and Planning A	46	5	207	0	6
Environment and Planning D	54	6	223	3	6
Geoforum	34	7	154	3	9
Journal of Economic Geography	4	0	23	1	0
Political Geography/ Political Geography Quarterly	37	10	212	4	18
Progress in Human Geography	37	17	208	4	19
Transactions of the Institute of British Geographers	38	7	118	0	6
Urban Geography	30	2	67	2	0
Total	514	115	2053	46	102

Note: *Political Geography Quarterly* became *Political Geography* in 1992.

of self-organization, voluntary association, and mutual aid are as old as humanity, and it is to time immemorial that he owed his intellectual debt.

Debates over the Paris Commune's policies and outcome solidified the divisions between anarchists and Marxists, fully realizing the fragmentation of socialist ideas, which had begun splintering even before the First International in 1864. Kropotkin ([1885] 1992, 97), for example, was dismayed by the Paris Commune's departure from Proudhon's antistatist ideas when, "in proclaiming the free Commune, the people of Paris proclaimed an essential anarchist principle … [but] they stopped in mid-course … [perpetuating] the old governmental principle by giving themselves a Communal Council copied from the old municipal councils." The main division between anarchism and Marxism consequently emerged out of differences in opinion over the need for leaders—or a vanguard—and the question of revolution itself (see later), as well as the degree of autonomy afforded to the workers in any postrevolutionary conjuncture and the closely related question of the monopoly of violence. Anarchists rejected any such monopoly on the premise that violence is first and foremost the primary dimension of state power and that, accordingly, any state, whether controlled by the bourgeoisie or captured by the workers, will inevitably come to function as an instrument of class domination. In contrast, Marxists believed that because a minority class rules most societies prior to socialism, the achievement of a classless society requires the previously disadvantaged class to acquire a monopoly over and superior capacity for violence. As Bakunin ([1873] 1953, 288) argued,

> they [Marxists] maintain that only a dictatorship—their dictatorship, of course—can create the will of the people, while our [anarchists] answer to this is: No dictatorship can have any other aim but that of self-perpetuation, and it can beget only slavery in the people tolerating it; freedom can be created only by freedom, that is, by … rebellion on the part of the people and free organization of the toiling masses from the bottom up.

The desire to overturn the state and create a liberated socialist system via despotic power is thus a contradiction, as is the related Marxian notion of withering away the state. Bakunin recognized this when he observed,

> If their State is going to be a genuine people's State, why should it then dissolve itself? … [Marxists] say that this State yoke—the dictatorship—is a necessary transitional means in order to attain the emancipation of the people: anarchism or freedom, is the goal, the State or dictatorship is the means. Thus, to free the working masses, it is first necessary to enslave them. (288)

Such vanguardism and noticeable inconsistency appalled anarchists and became the fundamental divide between socialists.

Marx's economic analysis is rooted in the notion of exploitation, where other forms of oppression, or what anarchists would call "domination," are reducible to the conflict of class relations. There is no space for gender oppression, homophobia, racial discrimination, or other social hierarchies to take on a separate analysis within a strictly Marxist view.

These struggles are not seen to have their own integrity beyond the os-tensibly more fundamental problem of capitalist exploitation, and thus the force of Marx's view is its insistence that the ultimate analysis of a society is that of its economic relations. To carry this idea forward, "if there is a single site of oppression, an Archimedean point about which history and struggle turn, then those who are more conversant with that point are the ones best positioned to oversee struggle and resistance" (May 2008, 80). Thus the idea of the vanguard is inextricable from Marxism precisely because it maintains a class-centric outlook wherein Marxists maintain that economic exploitation should monopolize our analyses of oppression. But if, in contrast, domination is considered multifarious, a reading that geography actually demands, as there is no single site of oppression and capitalism can never claim a totalizing and monolithic hegemony, then the distinction between an intellectual class and the masses is more difficult to sustain. Once we recognize multiple sites of oppression, patterns of domination that fold into, out of, and across the everyday, the geographies of rebellion become much more diffuse than a single class-based revolution. This is not to say that networks of solidarity cannot and should not be constructed on a voluntary basis of affinity, but it is an indictment of the idea that a vanguard somehow represents our collective hope rather than its own self-serving interests.

This line of critique reveals an additional sense of monopoly to which Marxism subscribes in the form of universalizing the proletariat and claiming such ontology as the engine of emancipation for all of humanity. Such a class-centric outlook is problematic precisely because identity is far more fractious than many Marxists care to admit, and yet Marxism as a philosophy presents itself as having a firm hold on how solidarities may be mobilized and from where they should be impelled. In this respect, its vanguardism once again becomes apparent. As Bellegarrigue (1848) succinctly put it, "one cannot redistribute wealth without first becoming master of all wealth; redistribution is first and foremost monopoly." This also hints at the limits of Marxian thought, which emerge from and have consequences for how it explains the transition from capitalism to socialism or from a class society to a classless society. It is impor-tant to remember that the Marxist explanation was developed almost entirely out of analogy with the transition of feudalism to capitalism, that is, from one class society to *another* class society. This raises a key question about the utility of Marxian analysis, namely, is it possible to explain and account for the transition from a class society to a classless society by means of the same dialectic that accounts for the transition of one class society to another? As Murray Bookchin ([1971] 2004) notes, there are very significant differences between the development of the bourgeoisie under feudalism and the development of the proletariat under capitalism, which Marx failed to anticipate or acknowledge. This is a powerful critique of Marxist epistemology that goes beyond abstraction to penetrate the concrete materiality of how revolution is actually operationalized. It also goes some way to explaining why the state does not actually wither under Marxism once it is put into practice and why a bourgeois character remains entrenched in the new socialist state. As soon as the reins of the state are captured, Marxism becomes mere ideology, assimilated into advanced forms of state capitalist movement, as we saw in the Soviet Union and its eventual collapse and as has become abundantly clear in contemporary China. Thus, when Bookchin argues that, "by an incredible irony of history, Marxian 'socialism' turns out to be in large part the very state capitalism that Marx failed to anticipate in the dialectic of capitalism" (117), it is hard to dismiss his charge when the empirical record verifies his assessment.

Whereas Marxism represents the vanguardist-cum-statist edge of the socialist political spectrum, or at the very least accepts the state in utilitarian terms as a means to an end through a supposedly "provisional" dictatorship of the proletariat, anarchism is the domain of libertarian socialism and rejects the idea that violent means can justify or ever possibly lead to an emancipated condition. Put differently, to be antistatist within the domain of socialist thought is to be anarchist. Although autonomist Marxists would undoubtedly object, I would nonetheless critique libertarian categories of ostensibly Marxian affiliation as being to a significant extent synonymous with socialist anarchism and, at the very least, "anarchistic" in their outlook. In particular, there is significant correspondence between the anarchogeographies of Kropotkin ([1902] 2008) and Ward ([1973] 2001), wherein the potential for a new society is seen already to exist within the materiality of capitalism and the analyses of autonomist

Marxists, who actively seek to create the future by fostering alternative social relations and new forms of being in their everyday lives (Pickerill and Chatterton 2006; Katsiaficas 2006; Marks 2012). "As a replacement for an exhausted and failed orthodoxy," Harry Cleaver (1992) notes that autonomist Marxists offer a more vibrant and dynamic Marxism, "one that has been regenerated within the struggles of real people and as such, has been able to articulate at least some elements of their desires and projects of self-valorization." In searching for the future in the present, the approach taken by anarchist geographers to the issue of transcending capitalism thus finds a common ground with autonomist Marxists in emphasizing existing activities that embody the primary importance of creative forms of social cooperation and alternative ways of being. Anarchists and autonomists both attempt to organize their productive activities in ways that impede capitalism with a view toward eventually breaking its command over society (Gautney 2009).

Presumably, it is for political reasons stemming from the recent misuse of the word *anarchism* by the political right that autonomist Marxists have chosen alternative discursive framings to represent their ideas. Arguably, it is for similar reasons that the tag of "Marxist" is sometimes dropped in favor of the more straightforward referent of "autonomist." Whatever the reasons for its nomenclature, there is significant correspondence between autonomist and anarchist ideas. Clough and Blumberg (2012) provide a useful discussion that traces the nuances of these two dimensions of libertarian socialism to bring them into conversation, whereas Pierpaolo Mudu (2012, 413) traces the history of "how and to what extent the people linked to anarchist or autonomist orientations shared principles of action and how individuals sharing these principles interacted." These are critically important interventions in building wider solidarity for the same general principles of freedom, affinity, and the reorganization of society along a nonhierarchical, horizontal axis. Anarchists and autonomists both engage such a process through a reimagining of revolution, where its basis is to be found not in a profound moment of widespread social and political upheaval that originates from an allegedly universal experience of immiseration among a particular class but within the insurrectionary locus of the everyday and the contextual specificity of lived experience.

THE PROBLEM WITH REVOLUTION

Marxist geographers have traditionally viewed revolution as a means to an end for their political project. Yet a critical reading of the state has been challenging the more vulgar forms of Marxism as of late, particularly within autonomist Marxist circles, where the revolutionary imperative has been called into question. Hardt and Negri (2000; 2004) are perhaps the most well known proponents of an alternative reading to revolution, with their suggestion that our efforts should be focused on a certain spontaneity that already exudes from the populace and foments political disruptions within the small cracks that inevitably exist within hegemony. This interpretation has significant correspondence with anarchist sensibilities and aligns with those anarchists who have argued against revolution and for insurrection. Max Stirner ([1845] 1993, 316, emphasis original) was one of the first to articulate this idea, suggesting that whereas revolution aimed to create new arrangements, insurrection, in contrast,

> leads us no longer to *let* ourselves be arranged, but to arrange ourselves, and sets no glittering hopes on "institutions." It is not a fight against the established, since, if it prospers, the established collapses of itself; it is only a working forth of me out of the established. If I leave the established, it is dead and passes into decay.

Stirner accordingly ridiculed the traditional notion of revolution, viewing those social movements aimed at overturning the state as implicitly statist insofar as, from the ashes of the state, they aimed to establish a new one. The displacement of one government with another was not a viable option for Stirner, an idea that anarchists have held ever since. Although some anarchists have continued to employ the language of "revolution," its envisioned meaning is very different from that held by most Marxists. The intention of insurrection is what might be referred to as revolution of the everyday, where individuals become "insurgents" by refusing the existing structures of domination and walking their own way. Stirner accordingly intended *insurrection* in its etymological sense of "rising up" above government, religion, and other hierarchies, not necessarily to overthrow them, but simply to disregard these structures by taking control of one's own individual life. This approach is, of course, the very essence of direct action, which, in contrast to civil disobedience and its grand gesture of defiance, proceeds with no consideration of authority whatsoever, as all authority is deemed illegitimate (Graeber 2009b). As Gustav Landauer ([1910] 2005, 165) argues, "the State is not something which can be destroyed by a revolution, but is a condition, a certain relationship between human beings, a mode of human behavior; we destroy it by contracting other relationships, by behaving differently." Direct action and insurrection are accordingly synonymous inasmuch as they reject any notion of vanguardism and invoke a prefigurative politics wherein the spectacular moment of revolution is replaced with the ongoing process of actually creating alternatives in the *here* and *now* rather than waiting for a singular proletarian identity to congeal and the entire structure to be torn down and resurrected with new leaders.[4]

The Marxist spirit of vanguardism and a class-centric view of the proletariat take center stage in Jodi Dean's (2012a) *The Communist Horizon*, which, although being touted as a manifesto for a new collective politics, instead offers a reactionary response to the language of autonomy, autogestion, and horizontalism that has been so inspirational to contemporary social movements. The spontaneity of the "coming insurrection" (Invisible Committee 2009) is rejected, and in its place, Dean regurgitates the dead-letter idea that collective action must constitute itself as a political party and be marshaled by a vanguard to lead a revolution, which in her own words requires "discipline and preparation" (241). To Dean, "a communist party is necessary because neither capitalist dynamics nor mass spontaneity immanently produce a *proletarian* revolution" (242, emphasis original), which reestablishes a class-centric outlook for Marxism. Elsewhere, and in demonstrating ignorance for the history of socialism, Dean (2013) snipes that "anarchism just repeats the neoliberal ideology, except with an oppositional, kind of groovier flavor." Playing into the same oxymoronic rhetoric of those who call themselves "anarchocapitalists," anarchism is astonishingly caricatured by Dean as a cipher for capitalism. How anarchism's cooperative approach to social change (i.e., mutual aid) can be considered neoliberal is a mystery to which Dean fails to respond. What is obvious is that she has either never heard of Kropotkin and the anarchocommunist perspective he advanced or conveniently ignores it to score political points. Yet Dean does not stop at inexplicably severing anarchism from socialism and communism; she also recapitulates the state-centric caricature of anarchism:

> What matters today is what we identify as the primary enemy. Is the primary enemy capitalism or is the primary enemy the state? Communists and socialists rightly recognize the primary enemy as capitalism. The problem with anarchists is that many of them see the primary enemy as the state or the state form. So they don't think that seizing the state—or trying to expropriate it in various sorts of ways by winning parts of it—matters. They think more about just abolishing it completely. That is a mistake.

The real mistake is Dean's instance that the only true form of socialism is Marxist and the fallacious claim that all antistate perspectives are synonymous with, or at least complementary to, neoliberalism, an error that Harvey (2012b) repeats. Though, undeniably, anarchist theory has focused on individual liberty, where Stirner ([1845] 1993) set the tone with *The Ego and Its Own*, only intellectual distortion can read this as a precursor to the privatized tyranny of neoliberalism. Although Stirner is "pursued through seven hundred pages of heavy-handed mockery and insult" in the unabridged version of Marx and Engels's *The German Ideology* (Berlin 1963, 105–6), he is clearly not out to defend the privileges of the ruling class, as this is not his conception of egoism, which is instead meant as the destruction of idols of every kind. The direct action, DIY ethic of anarchism expressed through squatting (Ward 2004), autonomous indigenous organizing (Yashar 2005), social centers (Hodkinson and Chatterton 2006), worker cooperatives (Vieta 2010), and alterglobalization movements (Pleyers 2011) is accordingly a far cry from the homophobia, sexism, racism, and selfishness of the libertarian right, precisely because anarchism is rooted in notions of affinity, solidarity, and togetherness expressed *here* and *now* through everyday lived experiences.

The revolution of the everyday is a thematic that was taken up by the Situationists,[5] where for the Marxist-inspired Guy Debord ([1967] 1994) and Raoul Vaneigem ([1967] 2012), possibilities to break with capitalism occurred at the level of daily practice and lived experience. Yet this character is entirely absent from traditional Marxism. Friedrich Engels ([1872] 1978, 733) couldn't see past his particular version of revolution, which effectively served as an excuse for the authoritarianism of Marxist ideas:

> [The anarchists] demand that the first act of the social revolution shall be the abolition of all authority. Have these gentlemen ever seen a revolution? A revolution is certainly the most authoritarian thing there is; it is the act whereby one part of the population imposes its will on the other part by means of rifles, bayonets and cannon—authoritarian means if such there be at all; and if the victorious party does not wish to have fought in vain; it must maintain this rule by means of the terror which its arms inspire in the reactionaries.

Engels's goal was to discredit anarchists and lend credence to the idea that a proletarian dictatorship is the only viable socialism, and yet this critique rings hollow because it misses the mark of anarchist intentions, which had been far more reflexive about this situation than Engels ever let on. Proudhon addressed this criticism directly: in a letter to Marx (Proudhon 1846), he wrote,

> Perhaps you still retain the opinion that no reform is at present possible without a *coup de main*, without what was formerly called a revolution and is really nothing but a shock. That opinion, which I understand, which I excuse, and would willingly discuss, having myself shared it for a long time, my most recent studies have made me abandon completely. I believe we have no need of it in order to succeed; and that consequently we should not put forward revolutionary action as a means of social reform, because that pretended means would simply be an appeal to force, to arbitrariness, in brief, a contradiction.

In particular, it is the violence and authoritarianism of revolution that prompted Proudhon to rethink where an anarchist philosophy should be aligned, and revolution was accordingly dropped from his vocabulary.

A great number of anarchists have followed suit, where the violence of revolution and the contradiction this entails for anarchism's vision of a peaceful and egalitarian society is the primary concern. Benjamin Tucker (1926, 71) argued that "force cannot preserve anarchy; neither can it bring it. In fact, one of the inevitable influences of the use of force is to postpone anarchy"; in turn, Ethel Mannin ([1944] 2009, 73) wrote that "the history of bloody revolution everywhere is the history of failure. . . . People are not to be bludgeoned into it; only what is achieved through the great upsurge of the human spirit, out of the impassioned desire of the multitude endures; what is imposed by force has no roots, and cannot last." There is, nonetheless, ambivalence with respect to violence in the anarchist tradition, even if "all anarchists look forward to a peaceful and non-violent society" (Marshall 1992, 636). Though the history of anarchism shows moments of violent engagement, particularly during the "propaganda of the deed" era of the late nineteenth century, the bulk of anarchist activities (i.e., the practice of mutual aid) throughout history and into the present have been nonviolent. It was during the height of the propaganda of the deed era that anarchism became particularly distorted in popular opinion. The actions of the few saw anarchism misaligned from its egalitarian imperatives and cooperative principles in the judgement of the public, where it became vilified as nothing more than a pact among terrorists and assassins. Yet the notion that the whole of anarchism is rotten because of the actions of those anarchists who have employed violent tactics is unreasonable. Such thinking is no different than the contemporary witch-hunt against Muslims, as though the actions of a violent minority somehow reflect the thinking and practice of the peaceful majority. Because anarchists generally accept the idea that means and ends should be indistinguishable, and "given the anarchists' respect for the sovereignty of the individual, in the long run it is non-violence and not violence which is implied by anarchist values" (Marshall 1992, 637).

The meaning of revolution, if it is to be rescued at all, must be realigned away from the use of violence and the conquest of state power (Holloway 2002) and toward the insurrectionary potential of the everyday. Such a view is not without its critics, though, as Neil Smith (2010, 57) argued that it misinterprets the ambition of revolution as simply seizing state power and replacing one regime with another, wherein "only a willful misreading of Marxist political theory could make such an elementary mistake. It not only disavows a whole history of revolutionary thought but it also conveniently erases Engels and Lenin's argument about the withering away of the state." Smith is correct: revolution is more than just the capture of the state; it exemplifies a totalizing spatial logic of Promethean impulse that seeks to remake everything according to a rational plan (Newman 2011). Aside from the obvious authoritarianism of such a project, we should also recognize that not everything needs to be remade, and revolution is insensitive to the "other worlds" and "diverse economies" that already exist and are continually being remade through experimentation beyond capitalism (Gibson-Graham 2008; White and Williams 2012). Insurrection defies the blueprint imposed upon society by institutions—whether capitalist or Marxist—and consists of the voluntary assertion of autonomous self-arrangement so that one may immediately disengage from established discourses and structures, becoming emancipated from domination through a politics of refusal and the prefiguration of alternatives. As Hakim Bey (1991a, 2) argues, "ontological Anarchy proposes that we wake up, and create our own day—even in the shadow of the State, that pustulant giant who sleeps, and whose dreams of Order metastasize as spasms of spectacular violence."

Unlike Smith's (2010) revolutionary imperative, which sidesteps any discussion of Marxism's false promise of a withering state—an untruth that history has repeatedly exposed—insurrection embraces a mode of organization that spontaneously springs from self-activity. As we have already seen, Bakunin ([1872] 2002, 318) was well aware of the ruse of the dictatorship of the proletariat, and he revealed this through an understanding of the state as always having been an endowment of some form of privilege: "a priestly class, an aristocratic class, a bourgeois class. And finally, when all the other classes have exhausted themselves, the State then becomes the patrimony of the bureaucratic class and then falls—or, if you will, rises—to the position of a machine." Such reflection makes the withering argument, and thus revolution itself, untenable when expressed in the vanguardist terms of seizing the state apparatus. If revolution is ever to be salvaged as a viable idea, it must be refocused toward the particularities of the everyday and the insurgent possibilities that exist within the *here* and *now*. But such an alignment with anarchist–autonomist sensibilities doesn't seem to suit Smith:

> the invocation of political spontaneity as a means to a different future conjures up its own utopianism. A revolution of the discursive self is necessary, whether connected to political movements or not, but it is not a sufficient means to revolutionary social change. "Change yourself and the world will change with you" was a hopeful 1960s slogan, which had its genuine uses, but the need for political organization is not thereby dissolved. (57–58)

Unfortunately, this critique misses the mark, as anarchism is not opposed to organization: "It is about creating new forms of organization. It is not lacking in ideology. Those new forms of organization *are* its ideology" (Graeber 2002, 70). Anarchism is about the reinvention of daily life through the active creation of horizontal networks of affinity and mutual aid in the place of hierarchical structures.

Unlike the end-state politics of Marxism and neoliberalism, which both envision a moment where history ends and a harmonious global village of one sort or another is instantiated, the prefigurative politics of anarchism are considered as an infinitely demanding struggle (Critchley 2007). In other words, whereas a revolutionary imperative is a means to an end, an insurrectionary imperative is a means *without* end. There is an ageographical tendency to the revolutionary imperative that some Marxists have begun to reject, notably autonomists and the Situationists, which moves them closer to an anarchistic understanding of the world. As a political philosophy, anarchism fully appreciates the processual nature of space, where the politics of waiting—for the revolution, for the withering away of the state, for the stages of history to pass—is rejected in favor of the realism that comes with acknowledging that the everyday is the only moment and space in which we have any tangible control over our lives. Thus, far from being utopian, anarchism is precisely the opposite. It is an antidote to Marxian political deferral. Embracing the *here* and *now* of the everyday represents a deeper appreciation for space-time as a constantly folding, unfolding, and refolding story, whereby direct action, radical democracy, and mutual aid allow us to instantaneously reconfigure its parameters.

ANOTHER WORLD BECOMES POSSIBLE

Although there is some debate over Henry David Thoreau's ([1854] 2004, 248) position as an anarchist, when it came to highlighting a prefigurative sense of politics, his intentions seemed clear enough: "If you have built castles in the air, your work need not be lost; that is where they should be. Now put the foundations under them." This sentiment seems to contrast starkly with the politics of waiting that rests at the center of the Marxist project. Perhaps owing to texts like *The Critique of Everyday Life* (Lefebvre [1958] 2008), which had a profound influence on the Situationists, Edward W. Soja once asked Henri Lefebvre if he was an anarchist. "No. Not now," he replied, and when queried as to what he is now, Lefebvre replied, "A Marxist, of course ... so that we can all become anarchists some time in the future" (qtd. in Soja 1996, 33). Thus, despite the major impact he had on a more autonomist Marxian trajectory, Lefebvre's response exemplifies the politics of waiting that signifies traditional Marxism. It is an attitude that resides in the decomposing body of vanguardism and bears only the withered fruit of an idea that has been, on numerous occasions, proven thoroughly rotten. The vanguard is a cipher for a new dictatorship, a gambit so powerful that it even blinds its own advocates. "Our vanguardism will be different," they tell themselves. "We'll do things right this time, we're not like the Bolsheviks or the Khmer Rouge, and the eventual withering away of our temporary authority is assured." But the problem is not to be found in either the sincerity or the lack thereof of this sentiment; the problem rests within the very idea itself. Marxism does not appreciate that we cannot liberate each other but can only liberate ourselves, and so it places its faith in a proletariat led by a vanguard that inevitably reproduces that which it rails against. It does so precisely because it employs the same twisted methodology of the oppressor, reaping what it sows through its reliance on authority. Stirner (as qtd. in Kalyvas 2010, 351) recognized the folly of an outside agent being responsible for individual liberation when he suggested that "whoever will be free must make himself free. Freedom is no fairy gift to fall into a man's lap." Philosopher William James (as qtd. in Johnson and Boynton 2010, 19) asserted a similar sentiment when he insisted that "the greatest discovery of our generation is that human beings can alter their attitudes of mind. As you think, so shall you be." Thus, until the day arrives when we can individually find the courage to unchain our imaginations from the prisons of vanguardism and hierarchy, the specter of authoritarianism will continue to haunt our political organizations and social relationships, infecting them with its violence. Our performativity literally makes the world (Butler 1997). The roles we play and the scripts that we follow set the parameters of possibility. But when we venture into the realm of improvisation, traditional Marxism recoils with the same sense of horror as capitalism. There is a rational order that must be followed in both ideologies, and those who refuse to play by the rules of the game, who actively laugh in the face of authority, are shunned for their bravery or, worse, silenced through ridicule, imprisonment, or, most heinous of all, execution.

Contemporary radical geography needs a shot in the arm precisely because it remains indifferent, skeptical, and even hostile toward those unconventional geographical imaginations that fall outside of a traditional Marxian analysis. Consequently, anarchism, as an alternative socialism to Marxism, remains all but ignored by contemporary human geographers. When anarchism is considered, it is either misused as a synonym for violence and chaos or derided as a hopelessly utopian project, one that is ostensibly irreconcilable with "reality" or any practical application.[6] Yet it is incorrect to assume anarchism as a *project*, which instead reflects the domain of Marxian thought. Anarchism, as I have attempted to demonstrate, is more appropriately considered a continually unfolding *process*, a forever protean means without end that is perpetually being prefigured through direct action, mutual aid, voluntary association, and self-organization. Unlike Marxism's stages of history and its revolution-ary imperative, which imply an end-state politics, anarchism is a political philosophy that fully appreciates the essential dynamism of the social world. As such, explaining the passage from the current condition of neoliberal miasma to an emancipated future is the problem of utopian thought, not the "anarchism without end" I describe here, which abandons any pretext of achieving a completely free and harmonious society in the future and instead focuses on the immediacies of anarchist praxis and a prefigurative politics of direct action in the present. History has clearly demonstrated that revolution merely introduces new forms of tyranny, and accordingly, I advocate a distinction between permanent insurrection, which is supported, and final revolution, which is opposed. This is not to argue that dreams of a better tomorrow are an insignificant component of anarchist thought, as indeed prefigurative politics embraces the notion of an improved alternative world. Instead, I mean to suggest that anarchism, as a *process* rather than a *project*, is able to conceive of utopianism in terms that allow for perpetual revision through its attention to prefiguration and the fact that we only ever live our lives in the *here* and *now*.

It may be said that my argument presents an old version of Marxism, and certainly it is the traditional variant of Marxism that is the focus of my critique. But with all the "post" revisions that are still being made, why not pause and reflect on how this activity of tacking on appendages and amendments often simply brings Marxism closer to anarchism, as is the case with the autonomists? Moreover, what has history taught us about the implementation of Marxist ideas on a broad scale? "The attempt to rescue the Marxism pedigree by emphasizing the method over the system or by adding 'neo' to a sacred word," Bookchin ([1971] 2004, 112) wrote, "is sheer mystification if all the *practical* conclusions of the system flatly contradict these efforts." And yet this is the precise location where Marxian geographical inquiry finds itself today. Marx's writings on commodity relationships, alienation, and particularly the accumulation of capital are still brilliant exegeses that inspire a great number of radical geographers, myself included. There is no doubt that Marxism offers a luminous interpretation of the past, but what it has to offer the present and future is misleading given the fragmented identity politics that exist in our contemporary world, where the notion of a universal proletariat is pure delusion. Anticapitalist and antiwar protests have become increasingly diffuse in recent years, where the solidarities and affinities of which they are indicative point to the emergence of new forms of emancipatory politics, breaking with Marxism's traditional category of class (Newman 2007). Though the academy clings to Marxism, it has lost its appeal on the street, having been eclipsed within contemporary social moments, which are now largely inspired by anarchist principles of voluntary association, egalitarianism, direct action, and radical democracy (Epstein 2001). And yet radical geographers continue to hold fast to Marxism, owing perhaps to a deep affinity within academia that anarchism could never claim. Graeber (2007, 303) muses that this circumstance is a reflection of the vanguard spirit of the academy itself, where Marxism was, after all, invented by a PhD, while anarchism was never really invented by anyone, as "we are talking less about a body of theory than about an attitude."

I have no major qualms with autonomist Marxism, other than what is seemingly a lack of courage simply to call their ideas anarchist, as this has been the most autonomous domain of socialist thought all along. Yet such fear is somewhat understandable given that most academics continue to have only the faintest idea of what anarchism is even about. There are hundreds of academic Marxist geographers of various shapes, stripes, sizes, and shades, but hardly anyone is willing openly to call herself an anarchist for fear of ridicule. Anarchism is, even within the academy, continually dismissed through the crudest stereotypes, where its mere mention invokes an uncritical and reactionary image of disorder and violence. Among a crowd of intellectuals who take pride in attention to detail, this is tiresome, and it was evidently already tiresome more than a century ago, when Reclus (1884, 627) wrote,

> Public speakers on social and political subjects find that abuse of anarchists is an unfailing passport to public favor. Every conceivable crime is laid to our charge, and opinion, too indolent to learn the truth, is easily persuaded that anarchy is but another name for wickedness and chaos. Overwhelmed with opprobrium and held up with hatred, we are treated on the principle that the surest way of hanging a dog is to give it a bad name.

Radical geographers can do better. It is high time that we collectively look again at what we think we know about anarchism to begin exploring the horizontality, rhizomic organization, and decentralization of power that anarchism offers so that we might therein acquire a greater appreciation for what is already happening all around us, from the streets of Cairo to the community garden on our own blocks. The geographies of direct action, mutual aid, and prefigurative politics demand our attention precisely because we stare them in the face on a daily basis, but we scarcely recognize them for what they are. Every time you have ever invited friends over to dinner, jaywalked, mowed your neighbor's lawn, skipped a day at work, looked after your brother's kids, questioned your professor, borrowed your mother-in-law's car, disregarded a posted sign, or returned a favor, you have—perhaps unknowingly—engaged in anarchist principles.

Unfortunately, old habits die hard, and in his latest book, Harvey (2012b, 69) scorns what he refers to as the naive and hopeful gesturing of decentralized thinking, lamenting how the term *hierarchy* is "virulently unpopular with much of the left these days." The message rings through loud and clear: how dare anarchists (and autonomists) attempt to conceive of something different and new, when we should be treading water in the sea of yesterday's spent ideas. In his dismissal, what Harvey perhaps doesn't recognize is that he is not just denying "some magical concordance" (80); he is also denying the very possibilities of space, with its undetermined stories-so-far and continually receding horizon (Massey 2005), possibilities that he once argued so passionately in favor of (Harvey 2000). Lefebvre (1991) demonstrated how our productions of space stem directly from our visualizations and that whatever materializations and administrations of space we might procure cannot be separated from the way we think about geography, precisely because thinking produces action. For anarchists, "there is no difference between what we do and what we think, but there is a continual reversing of theory into action and action into theory" (Bonanno 1996, 2). As we think, as we act, as we write, so we shall be. To write the earth with the pen of our hopes and dreams is not merely to sketch an illustration without materiality. Its very composition refracts against the world in which we live and therein transforms its character. This is why a radical geography must be anarchist, for in its anarchy comes, not chaos and destruction, not hierarchy and vanguardism, not alienation and exploitation, but new geographies of organization, solidarity, community, affinity, and opportunity. This is a magic I have to believe in, because to refuse its enchantment is to stoke the funeral pyre of emancipatory politics and cede to the insanity of government. "Anarchism is not a romantic fable," said Edward Abbey (1989, 22), "but the hardheaded realization, based on five thousand years of experience, that we cannot entrust the management of our lives to kings, priests, politicians, generals, and county commissioners." And so I am an anarchist, of course, so that right *here* and *now,* another world becomes possible. The foundations are in place.

4

Emancipatory Space

If we are to carry the lessons of the past with us, then, we must conceive and practice struggle not with democracy as an end in view, but democratically in its very unfolding.
—Todd May

Politics is the sphere neither of an end in itself nor of means subordinated to an end; rather, it is the sphere of a pure mediality without end intended as the field of human action and of human thought.
—Giorgio Agamben

In establishing an anarchist framework for understanding public space as a vision for radical democracy, this chapter proceeds as a theoretical inquiry into how an agonistic public space might become the basis of emancipation. Emancipation, as it is understood here, means perpetual contestation of the alienating effects of capitalism and its contemporary expression as neoliberalism. Central to this is imagining new forms of voluntary association and mutual aid, where pluralism may blossom, democratic engagement might be enhanced, and a liberatory zeitgeist may emerge. The emancipatory thrust inherent to democracy calls for a reclamation of its etymology and a critical rereading of the diverse contexts and contents—social, cultural, local, national, and global—through which it finds its expression (Kothari 2005). I advocate radical democracy, which, contra aggregative and deliberative models, places politics on a path toward the co-constitutive promise of anarchism and nonviolence. I argue for a conceptualization of public space that emphasizes an anti-hegemonic, antisovereign current, thus offering an opportunity to surmount the technocratic elitism that characterizes the current moment of neoliberalism and the class war that is capitalism. A move toward democracy "from below" is recognized as an affront to both "local" elites and "global" capital. Accordingly, I examine the contested, forever-protean *process* of radical democracy conceived as public space. Public space is understood as the battlefield on which the conflicting interests of the rich and poor are set as well as the object of contestation. Within this realm, violence is often understood as both an outcome of attempts to impose an "ordered" view of public space originating "from above" and as an act of resistance "from below" by those seeking radical democratic spaces of "unscripted" interaction.[1] This violence reveals an apparent paradox of democracy, because although premised on the nonviolent mitigation of conflict, contemporary "democracies" are often antipolitical and antagonistic, which provokes the possibility of violent conflict.

Celebrations of modernity have resulted in a division between those cities seen as sites for the production of urban theory and those projected as objects for "development." This has provided fertile ground for problematic demarcations that divide cities into systems of hierarchy, where the West/First World/Global North is imagined through a positive frame of dynamism and innovation, while the non-West/Third World/Global South is portrayed negatively as stagnation and stasis. Binary thinking "remains much more a driving idea than a fact of geography" (Slater 2004, 9), which suggests that a single urban discourse is overdue. Jenny Robinson (2006, 1) encourages scholars not to ascribe prominence to certain cities or features of particular cities and instead suggests that "an ordinary-city approach takes the world of cities as its starting point and attends to the diversity and complexity of all cities." An ordinary cities approach is not meant as a universalization that denies distinctive elements by downplaying the diversity among cities. Rather, "in a world of ordinary cities, ways of being urban and ways of making new kinds of urban futures are diverse and are the product of the inventiveness of people in cities everywhere" (1). Given that binary categories continue to retain broad usage in urban theory, while nonetheless being called into question, David Slater (2004, 10) proposes that they be approached "as if there is a line running through them, canceling them out in their old form, but still allowing them to be read." This partial erasure encourages scholars to continue to problematize their validity, while remaining open to the possibility of new categories that are more aware of asymmetrical relations, enable collective engagement, and take seriously the imbrications between "inside" and "outside." Thus an ordinary cities approach forms a postcolonial framework for understanding cities, challenging urban theory's tendency to privilege the experiences of the "West."

Although the ideals of public space and the ways citizens conceive democracy are uniquely shaped by contingent sociocultural histories, my purpose is not to apply a Global North–Global South perspective. Instead, I want to question such dichotomies and bring a more relational approach, precisely because the processes of neoliberalization that are deleteriously affecting the very notion of the public are being challenged in a diverse range of contexts that encompass all areas of the globe. Urban scholars must recall that relational connections across space are established by and constitutive of ostensibly "local" cultures all over the world (Smith 2001). By employing radical notions of public space through an ordinary cities approach, we may improve our understandings of the relational geographies of capitalism, where each "local" contestation of public space can be read as a nodal point of interconnection in socially produced space (Massey 2005). Through this, Gillian Hart (2008, 684) argues, we may grasp "the slippages, openings, contradictions, and possibilities for alliances" that exist across space. My purpose, then, is to acknowledge these relational geographies, wherein incidents like the struggles over water privatization in Cochabamba, Bolivia, in 2000 (Kohl 2006) and the "battle for Seattle" during the World Trade Organization meetings of 1999 must be considered not as isolated events in a "Third World" or "First World" milieu but as moments tied to the broader assemblage of global contestations over the "right to the city" and alternative urban futures (Purcell 2008). An examination of the controversy of public space allows for an understanding of the ongoing struggle for a more radical democracy as fundamentally a clash between the machinations of global capitalism and the attempts of the poor and marginalized to insert their voices into the development policies and planning practices that adversely affect their lives.

This chapter begins by establishing a framework for understanding democracy in nonviolent and anarchist terms by arguing for radical democracy conceived through agonistic public space. I investigate the relationship between anarchism, democracy, and nonviolent politics and contend that a radicalization of democracy's content and meaning through an insistence on agonism challenges the antipolitical modes of aggregative and deliberative democracy that are considered to legitimize neoliberal rationalities and license hierarchical power structures. In the following section, I recognize the "space of appearance" as vital to democratic representation. Distinction is drawn between public space and the public sphere, the latter of which lacks physicality, an essential requirement for individuals to exert pressure in demanding answers to issues of public importance. I also confront the ongoing exclusions of public space, as marginalized groups often find themselves subjected to prohibitions of access, yet their struggles for presence reveal that the democratic potential of public space is never entirely lost. Building on this notion of perpetual struggle, I then examine public space as a domain of contestation. I begin by recognizing public space as the site where political actors, both rich and poor, and the stratagem of neoliberalized capital continually stake their claims. The inherently contested character of public space reveals that it is never free from the risk of disorder, an observation that places democracy in conflict with the need for "order" so that capitalism should flow smoothly. The following section examines the interface between public space, democracy, and violence. Public space, while having democratic potential, is often also paradoxically a space of violence. So-called violence that originates "from below" is frequently driven by a demand for equality and is thus sometimes considered the only endeavor that can democratize a political system, whereas actual violence "from above" intends to preserve the status quo of the established order. Yet we know violence begets violence, and accordingly, I examine whether democracy exists in a disquieting nexus or an irreconcilable schism with violence. In the conclusion, I contend that when radical democracy is conceived in anarchist terms and materialized through public space, it offers emancipatory potential from disciplinary neoliberal strictures. Democratic struggle grounded in public space offers a chance not only for those most oppressed by capitalism to demand social justice but for the integral totality of human society to seek a new way forward through agonistic politics.

Although protest movements necessarily occur in terrains that always exceed neoliberalism (Hart 2008; Leitner, Peck, and Sheppard 2007), it is important to think through how a rising tide of contestation can be reinterpreted through a shared sense of betrayal with what can be defined as "neoliberal policy goals," which speaks to a more general discontent with capitalism. In going beyond the "facts" of neoliberalization, I align my arguments to the growing recognition that transnational solidarity is inseparable from "local" movements and must be built upon *relational* understandings of both resistance to and the violences of capitalism (see Seoane 2004; Sundberg 2007; Wainwright and Kim 2008). This chapter contributes to this discussion by arguing that the realization of a radical democratic ideals grounded in public space is of primary importance to the achievement of any emancipatory goal that seeks to transform capitalism's violent geographies of exclusion, inequality, and poverty but cautions that this process of transformation itself lamentably runs the risk of violence precisely because the political terrain has been so sharply narrowed by neoliberal antipolitics.

RADICALIZING DEMOCRACY THROUGH ANARCHISM

It is difficult to choose criteria by which one may categorize a political regime as "democratic." The waters are muddied, and as Errico Malatesta (1924) noted, "there is something to be said for the criticisms made of democracy by dictatorial regimes, and the way they expose the vices and lies of democracy." Meanings ascribed to democracy vary from a way of life to a form of government (Arat 1991). Schmitter and Karl (1993, 40) corroborate this notion, emphasizing that "the specific form democracy takes is contingent upon a country's socioeconomic conditions as well as its entrenched state structures and policy practices." But such understandings actually degrade our conceptualization of democracy. Accepting a "cultural relativist" position denies universal meaning to democracy and thereby contributes to indemnifying dictatorships that appropriate the word. George Orwell (1993, 163) once stated,

> It is almost universally felt that when we call a country democratic we are praising it: consequently the defenders of every kind of regime claim that it is a democracy, and fear that they might have to stop using the word if it were tied down to any one meaning.

Democracy is thus sometimes said to have a crisis of meaning, used to justify everything from terror to compromise, revolution to mediocrity. Making matters potentially more confusing, Larry Diamond (1993, 4) suggests that "democracy may approach the 'equilibrium version' of the process but is open to improvement or deterioration," whereas Iris Marion Young (2000, 5) calls democracy "a matter of degree." Robert Dahl (1971) thus chose to eschew democracy altogether, employing the term *polyarchy* to acknowledge that democracy is never a complete project but rather always in a process of becoming.

Although Anthony Giddens's (1999) "third way" treatise was published more than twenty-five years later, in hindsight, Dahl's (1971) emphasis on proteanism can be seen as a preemptive strike on deliberative democracy and its atemporal declaration of the end of adversarial politics through an insistence on consensual politics. Dahl's ideas nonetheless still fall under the umbrella of aggregative democracy, which uses processes such as elections to solicit citizens' preferences to determine policy directions. In contrast to both aggregative and deliberative models, radical democracy emphasizes "agonistic pluralism," which acknowledges the role of hierarchical and oppressive power relations in society and allows for the ever-present possibility of difference and dissent. The aim of radical democracy is not to establish a rational consensus in the public sphere but to defuse the potential of human hostilities by providing the possibility for antagonism to be transformed into "agonism" (Mouffe 2004). Agonism refers to the idea that conflict cannot and should not be eradicated. Nor should confrontation take the form of competition between elites or struggle between enemies (antagonism); rather, contestation must be between adversaries (agonism). In its radicalized sense, democracy is understood not as a system of rule *(archy)* but as a particular mode of power. The etymology of *democracy* (*demos,* "the people"; *kratia,* "power") exposes how its institutionalization changes it into something entirely different, into "demoarchy"—a system of rule by multiplicity and, ostensibly, by "the people." The aggregative and deliberative approaches have negative consequences for democratic politics because they seek to eliminate agonism, which Chantal Mouffe (2006) appropriately recognizes as ineradicable in politics. Aggregative models strip the soul of democracy by transforming its basis as a *mode* of power into a *system* of procedural rule. We might accordingly relabel the oxymoron "representative democracy" as "electoral authoritarianism," because voting encourages one to reduce opposing positions to hostile caricature that must be suppressed (Graeber 2009a). Deliberative democracy in contrast is the "fulfillment of

EMANCIPATORY SPACE   103

a tendency, inscribed at the very core of liberalism, which, because of its constitutive incapacity to think in truly political terms, must always resort to another type of discourse: economic, moral or juridical" (Mouffe 2004, 124–25). Rather than opening political space for those at the margins (see Dryzek 2000), deliberative democracy contributes to an antipolitical view of society that reinforces the hegemony of the existing economic order by forestalling our ability to articulate political alternatives.

The belief that political questions are of a moral nature, and therefore susceptible to rational treatment, is paramount to deliberative democracy. Here the objective of democratic society is reduced to creating rational consensus, and those who question this by maintaining that the political is a domain where one should always expect to find discord are accused of undermining the very possibility of democracy (Mouffe 2004, 124).[2] Contra deliberative democracy, a well-functioning democracy calls for a confrontation of democratic political positions. This means that democracy always runs the risk of violence, but paradoxically, this potential is actually mitigated by allowing conflict to play an integrative role. In its absence, there is an ever-present danger that "democratic confrontation will be replaced by a battle between non-negotiable moral values or essentialist forms of identifications" (125). This makes any latency of violence much more manifest in "democratic" models that abandon agonism for antagonism, not only because of the hierarchies built into all versions of systematized rule, which institutional "democracies" advocate, but also because the "them" that contrasts the "us" cannot be viewed as respected political adversaries in nonagonistic models of democracy. The "them" can only be defined as moral, economic, and juridical enemies, or enemies of reason, making "them" a "savage them" rather than legitimate adversaries. Therefore, despite the pronouncements of a third way and its benign appearance, only radical democracy can lead to a society rooted in nonviolence, which aligns its content very closely to anarchism. Although anarchism is often portrayed as a symptom of mental illness rather than a valid political position, such sensationalism is a ploy by its detractors. Far from caricatural depictions of anarchism as the promotion of violence, it is instead, as I have been arguing all along, the rejection of violence in all its forms. Violence is antithetical to anarchy precisely because all violence involves a form of domination, authority, or system of rule over other individuals. Violence is thus a disavowal of freedom, not its pro-motion. Through the renunciation of all forms of *archy* (systems of rule), radical democracy can be conceived as a basis for emancipation because it emphasizes nonviolence and allows for dissent and difference. In con-trast, overemphasizing consensus, coupled with aversion to confrontation, "engenders apathy and disaffection with political participation" (125). So although consensus is necessary for societies to function, it must always be accompanied by dissent, which means that democracy is a forever-protean process, where resistance to the integral logics of sovereignty, law, and capitalism becomes a politics of gesture—a permanent *"means without end"* (Agamben 2000).

Mouffe (2004, 130) maintains that to "establish the conditions for effective democratic self-governance, citizens need to belong to a *demos* where they can exercise their rights of citizenship...[which] does not mean that political units must be identical with the nation-state." I agree with the rejection of sovereign power, but I also want to go beyond no-tions of citizenship by replacing them with the free associations, voluntary cooperation, and mutual aid of anarchism. As Simon Critchley (2004, 231) recognizes,

> the problem with much thinking about politics is that it is *archic,* it is obsessed with the moment of foundation, origination, declaration or in-stitution that is linked to the act of government, of sovereignty, most of all *decision* that presupposes and initiates a sovereign political subject capable of self-government and the government of others.

To Jacques Rancière (1999), this is the reduction of *la politique* to the or-der of *la police* and is precisely why, as will become clear in what follows, I develop a distinction between "unscripted"–democratic–anarchic and "ordered"–authoritarian–archic views of public space. Radical democracy should not be about governance, whether directed by the "self," as in governmentality, or otherwise. There is no "self" to refer to in an anarchic democracy.

Who are "the people" then? Emmanuel Levinas (1979, 294) discusses the "anarchy essential to multiplicity," a multiplicity that is itself essential to politics, where politics is the manifestation of the multiplicity that is the people, the *demos.* This is similar to the multitude of Michael Hardt and

Antonio Negri (2004), where the people cannot be identified or policed in any territorializing sense. Rather, "the people" comprise what Rancière (1999) describes as that empty space that exceeds any social quantification, precisely because a democratic politics emerges through a *presupposition of equality*, meaning democracy is a resistance against the mechanisms of an order that distributes roles hierarchically. As Critchley (2004, 231) contends, "the people are those who do not count, who have no right to govern whether through hereditary entitlement like aristocracy or by wealth and property ownership like bourgeoisie." In short, the people represent a contradiction to sovereign order and juridical power, being conceived as precisely those who are excluded from civil rights, or what Giorgio Agamben (1998) refers to as *homo sacer*. Radical democracy occurs when those who the sovereign deems not to count insist on being counted, not within the existing order, but within a new antiorder, an *anarchy*. Thus the antipolitical tradition (exemplified by neoliberalism) fears the people in its radical manifestation, not as *das Volk* shaped by the state but as *die Leute,* the people in their bare-life liberty and irreducible plurality. The convergence of *homo sacer* and the *presupposition of equality* turns existing power relations on their head and overcomes the dangers of "militant particularisms" (Harvey 1996). Identity politics can still function, but it becomes nonessential to politics as antagonism is transformed into agonism, where everyone is a legitimate and equal claimant through her preconceived equality. This is precisely the heterogeneity that Clive Barnett (2004a) misses when he homogenizes the work of Laclau and Mouffe (2001) in arguing that agonism spatializes politics because it relies on clear distinctions between "inside" and "outside."[3]

If the contemporary zeitgeist embraces an all-encompassing consensus and therefore the elimination of agonism (Mouffe 2004), then the activity of governance continually risks pacification, order, the state, and what Rancière (1999, 135) refers to as the "dark side of the idyll of consensus." Faith in universal consensus is not only antipolitical, it is also the exact mode that constitutes end-state thinking, as is exemplified by neoliberalism's grand narratives of a harmonious "global village" and the "end of history" (Fukuyama 1992). Anarchism in contrast represents the living, breathing essence of politics, the "primary reality of strife in social life" (Mouffe 2000, 113), embracing the openness that the forever protean nature of space-time demands.[4] Politics as such is materialized via the public display of *dissensus*, a dissensus that disrupts the depoliticizing order built by government. As Critchley (2004, 232) argues, "if politics can be understood as the manifestation of the anarchic *demos*, then politics and democracy are two names for the same thing," where democratization "consists in the manifestation of...demonstration as *demos*-stration." Democracy, then, is the "politics of the street," which necessitates a material grounding in public space (Ferrell 2001; Mitchell 2003b), aligning its content to the direct action of anarchist praxis. But to align democracy to direct action and a material public space is not to suggest a spatiality of limited means, which would reduce the demand for democracy to little more than a theoretical abstraction, unconnected to the complex histories and elaborate geographies that have unfolded to create democratic desire. Instead, when the word *democracy* is used in "the right place, at the right moment, it is fresh, clear, and true" (Lummis 1996, 15), precisely because its spatiotemporality takes *place* in a political *moment* of globalized expropriation and violent injustice. Consequently, the spatialities of radical democracy conceived as public space are relational, stretching inward and outward across a "global sense of place" (Massey 1994)[5] So whereas radical democracy *is not* about spatialization in the sense of territorialization, as Barnett (2004a) argues, it *is* about the intercalated geographies of space in the sense Doreen Massey identifies, as it allows us to "envision new forms of solidarity based on recognized interdependence" (Mouffe 2004, 131). The ethics of radical democracy cannot be conceptualized in moralistic terms, as is the current (neo) liberal democratic treatment, nor can they be bounded in any sense that implies a sovereign. Radical democracy represents a disturbance of the antipolitical order of sovereignty itself and is thus, in a word, *anarchy*.

THE SPACE OF APPEARANCE

It is in the making and taking of space and place that allows us to move toward a more radical model of democracy:

> If...place and self are mutually constitutive, then the means of creating the ideal self for sustaining the project of democracy have parallels in place-making. In constructing places we seek to have them match our

projects and ideals, both individual and collective. In democracies such ideals include the desire to build places that promote social justice, tolerance, and inclusion and that offer public gathering spaces or places reflecting collective values about community....Viewed as a form of life and as a process, democracy involves in part the making, unmaking, and remaking of places. (Entrikin 2002, 107–8)

Because democracy is meant to be inclusive, it is specifically those *public* spaces and places that are of primary importance. Thus public space can be understood as the very practice of radical democracy, including agonism, which might rid politics of hierarchy, technocracy, international patrons, government appropriation, and co-optation by the modern aristocracy. This relationship between radical democracy and space is crucial, because democracy requires not only spaces where people can gather to discuss the issues of the day (Staeheli and Thompson 1997) but also places where ideas can be contested. A democratic society must value public space as a forum for *all* social groups, where there should be no structural deterrents prohibiting the ability of individuals to participate in public affairs. Public space as such is the site where collective performance, speech, and agonism must be entrenched (Goheen 1998), thus allowing it to become the primary medium through which identities are created and disputed (Ruddick 1996).

The idea that public space is important for identity formation is well recognized in human geography (Lees 1994; Massey 1994). This creative process works both ways, as identity is important in forming the contours of public space.[6] Whereas public space allows individuals to join collaborative efforts and still maintain distinct voices, representation demands a physical space so that individuals and groups may make their needs known and show themselves as legitimate claimants to public considerations (Mitchell 2003b). Yet the right to representation is not always recognized, as is the case under authoritarianism, and accordingly, public space can also refer to the extent of sociopolitical interaction available to a person. Arendt (1958) calls this the "space of appearance" or the space needed for people to be seen. Action and speech require visibility because for democratic politics to occur, it is not enough for a group of private individuals to vote anonymously as in aggregative democracy. Instead, because belonging to any public requires at least minimal participation, individuals must physically come together and occupy a common space (Howell 1993). Though visibility is central to public space, theatricality is also required, because wherever people gather, the space of appearance is not just "there" but is actively (re)produced through recurring performances (Valentine 1996).

Theatricality recognizes that space is produced, an idea popularized by Henri Lefebvre (1991), who draws a distinction between the administration of space and its materialization. In Lefebvre's terms, public space that is controlled by government or other institutions, or whose use is regulated, is referred to as "representation of space," whereas public space as it is actually used by social groups is called "representational space." This distinction draws attention to the difference between the "official" status of a space and the ability of various individuals and groups to use it (Arefi and Meyers 2003). The power to deem particular spaces "official" runs concomitant to the power to exclude certain groups from such sites on the basis of this very ascription. When might we be certain that any particular space is "official," except when told so by those holding archic power? Yet Lefebvre's dichotomy also hints at the underlying contestation of public space and its essential condition of agonism by acknowledging its social constructedness or spatiality. Thus representation not only demands space but also creates it.

A further benefit of Lefebvre's theorization is the significance afforded to bodily representations or lived experiences of space (McCann 1999). This addresses the fundamental difference between public space and the public sphere, which are often mistakenly conflated. The public sphere, which in its original Habermasian sense is effectively silent on space (Howell 1993), can be defined as the abstract domain of social life, ideally separate from the coercion of state power, where public opinion is formed (Habermas 1989). In contrast, public space must be taken literally as a material space precisely because this dimension provides visibility to political action (Ferrell 2001; Mitchell 2003b). Even aggregative and deliberative democracies bear witness to protests launched "on the ground" in material spaces providing nonelectoral feedback into "virtual public space" (i.e., the public sphere) when democracy is no longer radical. Although a demonstration's goal may at times be to achieve greater visibility via the public sphere, the media cannot enable such visibility without a political claim being enacted in public space. Absent this initial physical dimension, claims may be audible or textual to become discursive within the public sphere, but they still lack a space of appearance. Thus, because public space cannot be established in the abstract, newspapers, radio, television, and the Internet are part of the public sphere and not public space.

One could further argue against the notion of abstract spaces as public space because they are often highly structured, dominated by corporate and/or government interests, and thus may enhance existing power structures (Calhoun 1998). The Internet in particular has been championed as a revolutionary tool with the potential to invigorate democracy (Crang 2000). Jodi Dean (2003) disregards such views, suggesting that corporate control has made the Internet a "zero institution," leading not to democracy but to "communicative capitalism." Yet the Internet and other media are still able to provide a network that allows social groups to disseminate information, organize, and mobilize (Castells 2000). The circulation of images, arguments, and ideas through various media, including individual actions carried out in private space, but gaining access to a wider public through the public sphere, can have important effects that may open or even close opportunities for political action. For example, although the public was rarely provided with unedited versions, the impact of Osama bin Laden releasing videotaped messages was enormous. Yet despite the power of such communications to rally support and opposition through public broadcast, both al-Qaeda and the U.S. "war on terror" recognized the importance of grounding their political objectives in physical space, hence the horrifying events of September 11, 2001, and the equally appalling invasions of Afghanistan and Iraq. All groups, whether subaltern or dominant, cannot constitute themselves unless they produce a material space. As Don Mitchell (2003b, 147) argues, "all the web communications in the world would not have nearly shut down the Seattle meeting of the World Trade Organization or destroyed the Genoa talks. But people in the streets did."

Nonetheless, Barnett (2004b, 190) takes issue with a so-called prevailing view that presumes that Habermas's conceptualization of the public sphere must be grounded in real, material public spaces:

The assumption is that Habermas's original conceptualization of the public sphere depends on a metaphorical understanding of material spaces.... However, the argument that Habermas's public sphere is insufficiently material seems wrong-headed. The problem with *The Structural Transformation of the Public Sphere* is not that it ignores real spaces, but that it conceptually constructs locals of co-presence as the norm for judging the publicness of historically viable practices of social interaction. Furthermore, geographers' determination to translate the public sphere into bounded public urban spaces of co-present social interaction ... illustrates a long-standing underestimation of the significance of communications practices in critical human geography.... Any stark opposition between real material spaces and virtual media spaces does not hold up because it fails to register the extent to which various social movements deploy a range of dramaturgical strategies of protest that construct "real" spaces as stages through which to mobilize media attention and thereby project their presence through spatially extensive media networks.

What Barnett is really describing is how social movements use material public space as a costrategy to achieving further attention via the public sphere, as noted earlier. Barnett continues by arguing that "the geography of the public sphere should not be narrowly defined in terms of selected spaces of co-present social interaction ... [because] the idealization of 'real' and 'material' spaces closes down a full consideration of the geographical constitution of those strategic practices of needs interpretation and legitimate decision-making that establish the broader conditions of possibility for social interaction guided by norms of civility and respect" (191). In fact, what is being suggested here is not novel, and it seems that Barnett is simply playing to semantics in wanting to label this nonmaterial "feedback" of strategic practice as "public space." Far from negating a thorough contemplation of the extended spatialities of strategic practice employed by social movements, many geographers (see Goheen 1998; Howell 1993; Mitchell 2003b) simply assign this work to the public sphere, which, contra Barnett's claim, is still not tantamount to public space, a concept that is always material. In short, there is no assumption that Habermas's conception of the public sphere demands a metaphorical understanding of material spaces. Rather, to many geographers, the Habermasian public sphere is always a realm of immateriality and simply cannot be confused with material space.

Moreover, though Barnett (2004b; see also Keith 1997) may view such promotion of the necessary physicality of public space as a fetish that romanticizes the "street," such critiques are misplaced, serving to undermine the potential radicalism of postmodern politics. As Lewis Call (2002, 7–8) argues, Habermas "use[s] the terms and categories of the debate about postmodern politics to reinforce the rapidly eroding theoretical and epistemological foundations of the modern liberal state"; he hopes to do this "by placing instrumental rationality—the 'rationality' of concentration camps and hydrogen bombs—within the context of a broader and more hopeful 'communicative rationality' which, Habermas asserts, can operate within a kind of cultural and political 'public sphere' to produce viable (and implicitly liberal) communities." What is at stake here is that

> Habermas rejects Marxism and the radical materialist perspective in favor of an amalgam of liberal rationalism, conservative sociological theory, and mainstream language philosophy, and he puts aside the revolutionary goal of earlier Frankfurt School thinkers like Marcuse in favor of social democratic accommodation with the "rational" realities of capitalism. (Ryan 1989, 27)

Thus invocations of Habermas as the alpha and omega of relevant political theory with regard to assessments of the public sphere (misunderstood by Barnett as public space) should be treated with a deep skepticism that recognizes this view's contribution to reinforcing (neo)liberal rationalities. Ultimately, the Habermasian theory of immateriality cannot be accommodated within the politics of radical democracy, which is necessarily rooted in direct action and the materialism of public space. As Lefebvre (1991, 416–17) argues, those ideas, values, or representations that fail to make their mark in space "lose all pith and become mere signs, resolve themselves into abstract descriptions, or mutate into fantasies."

The exclusion of some groups from democratic processes via their failures to attain recognition in public space underlines the critical importance of materiality. Although many scholars recognize the democratic character of public space (Barnett and Low 2004; Hénaff and Strong 2001; Howell 1993), this idea is contested, as public space has paradoxically also long been a site of exploitation, oppression, and prohibition for women (Bondi 1996; Massey 1994), ethnic minorities (McCann 1999; Ruddick 1996), gay men and lesbians (Duncan 1996; Hubbard 2001), the elderly and young (O'Neil 2002; Valentine 1996), the homeless (Del Casino and Jocoy 2008; Mitchell and Staeheli 2006), and people with disabilities (Butler and Bowlby 1997; Freund 2001). Feminist scholars further contest the idea of public space because the public–private dichotomy relates problematically to social constructions of gender and sex (Bondi 1996). In contrast, Nancy Fraser (1990) contends that many feminists refer to public space as everything outside the domestic sphere and thus conflate three analytically distinct spheres: the state, the official economy of paid employment, and arenas of public discourse. Aside from their apparent malleability, notions of private and public are further complicated insofar as their meaning and usage are embedded within local specificities of time and place, differing across cultural contexts. This is not to advocate a position of relativism, and we should reject any suggestion that participation, and hence public space, is a distinctive "cultural value." A desire to participate in community affairs is intrinsic to the human animal as a social being, where recognizing specific contexts of public space requires understanding that any social organization is both the outcome of the "local" politics of the street and their relational geographies to the wider power geometries of "global" space.

In negotiating the private–public dichotomy, Hénaff and Strong (2001) look to the entrance criteria of a particular space. A space is deemed private when an individual or group is recognized as having the right to establish such criteria, where meaning is imbued through acknowledged "ownership." A space is public by contrast, precisely because whereas there are admission criteria, the right to enforce those criteria is always in question. Public space is open to those meeting the criteria, but it is not controlled in the sense of being owned and is thus always a contestation over the legitimacy of inclusion and exclusion. Yet, as Kurt Iveson (2003, 215) argues, "exclusions should be interrogated with respect to the processes through which they are politically justified, thus enabling critical theorists to distinguish between different kinds of exclusion." In particular, the liberal rhetoric of publicness actually reinscribes particular forms of subordination and exclusion as open, and supposedly "equitable" access to the public by all individuals is conceived only insofar as they leave their particular subjectivities behind in the private sphere and out of the public realm (Iveson 2003). In the liberal formulation, gay men and lesbians are, for example, deemed to possess the same access rights so long as they keep their sexuality private. This bracketing of status and identity effectively excludes what are some of the most important concerns by suppressing, devaluing, and truncating the exploration of possible identities (Calhoun 1997) and reinforcing normative subjectivities as universal. Therefore, because Habermas's liberal impression makes *a* public look like *the* public, the public sphere should not be considered as a universally accessible public space; rather, it should be regarded as "the *structured* setting where cultural and ideological contest among a variety of publics takes place" (Eley 1992, 306, emphasis added).

Supporting this perspective, although still finding value in deliberative democracy, Young (1990) emphasizes that the primacy of a material and embodied conception of public space rests in its *potential* to be a site of political participation where diverse publics can interact, thus engendering a more radicalized version of democracy. Arguing against the idea of democracy as public space, Malcom Miles (2002, 256) inadvertently lends his support when he asks, "When was public space ever a site of mass democracy, except when crowds . . . took matters into their own hands?" Although public space may be exclusionary to certain social groups, whereby some groups may even struggle to gain access in ways that impede its usage by others, public space remains the most important site where public claims can be made visible and contested. If at times spaces may change in their role for accommodating different social groups (Atkinson 2003), surely contesting one's exclusion and taking public space can potentially secure such accommodation and change. To demand inclusion in a space often means forcibly occupying the space of exclusion, reinforcing the idea that public space has never been guaranteed and, by its very definition, must be contested. In this sense, an agonistic approach to the political becomes an essential condition for conceiving a more inclusive public space that accepts and celebrates difference (Watson 2006).

CAPITALIST MACHINATIONS AND ANARCHIST CONTESTATIONS

Radical democracy is a messy process with an inherent uncertainty reflecting the essential agonism of open public discussion concerning community principles and the possibility of sudden changes, conflicts, and contradictions in collective goals. The spaces of democratic societies must always be in process, constructions to be maintained and repaired as the collective interest is defined and contested (Entrikin 2002). This processual nature of public space explains why it is and *must* be the subject of continuous contestation, spanning a fluid spectrum between debate, protest, agonism, and, at times, lamentably, antagonism and violence. Accordingly, it is paramount to view public space as a medium allowing for the contestation of power, focusing on issues of "access" ranging from basic use to more complicated matters, including territoriality and symbolic ownership (Atkinson 2003). Public space is never a complete project but is instead both the product and site of conflict between the competing ideologies of "order" (authoritarianism–archy–representation of space) and "unscripted" interaction (democracy–anarchy–representational space) (Lefebvre 1991; Mitchell 2003b).[7] These competing approaches do not result in dichotomous public spaces. Rather, emphasis must be placed on the processual and fluidic character of public space, where any recognizable "outcome" from either the ordered or the unscripted is necessarily temporary, that is, a *means without end*.

Although claiming to advocate democratic public space, Carr et al. (1992, xi) exemplify the ordered approach by suggesting that public space is "the setting for activities that threaten communities, such as crime and protest." The ability to protest is what makes public space democratic, as it provides those without institutionalized power the opportunity to challenge the status quo. Crime, for its part, is most often conceived in terms of property rights, and accordingly the poor and propertyless are repeatedly cast as transgressors of public space. Hee and Ooi (2003) take a different approach to the ordered view, contending that the public spaces of colonial and postcolonial cities are constructions of the ruling elite. Certainly colonial administrators and incumbent regimes enforce their representations of space, but this ignores the element of contestation and the possible emergence of representational space. Beijing's Tiananmen Square offers a case in point, as the people took this controlled space, and, although recaptured by the state, it remains ideologically contested in the public sphere, continuing to fire the imagination of social movements in China and beyond (Lees 1994). Thus the values embedded in public space are those with which the *demos* endows it (Goheen 1998), not simply the visualizations and administrations of reigning elites.

States and corporations may challenge collectively endowed values and espouse the ordered view because they seek to shape public space in ways that limit the threat of democratic power to dominant socio-economic interests (Harvey 2000). Although total control over public space is impossible, they do attempt to regulate it by keeping it relatively free of passion (Duncan 1996). To remove the passion from public space, corporate or state planners attempt to create spaces based on a desire for security more than interaction and for entertainment more than democratic politics (Goss 1996), a process Sorkin (1992) calls the "end of public space." Under the ordered view of public space, premised on a need for surveillance and control over behavior, representations of space come to dominate representational spaces. The processes of increasing surveillance, commodification, and private usage are known in the literature as the "Disneyfication" of space, where the urban future looms as a "sanitized, ersatz architecture devoid of geographic specificity" (Lees 1994, 446). In this light, the struggle for democracy is inseparable from public space, as *where* something is said is at least as important as *what* is said, *when* it is said, *how* it is said, and *who* is saying it. Thus shielding oneself from political provocation is easily achieved when all the important public gathering places have become highly policed public space or, its corollary, private property (Mitchell 2003a). It is consequently "time to move from protest to politics, from shutting down streets to opening up public space, from demanding scraps from those few in power to holding power firmly in all our hands" (Milstein 2000, 6).

Relentlessly confronting the arrogation of public space is imperative, because the entrenched power of capital can only be repealed through agonism, whereby a multiplicity of subject positions may be recognized as legitimate claimants to the spaces of the public (Mouffe 2006). When the seemingly everyday yet "Disneyfied" performances of capitalism are ignored as normative values, unexceptional practices, and quotidian sequences, they are lent the appearance of insignificance. This is the center of Lefebvre's (1984, 24) critique of everyday life, where such taken-for-granted succession helps to explain why neoliberalism is often understood as an inevitable, monolithic force. Such a view ignores how hegemony, understood in the sense advocated by Laclau and Mouffe (2001), is a discursively constructed strategy, reproduced through "everyday" practices that are often oppressive yet frequently go unnoticed as such. This suggests that neoliberalism proceeds through a dialectic of coercion and co-optation, which has significant implications for public space. Most often, public space is not the site of momentous clashes between *archy* and *demos* but rather a site of mundanity and routinized conduct. Consequently, everyday life as it is mediated through the continual (re)production of space (Lefebvre 1991) is also the terrain in which power is reified, manipulated, and contested (Cohen and Taylor 1992). It is the everyday forms and uses of public space that inform those moments when extraordinary contestation becomes manifest. So though public protests may initially appear limited in scope, they are often expressions of latent dissatisfactions with capitalism, which, in the current moment, are related primarily to the strains of neoliberalism.

The neoliberal assault on all things public is unabashed in the contemporary city (Brenner and Theodore 2002), where control of public space represents a central strategy (Smith and Low 2006). In a world of widespread aggregative-cum-deliberative (neo)liberal democracy, the contestation of public space, although filtered through cultural, religious, national, ethnic, and gender issues, has come to be predominantly about contesting the machinations of capitalism (Brand and Wissen 2005). So while opportunities for taking space steadily diminish as new forms of surveillance, revanchism, and control are implemented, in contrast to the death knell rung by Sorkin (1992), the Disneyfication of public space is fiercely contested on a global scale, from Quebec City to Cancun and Seattle to Genoa. Occasionally the reclamation of public space is so fierce that it can bring down a government, as happened during the Arab Spring movements in Tunisia, Egypt, Libya, and Yemen. Such events undoubtedly contribute to the ongoing profiling of the so-called Third World as a site of instability and hence a threat to First World security. Yet far from being a reflection of conditions inherent to non-Western peoples, the underscoring of a thinking, reasoning Western subject is synchronous to a general avoidance of the devastating impacts of colonialism and the violence it visited and continues to inflict on non-Western peoples. This suggests that the entire notion of the Third World (and hence of a First World) was called into being through an imperial gaze that was only able to make a Third World flesh insofar as it represents an object of colonial expansion. By analyzing the contestation of public space through an ordinary cities approach, we are able to move beyond essentialist accusations of "cultures of violence" as responsible for ongoing authoritarianism and conflict in the Global South (Springer 2009). Instead, any latent potential for violence should be read not only as a reflection of colonial legacies both past and present, in the form of intensive IFI conditionality and "peacekeeping" missions (Gregory 2004), but also as a discursive ruse invoked to invalidate the legitimacy of entire societies in public politics. Hence we have exclusive groupings, such as the United Nations Security Council within an institution that supposedly represents all nations as equal.

Part of the problem with contemporary development is that, rather than seeking similar patterns to diverse struggles that might offer a foundation for solidarity across space and between heterogeneous groups, the entire encounter is frequently seen through an Orientalist lens (Said 2003), framed not only as a process of "*self*"-affirmation but also as a denial of potentially beneficial associations with "*others*." In Slater's (2004, 11) view, "this sense of self-affirmation is often associated with a posited superiority which has permeated many discourses, from progress and civilization through to modernization and neoliberal development." The categories of First World–Third World, West–non-West, Global North–Global South, and so forth, can accordingly be seen as outcomes of the presumption that reason and reflection are qualities of the former in these pairings, whereas the latter are defined by their supposed lack of these attributes. There is almost no acknowledgment of what has been or might be gained by the "West," which is insistently imagined as the bearer of progress, civilization, and modernity, in contrast to the "non-West," conceived as a passive or recalcitrant recipient. The perpetuation of colonialism means that while the experiences of the Global North have been protracted over several centuries, "development" and the contestation of public space that coincides with this "rationalizing" project have been much more acute in the Global South (Escobar 2004). What this suggests is that contestation in the Third World is *potentially* more agonizing (in its double sense) as societies attempt to cope with the rapidity of this change, which opens the *possibility* that contestation in these sites may also be more transformative.

The importance of this potential and possibility in terms of anarchism's promise to radicalize democracy is that the historical record demonstrates that actual everyday revolutions tend to occur when the categories of "least alienated" and "most oppressed" vis-à-vis capitalism overlap (Graeber 2009a). This hints at the importance of indigenous movements like the Zapatista, as they seem to synchronize these two categories. In building relational geographies that seek to understand the similar difficulties different groups face in various sites of neoliberalization, it appears that the antiglobalization movement in the West has as much, if not more, to gain than the non-West from such solidarities. Given the positioning of indigenous groups in the hierarchy of global capitalism, it seems only fitting that they take a primary role in countering its hegemony, the paradox of which is that securing an urban "right to the city" through an agonistic, anarchic, and radical public space has a lot to learn from rural experiences. Nonetheless, as relational solidarities increasingly recognize space as a complex lattice of symbolism and power (Massey 2005), so too grows awareness that hegemony is never fully achieved. As the struggle for radical democracy emerges, the weapons of the weak will inevitably become more manifest once the visible battle for space begins to take shape, transforming covert hidden transcripts into overt protests, rallies, and other spatially defined arts of resistance (Scott 1990). Furthermore, whatever rights to public space have been won, people willing to break existing laws by exposing them to be oppressive in their geography have often only achieved them through concerted struggle. In this sense, public space is always a dialectic between its beginning and its end (Mitchell 2003a).

DISQUIETING NEXUS OR IRRECONCILABLE SCHISM?

The preceding interpretations highlight one central theme: public space is ideally a medium that allows for embodied self-representation.[8] When public space is deprived, individuals cannot situate themselves existentially. Consequently, as contestation becomes impermissible, self-representation is disembodied. Public space is in constant flux between those who seek to deprive it and those seeking to expand it, and where the ordered view comes to dominate, the resulting deprivation has two consequences: (1) the erosion of individual volition resulting in acquiescence, presumably the desired effect by those seeking to undermine public space, or (2) violent outbursts against those who suppress public space and the undesired effect of the ordered view. Through the privation of public space, an individual "acquires an eerie sense of unreality, as happens in a mass society and under tyranny when isolated individuals, thrown back on themselves, live a 'shadowy' existence and search for reality in intense private sensations or acts of violence" (Parekh 1981, 95). To the extent that Arendt (1958, 30–31) viewed the public and private realms as related to each other, she argued,

> It was a matter of course that the mastering of the necessities of life in the household was the condition for freedom of the *polis.* Under no circumstances could politics be only a means to protect society....In all cases, it is the freedom (and in some instances so-called freedom) of society which requires and justifies the restraint of political authority. Freedom is located in the realm of the social, and force or violence becomes the monopoly of government. What all Greek philosophers, no matter how opposed to *polis* life, took for granted is that freedom is exclusively located in the political realm, that necessity is primarily a prepolitical phenomenon, characteristic of the private household organization, and that force and violence are justified in this sphere because they are the only means to master necessity—for instance, by ruling over slaves—and to become free. Because all human beings are subject to necessity, they are entitled to violence toward others; violence is the prepolitical act of liberating oneself from the necessity of life for the freedom of the world.

In other words, in the search for reality (i.e., political meaning in the world), the expression of violence becomes the only practicable form of public self-representation available. Meaning, in Arendt's view, one must engage in violence to enter the public and to be free, and in this sense, "violence" can be a liberating process for those who participate. Yet I would hesitate in calling this violence given that it lacks the character of domination.

Outbursts of violence can be conceived as violence "from below," frequently referred to as political violence, which serves to counteract violence "from above," often called state violence. Because both the dominant and subordinate poles can engage in violence, and both sides may be politically motivated, each source is appropriately considered as political violence. Likewise, the internationalized and internationalizing character of the contemporary state (Glassman 1999) alerts us to the ambiguity of contemporary expressions of state violence, rendering this term equally problematic. Violence from above refers to the methods, including both acute and structural violence, used by the established social–political–economic order to safeguard its privileges. An acute example is the deployment of military force against potential challengers to the existing order's sovereignty, while a structural example is the prevailing hierarchical political–economic system itself. In contrast, violence from below refers to the anger and resentment felt by the general population toward the structures of the existing political economy, which again calls into question whether it is violence at all considering the intention of coercion is absent. Although violence occurs in public and private spaces, may be categorized in myriad ways reflecting the pursuit and exercise of power, and the dualism cannot capture all conceivable expressions or intents of violence, it nonetheless heuristically points to where so-called violence is impelled within the existing local-cum-global socioeconomic hierarchy. It also hints at the underlying values being promoted or defended in relation to the furtherance or hindrance of democracy.

For outbursts of violence from below to have meaning to both the deprived and the deprivers, they must necessarily occur in public and are thus reassertions of the perpetual contestation of public space. It is often through means or threat of "violence" that excluded groups have gained access to public space (McCann 1999). This is the paradox of democracy, because without confrontation manifested through an agonistic public space, there cannot be a democratic polity (Mouffe 2000). Yet any society that sanctions political conflict runs the risk of it becoming too intense, producing discordance that may jeopardize civil peace. Keane (2004) argues that violence is anathema to the spirit and substance of democracy, a position I advance in conceptualizing democracy in anarchist terms. On one hand, democracy and anarchism are predicated upon the idea of nonviolent confrontation, that is, agonism rather than antagonism. Conversely, many so-called democracies are born in the violence of revolution (Rapoport and Weinberg 2001), whereas anarchy is frequently sensationalized as violence incarnate. The problem with violence as a means for either democracy or anarchism is precisely the recognition that public space is a *means without end,* and thus any achievement made on the back of violence will only see that violence replicate. Since anarchism and democracy are recognized here as the negation of violence; any use of violence necessarily marks their erasure.

Nonetheless, violent revolution hints at the *seemingly* emancipatory potential of violence, as violence from below may generate reallocations of wealth and open paths to political empowerment (Iadicola and Shupe 2003). While this view acknowledges how subordinate groups at times use violence in their attempts at democratization, any "liberationist" use of violence is self-defeating. Violence is an act of domination, and its use aligns an emancipatory agenda to the *nomos* of the oppressor. In other words, violence is an archic force that defiles the ethos of anarchism and democracy. Moreover, I do not want to imply spontaneity to any such attempts at redistributive violence, as invocations of violence are never performed as sudden inclinations without predetermination or external impulse. Massey's (2005) relational understanding of space forces us to recognize that any seemingly particular "acts" of violence are always snapshots of existing political, economic, and social relations. Thus expressions of violence actually represent interlinking nodes along a continuum (Scheper-Hughes and Bourgois 2004) whose relational geographies represent a complex interlacing of local-meets-global, sociocultural, and political economic practices (Springer 2008), which tendentially links such manifestations to neoliberalism in the contemporary zeitgeist.

Although violence is antithetical to democracy and anarchism, what constitutes "violence" is often defined from above, thus enabling the mistaken idea that some violence is impulsive and irrational. That is, violence is frequently defined as legitimate or illegitimate depending on whether it furthers or threatens the social order of a society. Violence from above is often labeled as "defensive" or "peacekeeping," allowing archic elites greater ability to commit violence, and the violence they commit more likely to be defined as legitimate (Escobar 2004). Consequently, the exclusion of what is labeled as "violence" from below in public space is frequently not actually violence at all.[9] Instead, this represents a moralistic attempt to remove the "political" and so exclude "disobedient" adversaries, or those a priori defined as illegitimate and thus threatening to the existing order (Mitchell 1996). It is important to recognize that what (neo)liberals call an "adversary" is actually a "competitor." Liberalism, as Mouffe (2004, 126–17) explains, "envisions the field of politics as a neutral terrain in which different groups compete for power; that is, their objective is to dislodge others to occupy their place, without challenging the dominant hegemony and attempting to transform the existing relations of power." Politics is thus reduced to little more than competition among elites. Such ideas speak not only to the fundamental flaw of deliberative democracy (Mouffe 2000) but also to the deceptive antipolitical discourse authority invokes in demonizing anarchism.

Moreover, because the existing order increasingly means the economic order, there is an intensifying corporate imprint on the monopoly on violence (Atkinson 2003). In the contemporary context of global capital flows, the corollary of the corporatization of violence is neoliberalism. Thus the very understanding of "publicness" as something inherently good is increasingly threatened everywhere neoliberalism spreads its wings. The biggest threat to public space comes not from "disorderly" homeless and poor, as (neo)liberal discourse suggests, but from the ongoing erosion of the principle of the collective and from the use of corporate control as an apparent solution to social problems (Mitchell 2003a). Amid widespread privatization, cuts to public expenditure, and reduced social transfer programs, violence has become both a conduit of societal bigotry and an attempt by beleaguered states to regain their footing (Goldberg 2009). Violence from above comes attendant to both "roll-back" neoliberalism, where regulatory transformation sees the state narrowly concerned with expanding markets to the peril of social provisions, and "roll-out" neoliberalism, which concentrates on disciplining and containing those marginalized by earlier stages of neoliberalization (Peck and Tickell 2002).

While neoliberal proponents suggest that absolute poverty levels have declined since the early 1980s (Dollar and Kraay 2002), the reliability of such statistics has come under fire (Wade 2003). Poverty reduction statistics do not recognize spatial and temporal variations in inflation or purchasing power, and if China is excluded, the 1990s actually show an increase in global poverty (UNDP 2002). Nevertheless, "violence" explodes most frequently in a sociopolitical atmosphere where programs of regulatory change have been implemented, particularly when the social, economic, or political position of the subordinate group has been improved (Bill 1973). Thus, even if we accept the validity of the "official" statistics, the potential for violence is not abated, as neoliberalism ignores the "paradox of prosperity" in assuming that absolute rather than relative affluence is the key to contentment (Rapley 2004). Socioeconomic inequality is on the rise and has been so marked under neoliberalism that Harvey (2005) contends that it is structural to the entire project. Accordingly, as egalitarian dreams are continually broken under neoliberalism, violence is an inevitable outcome. It is not poverty that provides an impetus for violence, a problematic notion not least because poverty *is* violence (Galtung 1996); rather, it is relative inequality and its associated humiliations that often spark violence from below, which may proliferate where its use opens avenues to political and economic power (Tilly 2003).

Attempts to achieve the ordered view of public space through prohibition of assembly may reduce the frequency of protests in the short term. Likewise, deliberative democracy's rejection of agonism in favor of a consensual vision of antipolitics may produce an immediate reduction in confrontation. However, on an extended timeline, such practices function to alienate the population, suppress differences provoking more exclusions, increase the likelihood of clashes between police and activists, and, ultimately, induce an antagonistic politics that is more likely to result in violence (Mouffe 2000). This is why any distortion in access to public space can be so ominous, leading people to feel powerless and frustrated. Violence has a self-replicating character, which counteracts the goal of realizing a nonviolent society. So while violence can appear to be an act of liberation that serves to include the excluded, even under the best circumstances, violence is morally ambiguous (Keane 2004).

The brutality of violence not only desecrates those directly affected; it also tears the social fabric by subverting the level of trust, the interconnectedness, and the very publicness necessary for societies to function. Public space ideally allows for embodiment of the self, but the publicity of violence "brings one to experience one's own embodiment in a totalizing way that language fails. Violence turns a speaking body dumb" (Bar On 2002, 14).

Conceptualizing democracy as processual is fitting in this light, as there is always the threat (either latent or manifest) that public violence will ultimately tear it apart. To break this cycle, Mitchell (1996) argues that a democracy must recognize the right to protest, which he suggests is paradoxically often only ever achieved through so-called violence. Yet this rendering makes little sense when violence is considered antithetical to democracy. Despite the liberatory potential of violence recognized by Arendt in her earlier work (indicated earlier), her stance shifted when she wrote *On Violence* (Arendt 1970) during the height of the Vietnam War. Arendt adopted a more pacifist position, as she was unable to reconcile justifications for violence with actual legitimacy:

> Legitimacy, when challenged, bases itself on appeals to the past, while justification relates to an end that lies in the future. Violence can be justifiable, but it never will be legitimate. Its justification loses in plausibility the farther its intended end recedes into the future. (52)

Scholars such as Barnett (2009), Keane (2004), and Young (2007) have picked up on Arendt's distinction in advancing their own understandings of when violence might be justified by democracies. These are important critiques in going beyond the notion that explanation of violence is tantamount to its legitimation. However, when the idea of revolution is reconceived as permanent resistance, a *means without end,* it becomes clear that any and all forms of actual violence, meaning the expression of domination, lack both legitimacy *and* justification. Thus an anarchist model of radical democracy, where agonism replaces antagonism, is precisely the realization of nonviolent politics.

A *means without end* view, in conjunction with a relational understanding of geographies, answers Barnett's (2009) concern for the "ontologization of violence" and the shared insistence of Keane (2004) and Tilly (2003) that violence must be understood in acute terms. Disregarding the profusion of literature that points to the importance of understanding a continuum between the structural, aesthetic, symbolic, and epistemic conditions of violence and its direct expression as physical force (Cockburn 2004; Scheper-Hughes and Bourgois 2004; Turpin and Kurtz 1996), Barnett (2009) suggests that such an integral view does not "address the difficult question of whether it is ever possible not only to recognize violence in human affairs, but to justify the use of violence for political ends." Contra Barnett's limited conceptualization of the geographies of violence, one that privileges the compartmentalized view of isolated yet "meaningful" places within an immaterial, "meaningless" space that Massey (2005) rebukes, the confounding effects of violence ensure that it is a phenomenon shot through with a certain perceptual blindness. Benjamin ([1921] 1986) exposed the unremitting tendency to obscure violence in its institutionalized forms and, because of this opacity, the enduring inclination to exclusively regard violence as something we can see through its direct effects. Yet the structural violence resulting from our political and economic systems (Galtung 1996; Iadicola and Shupe 2003) and the symbolic violence born of our discourses (Bourdieu 2001) are something like the dark matter of physics: "invisible, but [they have] to be taken into account if one is to make sense of what might otherwise seem to be 'irrational' explosions of subjective [or direct] violence" (Žižek 2008, 2). It is surprising, then, that Barnett insists that his position enables violence to be understood as rational and thus he is able to better answer questions of legitimacy, justification, and responsibility. In its instrumental and strategic capacity, violence is undoubtedly a rational phenomenon (Arendt 1970; Foucault 1996), but insisting on an acute understanding of violence does not bring us closer to recognizing violence in human affairs; it actually pushes us further away by treating violence as an "act," an occurrence without a history or a geography, decontextualized from the complex social processes that have informed its expression (Springer 2012a). When we read violence in this way, we can start to question whether violence from below is even violence at all, particularly when it lacks any impulse for domination and is mounted as self-defense.

MEANS WITHOUT END AND THE (RE)DISCOVERY OF POWER

Jeff Ferrell (2001, 222) provides an insightful and critical assessment of the challenge of public space in our contemporary moment:

> All of these identities, all of these conflicts over public space and public meaning are in turn undergirded by deeper oppositions, as fundamental as they are complex: inclusion versus privilege, anarchy versus authority, emergence versus order. As the latest arrangements of spatial authority are made, as ever more exclusionary patterns of privilege are encoded and enforced in the space of the city, street denizens and street activists regularly move to unravel this emerging spatial order.

When a society lacks a dynamic public space that allows for agonistic confrontation among diverse political identities, a more nefarious space may open, where alienation fosters alternative identifications along antagonistic divides like nationalism, religion, and ethnicity (Mouffe 2004). This is the "dark side of democracy," where *demos* becomes confused with *ethnos,* and is responsible for some of the worst cases of ethnic cleansing, mass murder, and genocide in human history (Mann 2005). Yet the most extreme human mortality has occurred under authoritarian regimes, not democratic ones (Keane 2004). When democracy is radicalized, such comparison of regime types becomes irrelevant, as the desired change is not for a new regime but an end to systematized rule and the complete renunciation of archy in all its forms. Radical democracy accordingly has the potential to repeal the violence that archies engender by dispersing power more evenly across the entire social body. This occurs when "politics" conceived as an *ends*-oriented project of consensus is replaced with the perpetual *means* of democratic process through the "political" and its acknowledgment of agonism. Powerful elites, both authoritarian and those claiming to be "democratic," will fervently try to impede any move toward a radical vision of democracy. Radical democracy diminishes their institutionalized, hegemonic, and archic grip, reorienting power from hierarchical constructions founded on moral, juridical, and economic frameworks, toward the fluidic voluntary associations and antihegemony of anarchism, which recognizes the legitimacy of *all* political adversaries and not simply other (capitalist) competitors who wish to play within a system that favors entrenched elites.

Radical democracy demystifies democracy by acknowledging that its achievement is not attained through processes of "development" that bring about supposedly necessary economic "prerequisites." Radical democracy does not look to cultural relativism in suggesting that it is an exclusive outcome of Western experience or a transplanted practice to be habituated in the Global South. Instead, radical democracy proceeds though an ordinary cities approach, where it is recognized as a latent energy found in all cities, a vitality waiting to be set in motion through struggle and the contested politics of the street. Framed within agonistic public space, radical democracy is the very process of exertion, where a *path* toward social justice might be opened in place of an end-state antipolitics, as this is a passage without destination, a permanent *means without end*. If violence is recognized as more likely under archy (whether hierarchy, oligarchy, patriarchy, or otherwise), then radical democracy founded on anarchism offers a lasting preventive measure against such violence. Freedom from violence is something the institutionalization of power and its closed systems of bounded territories and sovereign protections has always promised but only the openness of anarchism can potentially achieve, through emphasizing continuous contestation, rejecting enclosure in all its forms, and insisting on the protean, anarchist horizon of space-to-come.

As the contemporary zeitgeist of neoliberalization continues to exacerbate the concentration of wealth, reshape political sovereignty, and reorganize economies along increasingly exclusionary lines, the need to establish democratic public spaces is intensified. There is a clear need for a vision of public space that extends beyond the market to communicate alternatives to capitalism and the current moment of neoliberal hegemony with its antipolitical version of politics that privileges moralistic, econometric, and juridical applications of power. Recognition of capitalism's geographies of poverty, inequality, and violence as intertwined across a multiplicity of sites (Springer 2008) impels us to view its geographies of protest, resistance, and contestation in the same light. It may be the case that effective transnational solidarity can only be built on an emancipatory agenda lodged in such a relational understanding of space. Although informed by contextually specific meanings of inclusion and liberation, the struggles that occur in the public spaces of diverse cities across the globe can also be recognized as expressions of profound betrayal with capitalism and its "actually existing" circumstances of neoliberalization (Brenner and Theodore 2002). The challenge, to paraphrase Hart (2008), is in coming to grips with how such contestation to neoliberal practices operates on terrains that always exceed neoliberalism yet nonetheless still extend beyond "local" grievances.

Public space offers a spatial medium to the frustrations subalterns feel with regard to systems of archy. It allows them to locate their anger in a material sense, thereby opening public space to new visualizations, which may initiate new organizations rooted in the idea of system and management without rule, and co-operation and contestation without repression. If those "from below" perceive those "from above" as unwilling to listen, evidenced through a denial of public space and a refusal to recognize them as legitimate political adversaries, then tensions will mount and may erupt into violence. Contestation of public space is paramount because, though elite challenges may be fierce, they are never insurmountable. Dahl's (1971, 15) axiom that "the likelihood that a government will tolerate an opposition increases as the expected costs of suppression increase" illustrates that violence from below may not always be necessary to overcome an oppressor, as the threat of civil disobedience or direct action may be enough to impel respect for the necessity of agonism. Employing nonviolent principles ensures that the reciprocity of reinforcement engendered by violence does not come to characterize the emancipatory process, thereby turning agonism into antagonism. Nonetheless, pressure for democratization still demands ongoing physical presence in public space if dissidents are ever to be seen and heard, which always risks the potential for violence (Mitchell 1996).

The predominance of neoliberalism means that the ordered vision of public space has become the primary model available to ordinary cities insofar as it represents the interests of capital. What this implies is that the answer to a continuing proclivity for authoritarianism in the Global South is not to be found in culture but in the contextual embeddedness of neoliberal reforms and the resultant unequal political–economic arrangements of neoliberalization (Springer 2010a; 2015). The corollary is that neoliberalization may also help to explain the increasingly authoritarian tendencies found in other settings with an ostensibly long-standing "democratic" tradition (Giroux 2004). Yet despite such adverse conditions, through the struggle for social justice and the radicalization of democracy via anarchism, even a people who have been oppressed or mystified into believing that the power of government is a monarchial attribute, a divine punishment, a colonial inheritance, a market commodity, an IFI provision, or something that grows from the barrel of a gun may still make the discovery that the real source of power is themselves (Lummis 1996). It is in spaces of the public that the discovery of both *power* and *demos* is made, and it is in the contestation of public space that democracy lives. Emancipation must accordingly be understood as an awakening, a (re)discovery of power that is deeply rooted in processes of mobilization and transformation, and in this sense, emancipation cannot be conceived as a subject–object relationship in which some are emancipators (revolutionaries, mavericks, academics) and others are being emancipated (the poor, the propertyless, the marginalized) (Kothari 2005). Either the whole of humanity is liberated or no one is. This may seem an impossible goal to achieve, but thinking so misinterprets what is at stake. It is not an end state resulting from revolution or consensual deliberation that should be pursued. Instead, through a relational, processual, and forever-protean understanding of space, the aspiration becomes radical democracy viewed as an agonistic *means without end.* Such is the promise of space and the life it breathes into anarchism.

5

Integral Anarchism

The Anarchists are right in everything; in the negation of the existing order, and in the assertion that, without Authority, there could not be worse violence than that of Authority under existing conditions. They are mistaken only in thinking that anarchy can be instituted by a violent revolution. . . . To use violence is impossible; it would only cause reaction. To join the ranks of the Government is also impossible—one would only become its instrument. One course therefore remains—to fight the Government by means of thought, speech, actions [and] life.
—Leo Tolstoy

By proclaiming our morality of equality, or anarchism, we refuse to assume a right which moralists have always taken upon themselves to claim, that of mutilating the individual in the name of some ideal.
—Peter Kropotkin

I used to think that my path toward anarchism was above all informed by a commitment to nonviolence, a conviction that was initiated by reading the works of renowned Russian novelist and thinker Leo Tolstoy, whose masterpiece *War and Peace* (Tolstoy [1869] 2006) served as a point of inspiration. Given that the popular geopolitical imagination—in a convenient ruse for legitimizing sovereign authority—sees anarchism as a synonym for violence, positioning anarchism as a nonviolent practice may seem counterintuitive to those uninitiated in anarchist philosophy, and perhaps even to those who have engaged in this literature. Such misgivings are hinted at in the epigraph from Tolstoy, where he maintains a certain ambivalence toward anarchism. Yet, though violence has informed many historical anarchist movements, and it would be disingenuous to ignore or deny this constituent, "historically anarchism has been less violent than other political creeds. . . . It has no monopoly of violence, and compared to the nationalists, populists, and monarchists has been

comparatively peaceful" (Marshall 1992, ix). Moreover, my conceptualization of anarchism—which owes much to the pacifism of Tolstoy
and finds contemporaries in Jeff Ferrell (2001), David Graeber (2002),
and Randal Amster (2010)—is such that the moment violence enters
into the equation of whatever social action is being called forth under
the name of anarchism, it ceases to actually be anarchism and instead
recapitulates authoritarian modes of practice. In other words, because
violence is fundamentally coercive, anarchism at the instant of violence
is transformed into something altogether different: it becomes "archism."
Though a concern for nonviolence has undoubtedly shaped my political
thought, after spending the last few years reading anarchist philosophy, I
now realize that I was born an anarchist. In fact, we all were. In my reading, I was not actually learning to be an anarchist; I was instead engaged
in a process of unlearning all the archist ideas that had been inculcated
in me since childhood.

If anarchism is literally an-archy, and archy is generically understood
as systematized rule, it stands to reason that any version of archy (i.e.,
hierarchy, patriarchy, monarchy, anthroparchy, oligarchy, etc.) must be
learned. Thus, however much people might like to, or more accurately
are compelled to, think that children are born into preconfigured identities like "American," "Muslim," "Harijan," "royalty," "Tutsi," or even
"female," and however much existing institutions attempt to confer such
prescribed identities onto individual babies, there is no essential truth to
such ascriptions. Babies are born babies and know nothing of the political,
economic, social, and cultural structures and strictures into which they
have arrived. At the precise moment of our birth—before our bodies are
judged, categorized, measured, designated, registered, enrolled, numbered,
managed, licensed, and assessed, that is, before being "governed" (Proudhon [1851] 2007, 294)—we therefore exist in the world as "radical equals,"
which I interpret as the sine qua non of peace. The problem is that in
the contemporary zeitgeist, almost every event that follows a person's
birth is a process whereby the person becomes ever more "mutilated"
into the "ideals" of nationalism, religion, class, ethnicity, gender, and so
forth, which are the fragmented *pieces* that are antecedent to *war*. This
is not to suggest that there is a direct translation of identity formation
into violence but rather to acknowledge that the politics of difference, as

it is currently practiced and understood in our ostensibly "postpolitical" moment, makes "othering" possible. When identity is held up to ageographical and ahistorical notions of imagined stasis and rigidity—as is the assumption and intention of postpolitical thought—rather than being properly acknowledged as a mercurial, fluidic, and forever-protean process of becoming, difference grows into the mutilated ideals of war instead of the potential poetics of peace.

Human geographers are increasingly cognizant that conceptualizing the spatiality of peace is a vital component of our collective disciplinary praxis (see Le Billon 2008; Kobayashi 2009; Koopman 2011; Springer 2011; Williams and McConnell 2011). Elsewhere in the literature, a great deal of attention has recently been afforded to the ethical, emotional, and affective sensibilities of geographical practice and thought (see Davidson, Bondi, and Smith 2007; McCormack 2003; Pile 2009; Popke 2009; Proctor 2005). Within these emergent literatures, I want to position anarchism as an ethical philosophy of nonviolence that enables a more emancipatory worldview through the absolute rejection of war in all its myriad forms. Such an interpretation does not attempt to align nonviolence to any particular organized religious teaching, as has recently been advocated by Nick Megoran (2007). Instead, in the section that follows this introduction, I set out to argue that the current practices of religion undermine the geographies of peace by fragmenting our affinities into discrete pieces. I contend that anarchism is a far more emancipatory process and practice toward achieving nonviolence precisely because it enables us to conceptualize peace as both the unqualified refusal of the manifold-cum-interlocking processes of domination and a precognitive, prenormative, and presupposed category rooted in our inextricable entanglement with each other and all that exists. I then turn my attention toward the ways in which religion continues to structure a sense of bondage, advocating for spirituality in its place. I address how my own view of spiritualism aligns with atheism and reject the fallacious idea that atheism is but a cipher for nihilism. Indeed, it is precisely an anarchist ethics rooted in atheism that demonstrates a path toward living in a more just and inclusive world. In short, anarchism insists that affinity and common bonds can be built as a foundation for connectivity through an insistence on integrality. Far from proposing an essentialist view of humanity or engaging a naturalized argument that reconvenes a "noble savage," in the section that follows, I contextualize my arguments within the processual frameworks of radical democracy and agonism and seek to redress the ageographical and ahistorical notions of politics that comprise the contemporary postpolitical zeitgeist, before offering some final thoughts.

NONVIOLENT GEOGRAPHIES AND INTEGRAL ANARCHISM: BEYOND THE FRAGMENTARY PRACTICES OF RELIGION

Nick Megoran's (2007; 2010) articles outlining an agenda for peace research and practice in contemporary human geography are necessary interventions if we are ever to reconfigure the discipline in such a way that Yves Lacoste's (1976) claim that geography is first and foremost an art of war no longer makes sense. In his article, Megoran's (2011) starting point is a critique of Derek Gregory's (2010) plenary lecture for the Royal Geographical Society–Institute of British Geographers 2008 conference titled "War and Peace." Megoran laments that although peace is gestured at in Gregory's account of the ongoing horrors of war waged by the Global North, it quickly falls out of view. In Gregory's defense, he explicitly states that his emphasis is on war, yet he nonetheless wants to remind his audience of the mutually reinforcing processes that shape the contours of both war and peace. Nancy Scheper-Hughes and Philippe Bourgois (2004) attempt to do much the same in the introduction to their anthology *Violence in War and Peace,* in which they set out to "trouble" the distinctions between war and peace by demonstrating how often the most violent acts consist of conduct that is socially permitted, defined as virtuous, and enjoined as a moral duty in the service of conventional political economic and sociocultural norms. Likewise, drawing on Giorgio Agamben's (1998) exposition on sovereign power, within my own work, I have sought to acknowledge that what may at first glance appear as exceptional violence in fact comes to form the rule; it becomes exemplary (Springer 2012a). Yet there is much to be gained from Megoran's analysis, not least of which is the recognition that it is one thing to critique how war and peace are entangled in a reciprocating arrangement but something else to attempt to tear this dialectic apart at its seams and therein fasten something altogether new and emancipatory. Like Megoran (2008;

2011), I am convinced that the continual performance of nonviolence in all areas of one's life is the answer, but I take issue with his invocation of Christian morality as the means to achieving this.

To make his case, Megoran curiously draws on Peter Kropotkin, an individual remembered today more for his influence on the development of anarchist philosophy than for his contributions to geography. Writing at a time when geographers like David Livingstone, Friedrich Ratzel, and Halford Mackinder were content to perpetuate the discipline's relationship to colonialism (see Driver 2001; Godlewska and Smith 1994; Kearns 2009a), Kropotkin (1885) passionately argued that dissipating all manner of prejudice is "what geography ought to be." If the standard postcolonial critique is that colonialism attempts to universalize and impose a particular version of morality (Sidaway 2000), my skepticism leads me to question what prejudices remain hidden beneath a version of peace rooted in Christianity. I do not mean to call Megoran's own character to account here, as I do not doubt that his heart is in the right place. Instead, I think it is important to remember that all religions are the product of particular cultural developments, and so it follows that their versions of morality are informed by situated knowledges (Haraway 1988). For Kropotkin (1897), morality had nothing to do with the cultural prejudices of religion, and far from requiring a proselytizing imperative, he argued that

> the moral sense is a natural faculty in us like the sense of smell or of touch. As for law and religion, which also have preached this principle, they have simply filched it to cloak their own wares, their injunctions for the benefit of the conqueror, the exploiter, the priest.... Each of them covered themselves with it as with a garment; like authority [the state] which made good its position by posing as the protector of the weak against the strong. By flinging overboard law, religion and authority [the state], [hu]mankind can regain possession of the moral principle which has been taken from them. Regain that they may criticize it, and purge it from the adulterations wherewith priest, judge and ruler have poisoned it and are poisoning it yet.

Although I want to distance myself from the idea of morality being a "natural faculty," in identifying the series of mystifying erasures on which authority and its own morality are premised, Kropotkin amply demonstrates his antipathy for the state, law, *and* organized religion, considering them as a trident in the perpetuation of prejudice and domination. In this sense, Megoran's invocation of Kropotkin is peculiar, as he rooted his morality not in religious teachings but in nothing more and nothing less than the presupposition of equality, an ideal we should recognize as being in perpetual need of verification and as the single most fundamental tenet of anarchism.

James Sidaway once told me that my version of anarchism seems to find something in common with certain elements of religion. While I am generally quite adverse to this comparison, I have identified Tolstoy as a key influence on my thinking. This necessitates some critical reflection on my part, as Tolstoy was often labeled a "Christian anarchist." Yet Tolstoy's version of Christianity was far from doctrinaire, so much so that he was labeled a heretic and excommunicated from the Russian Orthodox Church in 1901. In his monumental *The Kingdom of God Is within You,* which was banned from publication in his home country, Tolstoy ([1894] 2004) bases his scathing critiques of private property and statist violence on the teachings of Jesus Christ, yet he also rails against the institution of the Church and its entrenched ecclesiastical hierarchies. If Christianity is to mean simply an unwavering commitment to nonviolence and the absolute condemnation of war, as is Tolstoy's sense, then I can concede that my version of anarchism aligns to this. Taking this religious analogy one step further, the promise I see in Élisée Reclus's (1894) universal geography shares a lot with so-called Eastern religious philosophies. Far from an essentializing sense of the universal, human phenomena such as "culture," "economics," "politics," and "the social" are considered false dichotomies, necessarily imbued within and co-constitutive of the natural "environment." Such thinking coalesces both with the concept of Indra's Net from Buddhist philosophy and with Taoism's view of humanity's imbrication within the cosmos (Marshall 1992; Rapp 2012). This goes further than Noel Castree and Bruce Braun's (2001) conceptualization of "social nature" inasmuch as it seeks to recognize how humanity is intimately intertwined within all the processes and flows of the entire planet and, indeed, the universe at large. In many ways, this necessitates an affective or even spiritual approach, one that goes beyond simply crossing interdisciplinary boundaries to initiate a process of "undisciplining" by engaging both critical geopolitics and geopoetics to suture together all the ostensibly separate *pieces* in articulating an "integral anarchism."

Perhaps somewhat paradoxically, this view is not exclusively confined to a metaphysical exegesis, as Albert Einstein (2003, 10), the father of modern physics, conveyed a similar vision:

> A human being is a part of the whole called by us "Universe," a part limited in time and space. He experiences himself, his thoughts and feelings as something separated from the rest, a kind of optical delusion of his consciousness. This delusion is a kind of prison for us, restricting us to our personal desires and to affection for a few persons nearest to us. Our task must be to free ourselves from this prison by widening our circle of compassion to embrace all living creatures and the whole of nature in its beauty.

Although the methodological approach of science claims objective detachment, the ongoing scientific search for a unified theory of everything, which Einstein initiated, is actually shot through with emotion. The unknowable mystery at the end of the universe and the fundamental significance of human consciousness have led some of the most scientific minds to accept the morality of existence, but without the need to invoke God (see Davies 1993; Hawking and Mlodinow 2010). David Bohm, for example, argued that "deep down the consciousness of [hu]mankind is one. This is a virtual certainty because even in the vacuum matter is one; and if we don't see this, it's because we are blinding ourselves to it" (Bohm 2003, 149).

Human geography is in the midst of an affective turn (Thien 2005), where Catherine Nolin's (2010) "geography that breaks your heart" and Vicky Lawson's (2009) "caring geography" are welcome antidotes to the neoliberal myth that our successes are achieved as autonomous individuals, helping geographers to visualize how we can bring the *pieces* of humanity back together through a solidarity rooted in affection. Advocacy, activism, and affect are precisely what the discipline needs to shed its colonial skin, not more of the detached masculinist scholarship that Edward Holland (2011) seemingly promotes when, in critiquing Megoran's religious positionality, he writes, "To take a commitment to non-violence as the consistent point of departure for our analysis leads us too closely toward advocacy and away from the independent, unbiased perspective which is the foundation of the academy." This is a bewildering regression that ignores the beautiful vitality that feminism has breathed into the discipline. Even more confounding is that Holland actually recapitulates the very notion he critiques. In defending the oxymoronic notion of "just war," as if a person could ever remove *him*-"Self" enough to determine where and when violence is moral, Donna Haraway's (1988) god-trick takes center stage in Holland's argument. Intellectual mastery, masculinist reason, and disinterested appraisal stand in for divine omniscience to determine our morality for us. Does this really help geographers escape the prejudice Kropotkin disavows, or is it simply a delusion that chains geography even more tightly to its colonial past? My answer is the latter, and contra any feigned sense of objectivity, I embrace the emotional turn as a much more honest assessment of how our inescapable humanity influences our scholarship. Yet I do so with my skepticism for organized religion intact, because within its contemporary practices, religious affection encounters, takes on, and at times and within particular places even provokes a divisive quality. The dictates of most organized religions maintain that care is extended unconditionally to all members of humanity. In actual practice, when it comes to "Others" in the form of nonbelievers and those from differing faiths, there is often a considerable degree of suspicion and doubt.

Setting aside Dharmic and Taoic religions, we have discourses of "infidel" and "heathen" emerging from and circulating between the various fractures of Abrahamic faith, to say nothing of the splintering, ridicule, and contempt that have arisen and continue to proliferate within the manifold denominations of Christianity, Islam, and Judaism. These broken *pieces* in and of themselves seem to tell us something important about the systematic hierarchies embedded within the practice of organized religion, where organization in this sense entails a considerable dose of discipline. In *God and the State,* Mikhail Bakunin ([1882] 2010, 13, emphasis added) was unforgiving in identifying this relationship, isolating Christianity as the primary recipient of his ire:

> Christianity is precisely the religion *par excellence,* because it exhibits and manifests, to the fullest extent, the very nature and essence of every religious system, which is *the impoverishment, enslavement, and annihilation of humanity for the benefit of divinity.* God being everything, the real world and man are nothing. God being truth, justice, goodness, beauty, power, and life, man is falsehood, iniquity, evil, ugliness, impotence, and death. God being master, man is the slave. Incapable of finding justice, truth, and

eternal life by his own effort, he can attain them only through a divine revelation. But whoever says revelation says revealers, messiahs, prophets, priests, and legislators inspired by God himself; and these, once recognized as the representatives of divinity on earth, as the holy instructors of humanity, chosen by God himself to direct it in the path of salvation, necessarily exercise absolute power.

While I would hesitate in singling out Christianity in identifying an apex to the ways in which organized religion functions as the ultimate sovereign authority, I think the case for theistic domination and hierarchy is well made by Bakunin. In getting back to Megoran, the problem I see in some of his work (see Megoran 2007) is that it attempts to position itself as emancipatory, but without fully coming to terms with the prejudices organized religion so often entails and the *pieces* it produces in its actual practice. From the wars of extermination in the Tanakh to the Reconquista to the Crusades to the Thirty Years War to the Taiping Rebellion to the Israeli–Palestinian conflict, to the Troubles in Northern Ireland, and to the contemporary war on terror, organized religion has repeatedly revealed its capacity to divide us.

NO GODS, NO MASTERS: BONDS WITHOUT BONDAGE

Religion is bondage. The etymology of the word *religion* reveals such intentions, coming from Old French *religiō,* meaning "obligation, bond, reverence," and earlier still from the Latin *re-ligāre*, "to bind, to tie." It takes very little effort to see how such a proposition contradicts anarchism's general impulse for freedom. Some may protest that I am being too harsh. One might contend that I am making a transhistorical and singular entity out of variegated and diffuse phenomena or that my conceptualization of religion is monolithic and hence deeply flawed. Surely "to bond" can also have positive connotations of kinship, association, and a sense of belonging. Indeed, the single most important contribution that a geographer has made to the theorization of anarchism is rooted in such an understanding of what it means to bond, as Peter Kropotkin's concept of mutual aid is a critique of the "all against all" interpretation of evolution, advocating instead that the bulk of human organization, both historically and into the present, has revolved around the reciprocal exchange of resources for common benefit (Kropotkin [1902] 2008). But unlike anarchism, which never shackles its followers to dogma and is instead open to the spirit of perpetual revision and experimentation, maintaining that any relationship, organization, or affiliation should be entirely voluntary, religion—and particularly organized religion—in contrast sets out incontrovertible principles of how life is to be lived. Such arrogance comes most overtly through monasticism, having ostensibly been handed down from the so-called supreme authority as a divine ordinance. To Émile Durkheim ([1915] 2008, 10), religion differs from private belief in that it is "something eminently social," which is not at all a bad thing. The problem rests with the current workings of religion, particularly the ways in which its organization has been oriented around structures of obedience, arrangements that often belittle and divide. In other words, as anarchism critiques vis-à-vis political organization, it is not organization itself that requires undoing, for anarchism is not chaos (Graeber 2002); rather, it is the way in which organization proceeds that needs to be remade, ideally along a horizontal rather than vertical axis. Hence there is a real need to align spiritual affinities in inclusive ways, but without any sentiment of coercion or hierarchy—in short, promoting bonds without bondage.

William Cavanaugh (2009, 4–5) contends that the entire notion of something called "religion" was fashioned by the arrival of the modern state system, justifying the violence of the state and the belief that "killing and dying in the name of the nation-state is laudable and proper." To me this reveals exactly what is so problematic about religion. Religion, in its organized form, has become one and the same as the institution of the state. Autocracy becomes theocracy, jurisdictional hierarchies become ecclesiastical hierarchies, law becomes dogma, and, in the supposedly secular context of the United States, "in God we trust" prevails as a cultural axiom. Emma Goldman would surely agree: "Religion, the dominion of the human mind; Property, the dominion of human needs; and Government, the dominion of human conduct, represent the stronghold of man's enslavement and all the horrors it entails" (Goldman 1917).

This is not to say that useful connections between religion and anarchism have not been developed, but for something like a "Christian anarchism" to be viable, it must move outside of the domain of religion and into the realm of spirituality. This is how I read Tolstoy ([1894] 2004), whose excommunication from and antipathy for the institution of the Church positioned him within the category of spirituality, as he sought a new mode of organization for his beliefs that was far more personal. Spirituality also requires some unpacking because of its slipperiness in terms of how it has been deployed and understood. Sometimes muddled with religion, but more often used to broadly reflect the search for the "sacred," spirituality as understood here refers to personal well-being and fulfillment (Wong and Vinsky 2009). Spirituality rejects the dualistic, insider–outsider worldview that is common in religion and is instead aligned to compassion and reciprocity rather than to clergy and rules. The two are not necessarily antithetical, but I draw a distinction to emphasize the difference in patterns of organizing. This is akin to the difference between society and the state, which are often problematically conflated but still not diametrically opposed, as the existence of the latter depends on the structure of organization found in the former. Just as a society that is organized hierarchically produces a state, while society organized voluntarily through rhizomic patterns facilitates anarchism, so too do I consider spirituality organized hierarchically to produce religion, while spirituality organized without submitting to the authority of scriptures or priests to have anarchistic potential. One can conceivably follow the enlightenments of Buddha, Krishna, or—as Tolstoy did—Christ, without subscribing to these teachings in the form of organized religion. Yet just as being inculcated in the ideology of nationalism leads to a credulous acceptance of the state, so too does religious ideology lead to an unreflexive deference to the church, wat, mosque, temple, gurdwara, or synagogue. Religion is spirituality in chains.

One of the key maxims about the contemporary anarchist movement is the recognition that there are as many anarchisms as there are anarchists, and as someone who embraces the notion of "anarchism without adjectives," I don't seek a "pure," "singular," or "true" anarchism but instead welcome plurality. I don't deny Christian anarchism exists, but nor do I want to prioritize it. My argument is specifically concerned with how—much like nationalism—under its current practices, religion possesses significant capacity to fragment our affinities into discrete *pieces* because of the hierarchical modes it assumes. A great number of anarchists have recognized the domination of religion, making a strong case for anarchism as a form of atheism. To Emma Goldman, the philosophy of atheism was irrevocably linked to anarchism, having shared roots in the Earth and life itself. Like anarchism, atheism was seen to offer "the emancipation of the human race from all God-heads, be they Judaic, Christian, Mohammedan, Buddhistic, Brahministic, or what not," thereby enabling people to "break [the] fetters that have chained [them] to the gates of heaven and hell, so that [they] can begin to fashion out of [this] reawakened and illumined consciousness a new world upon earth" (Goldman 1916). I can happily accept that a Christian version of anarchism exists, even if I fail to understand how certain hierarchies can be reconciled within this view. I do, however, take exception with the way in which some Christians have positioned a Christian morality as the only viable path toward nonviolence. Such a rigid view reflects a hardened position that is ultimately divisive. "If atheism is correct," Megoran (2013, 103) writes, "then there is no more inherent value to human life than there is to raindrops or asteroids." Not only is this a red-herring argument, given that the points of reference are inanimate objects, but it also unfortunately seems somewhat sanctimonious when coupled with the statement that "the Christian (anarchist or otherwise) case for nonviolence is based on the Biblical assertion that human beings are made in the 'image of God' by a loving Creator" (103).

I have deep ethical concerns with the notion that humans were created in the image of an unseen deity. Should we only narcissistically refrain from violence toward others because they supposedly reflect "God"? Is that not a deeply divisive approach to understanding the world? Bakunin ([1882] 2010, 2) ridicules this exact proposition:

> Jehovah had just created Adam and Eve, to satisfy we know not what caprice.... He generously placed at their disposal the whole earth, with all its fruits and animals, and set but a single limit to this complete enjoyment. He expressly forbade them from touching the fruit of the tree of knowledge.... We know what followed. The good God, whose foresight, which is one of the divine faculties, should have warned him of what would happen, flew into a terrible and ridiculous rage; he cursed Satan, man, and the world created by himself, striking himself so to speak in his own creation, as children do when they get angry; and, not content with

smiting our ancestors themselves, he cursed them in all the generations to come, innocent of the crime committed by their forefathers.

I would again seek to moderate Bakunin's uncompromising view because, as an integral anarchist, I also embrace an epistemological anarchism (Feyerabend 2010), which means I am quite prepared to make space for a multiplicity of worldviews. But I also want to ask what happens to those "Others" who don't reflect an anthropomorphized deity. What then becomes the basis of the tradition of Christian vegetarianism, for example, which some consider to be a key teaching of Jesus Christ? The very idea that human beings are the "image of God" laid out a role for humans of dominion over nonhuman animals, which establishes a sovereign relationship with "Others," and a false dichotomy between humans and nature by way of a pyramidal ordering. If Megoran had suggested raccoons and alligators rather than raindrops and asteroids, I would have whole-heartedly agreed that there is no greater intrinsic value to human beings than other nonhuman animals, as my anarchism is integral, where I see speciesism as forming the same violent genus as racism, classism, sexism, and homophobia, meaning that I embrace veganism as a crucial component of my anarchism and my commitment to nonviolence.

Atheism means only the lack of theism, or the rejection of the notion that there is a transcendent being that is consciously active in the workings of the universe. Notably, atheism is not antithetical to spirituality; it is merely a rejection of religion, which can only be conflated with spirituality by virtue of metonymy and misnomer. All religions involve spirituality, at least to some extent, but not all forms of spirituality are religious (Comte-Sponville 2007). My atheism is spiritual insofar as it draws from Baruch Spinoza, who saw "God" and "nature" as being entirely indistinguishable, forming the "whole, infinite, eternal, necessarily existing, active system of the universe within which absolutely everything exists" (Nadler 2011, 86). This simultaneity of *being,* or the very essence of existence, is what I would simply call the "universe" as opposed to "God." Like Albert Einstein (qtd. in Hoffmann and Dukas 1972, 95), "I believe in Spinoza's God who reveals himself in the orderly harmony of what exists, not in a God who concerns himself with the fates and actions of human beings." This is the fundamental principle of Spinoza's ([1677] 2001) *Ethics,* which has no use for the supernatural precisely because there is already enough wonder, mystery, and beauty in the universe we actually encounter that I have no need for superstition and fantasy. As Alan Watts (1960) argued, we don't require God as a hypothesis:

> If you awaken from this illusion, and you understand that black implies white, self implies other, life implies death—or shall I say, death implies life—you can conceive yourself. Not conceive, but *feel* yourself, not as a stranger in the world, not as someone here on sufferance, on probation, not as something that has arrived here by fluke, but you can begin to feel your own existence as absolutely fundamental. What you are basically, deep, deep down, far, far in, is simply the fabric and structure of existence itself. . . . So in this idea, then, everybody is fundamentally the ultimate reality. Not God in a politically kingly sense, but God in the sense of being the self, the deep-down basic whatever there is.

Such a spiritual view aligns with anarchism because it has no points of authority and instead thinks integrally, or without *pieces*.

The biggest conundrum faced by Christian and other religious anarchists is how to overcome hierarchical thinking without abandoning their religious convictions. I'll leave that for those who identify in these terms to resolve, but I nonetheless want to alert readers to the parallels between this line of argument and the arguments put forward by those who favor the rule of law. Religion, like law, appeals to discipline (i.e., unquestioning commitment to certain principles) and punishment (i.e., incarceration or eternal damnation) as the pillars of our collective moral edifice. Religion, like law, supposes that only fear of its own authority keeps us from raping and murdering our fellow human beings. And religion, like law, views humans as inherently wicked and in need of salvation, which comes only via an unwavering faith in the righteousness of the rules that have been established. Lack of religion and law is clearly not the equivalent of being without values, and though atheism can be nihilistic, this is not ipso facto the case. A lack of belief in an intervening deity is not tantamount to saying that life is meaningless; it simply says that the meaning of life can only ever be discovered for oneself, indeed, that our reason for being is inseparable from the pervading whole of the universe. We are, quite literally, the pulse of immanence. The morality of this proposition, for anarchism, has come from suturing affinities together through tenets like voluntary association and mutual aid, not tearing them to *pieces* by suggesting that one person's ethics, faith, or convictions are somehow more authentic than another's:

> And man is appealed to be guided in his acts, not merely by love, which is always personal, or at the best tribal, *but by the perception of his oneness with each human being.* In the practice of mutual aid, which we can retrace to the earliest beginnings of evolution, we thus find the positive and undoubted origin of our ethical conceptions; and we can affirm that in the ethical progress of man, mutual support not mutual struggle—has had the leading part. (Kropotkin [1902] 2008, 181, emphasis added)

It is this very presupposition of equality as an aspiration to live into, and the tracing of mutual aid to time immemorial, that guides an anarchist ethics. Anarchism, in all of its many registers, has no need for fabricated hierarchies, whether divine or otherwise. The providence of anarchism is to be found not in bondage to a transcendent illusion but rather in our immanent connections to each other and a faith in the possibilities of the *here* and *now.*

REDRESSING THE POSTPOLITICAL ZEITGEIST: PEACE AS THE INFINITUDE OF ANARCHY

While I dream of a world without war, without domination, without bondage, and without violence, the suturing together of the various broken *pieces,* or integral anarchism, that I advocate is not tantamount to envisioning a global consensus without dissent or difference. This is not the mirror image to the neoliberalized "new world order" anticipated by the Project for the New American Century, nor do I seek to stoke the fires of anti-immigration and xenophobic sentiment through the misguided perception that diversity is a problem that threatens the unity of particular communities, municipalities, or nations. In the previous chapter, I argued in favor of radical democracy as a form of *dissensus* that powerfully disrupts the depoliticizing order built by government and the violence this evokes. Radical democracy—which I interpret as tantamount to anarchism—stands in stark contrast to the representative model of democracy and is accordingly the antithesis of the postpolitical consensus that reduces politics to organizational functions and governmental techniques. Bringing the fragmented *pieces* back together instead means to summon the repudiation of antagonism, which is not only the primary modality that conditions violence and provokes war but is also ingrained within consensus models of democracy (Mouffe 2006). The widely accepted process of voting, for example, encourages one to reduce opposing positions to hostile caricature (Graeber 2009a), where the unspoken implication—and sadly, at times, the manifest result—is that individuals are considered in black and white as either part of the consensus or as enemies to the "peace," "order," and "stability" of the community that has been administratively imagined, territorially demarcated, and electorally reified (Anderson 1991). Radical democracy replaces the latent enmity of representative democracy (read electoral authoritarianism) with agonistic pluralism, which is rooted in a form of mutual respect that mirrors Jacques Rancière's (1999) presupposition of equality while allowing for the ever-present possibility of difference and dissent. Dissent becomes the lifeblood of anarchism precisely because it is not treated as divisive, as is the view maintained by advocates of a postpolitical consensus as well as many organized religions, but is instead viewed as a continually unfolding process that embraces difference through the lens of "radical equality" (or equality as an axiomatic given). Put differently, dissent becomes a way of life, where its perpetuity represents the very practice of politics, an unremitting and unbreakable thread that ties the people *(demos)* together by recognizing, rebuking, and rescinding hierarchical and oppressive power relations in society as and when they form.

Presupposing egalitarianism does not require us to base this idea in naturalistic assumptions, as was the framework for Kropotkin's thought. Rather, as political philosophers such as Slavoj Žižek (1999), Jacques Rancière (2006), and Todd May (2009b), as well as human geographers such as Erik Swyngedouw (2011), have all shown, we can make claims about radical equality without essentializing humanity or falling victim to the postpolitics school of thought popularized by Francis Fukuyama's (1992) end of history and Anthony Giddens's (1999) third way. The aim of my anarchist political project is not to establish a rational or utopian consensus that is to stand for all time and thereby represent an apolitical, ahistorical, and ageographical end state. Rather, like Mouffe (2004), I

hope to calm the potential of human hostilities by allowing for the possibility of antagonism to be transformed into agonism. Opening such an
opportunity for mutual respect, accommodation, humility, support, and
compassion to germinate and flourish involves dismantling the administrative structures, apparatuses, and logics of archy that maintain the rigid
codifications of space and belonging that are antecedent to the multiple
lines of antipathy we see in the world today.

In his essay "Ten Theses on Politics," Rancière (2001) develops a
masterful exegesis of archy, or *arche*, by drawing from Hannah Arendt
([1958] 1998), who identifies the power of *archein* as the power to begin
anew: "To act, in its most general sense, means to take an initiative, to
begin (as the Greek word *archein*, 'to begin,' 'to lead,' and eventually 'to
rule' indicates)." From this Rancière (2001) contends that "the logic of
arche presupposes a determinate superiority exercised upon an equally
determinate inferiority," which he links to the original usage of democracy as a term of derision, where those arbitrarily "qualified" to govern
by virtue of their birth, seniority, wealth, and knowledge and, most of all,
their means to violence articulated the "power of the *demos*" (democracy)
as rule by those who have no specificity in common, apart from their having no qualification to govern. Democracy, from the vantage point of the
governing class, was an affront to the "order" they had constructed and
was thus akin to chaos. The parallels to the contemporary caricature that
informs mainstream accounts of anarchism should not go unnoticed. To
Rancière, the *demos* exists only as a rupture of the logic of *arche*, of being
ruled. Yet it should be emphasized that this rupturing does not require a
fragmentation into distinct *pieces*, as the *demos* "should not be identified
either with the race of those who recognize each other as having the same
origin, the same birth, or with a part of a population or even the sum
of its parts." Identity still matters and is accommodated for and indeed
celebrated through democratic practice, yet the *demos* is not about breaking humanity into ever more pieces but instead enters a radical equality
that sees no privilege assigned to any particular category of belonging.

Through Rancière we can begin envisioning how the idea of *arche*
allows us to develop a very rich idea of *an-arche*, which emphasizes the
project of autonomy rather than heteronomy. The participation proper
to politics is actually allowed for through the very rupturing of all those

logics of allocation and administration that are exercised through the matrix of *arche*. "The 'freedom' of a people that constitutes the *axiom* of democracy," Rancière avers, "has as its real content the rupture of the axioms of domination: a rupture, that is, in the correlation between a capacity for rule and a capacity for being ruled." *An-arche* thus becomes not the realization of a utopian end state without domination, nor, as we have seen, can *an-arche* be conceived of as having a definitive "beginning." Instead, *an-arche,* or anarchism, speaks of the "infinitely demanding" struggle of being active, of forging solidarities across space, of evading sovereign logics, of accommodating dissent, of denying authority, of ethical commitment, of resisting oppression, and ultimately of taking up the challenge of "ruling" ourselves (Critchley 2007). To Rancière (2001), this trial represents the very essence of the political, where politics is to be conceived as a very specific burst in the logic of *arche*:

> It does not simply presuppose the rupture of the "normal" distribution of positions between the one who exercises power and the one subject to it. It also requires a rupture in the idea that there are dispositions "proper" to such classifications.

This explication cuts to the very heart of anarchist geographies, which in the introduction I defined as the "kaleidoscopic spatialities that allow for multiple, nonhierarchical, and protean connections between autonomous entities, wherein solidarities, bonds, and affinities are voluntarily assembled in opposition to and free from the presence of sovereign violence, predetermined norms, and assigned categories of belonging." Anarchism is accordingly to be understood as the perpetual implementation (through thought, speech, and direct action) of a promise for something better, wherein it is not peace and the finitude of utopia that become synonymous but rather peace and the infinitude of *an-arche*.

Although I take radical equality as the basis of my emancipatory concerns, my arguments should not be interpreted as denying political responses that attended to the marginalizations that emerge through our lived experiences as differently situated actors. Indeed, at the root of a feminist ethics of care is the rejection of the masculinist and Kantian idea that we can or should treat everyone exactly the same. Janine Wiles and Audrey Kobayashi (2009) differentiate between "formal equality," which is concerned with the principle of treating individuals the same regardless of the outcomes, and "substantive equity," which conversely refers to the principle of achieving an equitable outcome. In this sense, the radical equality I support is compatible with the feminist tradition and its suggestion that it is, at times and in particular spaces, perfectly ethical to care for some more than others, given that

> lives are supported and maintained differently, and there are radically different ways in which human physical vulnerability is distributed across the globe. Certain lives will be highly protected, and the abrogation of their claims to sanctity will be sufficient to mobilize the forces of war. *Other* lives will not find such fast and furious support and will not even qualify as "grievable." (Butler 2004, 32, emphasis added)

Hence the ethical principle of substantive equity, which I take as a core constituent of the larger process of radical equality (as opposed to formal equality), is that selective priority should be given to improving the situation of the most socially disadvantaged groups in a society, which requires continual readjustment of existing structures and a recalcitrance toward processes that drive an inequitable system (Wiles and Kobayashi 2009). Consequently, the radical equality I propose is not something that can be implemented instantaneously as an ideational flash point that is subsequently assigned a finality or completeness. Rather, as a properly political process, radical equality is something that is in need of continuous confirmation precisely because, as Jacques Derrida ([1967] 2001) argues, normalizing codes conceptualize and materialize difference through the irreducible relationality and intertexuality of human experience. Subject positions and their distribution are always being made and remade, meaning that identity politics are both inexorable and insurmountable.

In this light, my arguments should not be misinterpreted as wanting to disavow any particular or all religious philosophies, as was the historical imperative of Communism and its practices of attempted censure and erasure. To deny religion tout court is to repudiate the freedom of particular categories of affinity, identity, and belonging, which is a step toward convening a normative frame for all of humanity, an idea I have been arguing against. This is the exact danger we currently face under globalized neoliberalism and its aspirations of a "global village" of properly neoliberalized subjects (Kingfisher 2007). Within the context of neoliberalism's aligned global "war on terror," Judith Butler (2004, 32) asks, "To what extent have Arab peoples, predominantly practitioners of Islam, fallen outside of the human as it is being naturalized in its 'Western' mold by the contemporary workings of humanism?" The amplification of religious fundamentalism on both sides of this divide should be recognized as an alarming trend that attempts to set rigid moral limits to what it means to be human, thereby renewing the notion of *homo sacer*—life that does not count as politically qualified and so may be killed but not sacrificed (Agamben 1998). My concern is thus for an honest appreciation of how the current workings of organized religion—as opposed to faith itself—engender particular forms of prosecution and hierarchy and the need to be attentive to refashioning spiritual affinities in ways that are more inclusive, compassionate, and forbearing without denying the identity and sense of belonging that religious affiliation fosters.

RADICAL EQUALITY AND OUR BEST POSSIBILITY FOR PEACE

If human geography is to convene a morality premised on the presumption of radical equality, which I have already suggested is akin to humanity's collective birthright, one might object to this being an "ordinary normativity" (Sayer 2003), no more or less a cultural prejudice than religion. My response is simply that the moment of birth knows no norms, where radical equality precedes any and all cultural content. We learn to perform our assigned and hierarchically organized roles of class, gender, ethnicity, nationality, religion, and so forth, through culture, which geographers by now know very well makes identities fluid and variable across space and time. What we cannot learn through any cultural program is how to be born, we just are. Put differently, while we come to learn to be different identities, we do not learn to simply *be*. Alan Watts (2006, 37) put this into perspective when he said,

> The meaning of life is just to be alive. That is to say, when I look at the color of your hair and the shape of your eyebrow, I understand that their shape and color are their point. And this is what we are all here for, as

well: to be. It is so plain and so obvious and so simple. And yet, everybody rushes around in a great panic as if it were necessary to achieve something beyond themselves.

Readers should not mistake my arguments as high Rousseau. It is not my intention to argue for the restoration of a precapitalist, precolonial, or premodern utopia, wherein only the proverbial noble savage exists. I am not convinced by anarchoprimitivist authors like Derrick Jensen (2006) and John Zerzan (2002), who explicitly prosecute such arguments, not least because in their imagined nostalgia they advocate all manner of violence to facilitate a supposed "return" to universal peace. So-called classical anarchists such as Proudhon, Kropotkin, Reclus, and Bakunin similarly advocated essentialist or naturalist views of humanity that—in light of the achievements of thinkers such as Rancière, Butler, Žižek, and Derrida—I find tremendously problematic. Accordingly, I place my views within the antiessentialist frame of postanarchism, which denotes a merging of anarchist and poststructuralist thought (May 1994; Newman 2010). To postanarchists, identity still unavoidably matters, and the notion of radical equality is intended to serve only as an ideological referent for our political engagements, not as an idealized reality of the workings of our present or as a fully realizable condition of our future. Though the presupposition of equality should be understood as self-evident, it is nonetheless a promise to relentlessly struggle toward and a hope that we should aspire to live into.

There is no precursory or future utopian state for humanity, only the continually unfolding of systems of organization that we ourselves construct, disassemble, and reconstruct anew. Unfortunately, the contemporary zeitgeist sees such structures unfold in ways that appear ever more hierarchical in composition, and yet such an orientation largely goes unchallenged because it has become so routinized and quotidian that we have come to accept *arche* as a given. The very idea of government itself has become the essential condition of the postpolitical conjuncture, wherein the emancipatory potential of anarchism has been demonized, admonished, caricatured, berated, and renounced as a dangerous "chaos" that threatens the existing consensus. The acceptance of the existing system of rule speaks to Arendt's (1963) "banality of evil," which views history's profoundest moments of malevolence as being executed not by fanatics or sociopaths but by ordinary people who simply accepted the premises of the prevailing order. As academics, we consequently have an ethical obligation to reveal and challenge the quagmire of contemporary orderings of *arche,* which at their root represent nothing less than the very fog of war. My appeals to radical equality should accordingly be read as an appreciation for the *potential* decentralization and diffusion of power, which is to be rooted in an affinity where difference is neither denied, essentialized, nor exoticized but embraced as potentially transformative (Day 2005; Mueller 2003). The project of anarchism is thus not at all about chaos but about creating new forms of organization that break with hierarchy and embrace egalitarianism (Graeber 2009a). We all make political choices, and the future of the thoughts expressed here resides in the notion that any praxis begins first and foremost with an introspective reflection on our own participation in the structures that facilitate and reproduce violence, and an unwavering commitment to unfastening these bonds. Our shared morality, then, should not be premised on the prejudices of life as it is currently lived through a politics of consensus that is antagonistic toward difference. Instead, we should allow the empathetic horizons of agonism to be our guide.

By aligning anarchism with the most emancipatory current of feminist thought, and in embracing our ultimate integrality to each other and all that is, the morality of peace should accordingly function as an ethics of intersectionality (see Grillo 1995; Valentine 2007). This entails a categorical rejection of all the interlocking systems of domination, including capitalism, imperialism, colonialism, neoliberalism, militarism, nationalism, classism, racism, ethnocentrism, Orientalism, misogyny, genderism, ageism, misopedy, ableism, speciesism, carnism, homophobia, transphobia, sovereignty, the state, *and* organized religion. The mutually reinforcing composition of these various dimensions of *arche* consequently means that to insulate any one of these *pieces* from our critical and vigilant interrogation is to allow the banality of evil to go unchecked and thereby to perpetuate the conglomeration of *war* as a whole. Freedom from bondage and the practice of mutual aid, which together represent the sine qua non of peace, rest in the promise of intersectionality to expand our circle of empathy in such a radical way that "Others" come to be seen as but extensions of ourselves. The very oneness of the universe implies spiritual purpose because it allows us finally to recognize that doing violence to others is no different than doing violence to ourselves. To be atheist is not a denial of the absolute; it is a denial of its transcendence and the realization of immanence. There is no salvation, only *nunc fluens*, the eternal flowing now, which represents the very fabric of existence, where space and time are united in the spectrum of eternity. The primal energy of the living infinite is integral, and it is this very integrality that affords possibility to nonviolence. My understanding of anarchism as a means without end that embraces an agonistic politics is not ahistorical but forever processual and infinitely demanding (Critchley 2007), where nonviolence is a possibility for anarchism to live into. Once we accept that a creative deity "is the most decisive negation of human liberty, and necessarily ends in the enslavement of [hu]mankind, both in theory and practice" (Bakunin [1882] 2010, 13), we no longer need to appeal to a higher authority to love, care for, and respect each other and ourselves, for this is the essence of bondage. All that we require is a willingness to accept that another world is not only possible but also our best possibility for peace.

6

The Anarchist Horizon

What happened to ethics along the way—especially among
radicals who profess to be antiauthoritarian, ethical socialists.
—**Murray Bookchin**

There are still empty maps, nameless places, places wild and free.
—**Tyra A. Olstad**

In *A Thousand Plateaus*, Gilles Deleuze and Félix Guattari (1987) intro-
duced the concept of the "arborescent" to describe a vertical, treelike
ontology of totalizing principles and binary thought. They contrasted
this with the notion of the "rhizome," which is marked by a horizontal
ontology, wherein things, ideas, and politics are able to link up in nonhierarchical patterns of association. It is fair to say that a certain arbores-
cence with respect to the political economic imagination marks contemporary geographical thought. This is exemplified in debates surrounding
neoliberalism. Here we find two competing visions, each blinkered in its
own unique way, which see either decentralization and increased flows of
capital as the salvation of humanity or, conversely, centralization and the
end of capital accumulation as our collective redemption. The former is
propagated largely outside of the academy by politicians, journalists, think
tanks, and popular authors such as Thomas L. Friedman (1999), whereas
the latter is advanced primarily within the academy as an attempt to stem
the public discourse that favors neoliberalism (Duménil and Lévy 2011;
Peck 2010; Smith, Stenning, and Willis 2009). Although scholars like
Michael Hardt and Antonio Negri (2000) and J. K. Gibson-Graham
(1996) offer intriguing alternatives to the simple reconstitution of a centralized authority, and there exists a progressive strain of understanding
neoliberalism through its governmentalities and discourses (England and
Ward 2007; Larner 2000; Lemke 2001; Springer 2012b), the bulk of the
critique that has been mounted against neoliberalization within human

geography problematically perpetuates the dichotomy that I have identified, falling back on Marxist conventions and "jumping scales" to make
its claims (Brenner and Theodore 2003; Glassman 2002; Smith 2005). As
Aihwa Ong (2007, 3) observes, "the newness of the neoliberalism word
does not disguise the classic method of relying on old macro political
distinctions....The main issue appears to be identifying the scale of neoliberal progression and the appropriate scale of analysis." David Harvey,
for his part, actually poisons the well of decentralization by preemptively
refusing its possibilities and positioning every movement toward a more
autonomous political arrangement as a device that somehow necessarily
greases the rails for a neoliberal future. In *Rebel Cities,* Harvey (2012b, 69)
sums up this problematic mode of thought when he argues,

> In some sense "hierarchical" forms of organization are needed to address
> large-scale problems....Unfortunately the term "hierarchy" is anathema
> in conventional thinking...and virulently unpopular with much of the
> left these days. The only politically correct form of organization in many
> radical circles is non-state, non-hierarchical, and horizontal.

But why exactly is it "unfortunate" that hierarchy is denunciated?

I suppose if we subscribe to a limited political economic imagination and dichotomous thinking, then sure, a Marxist state is arguably
a better option than unrestrained capitalism. Yet the problem is not so
easily resolved, and advocating political authority is (at least in my mind)
hardly a radical solution. Instead, it represents a problematic disregard for
the new possibilities that have emerged and a perpetuation of the same
weary politics that have been empirically proven false. At a historical
conjuncture where hierarchy is being actively questioned across such a
diverse range of political sites, where WikiLeaks cracked the possibilities of accountability wide open (Curran and Gibson 2013; Springer et
al. 2012a), where the Occupy movement seemingly unified 99 percent of
the population through affinities that transcend rigid identities (Chomsky
2012; Sparke 2013), and where the Arab Spring struck fear in the hearts
of dictators not just in northern Africa and the Middle East but across
the entire planet (Mamadouh 2011; Dabashi 2012), we are curiously presented with lamentations on the political left, coupled with a demand for
a "centralized movement" arranged around class lines and a reconstituted
hierarchy. Outside of geography, Jodi Dean (2012a) does much the same

in *The Communist Horizon,* calling for a return of the Communist Party, a renewed sense of vanguardism, and the cultivation of vertical structures, wherein she caricatures anarchist politics and the openness, horizontality, and diversity that it implies as being easily expropriated by what she calls "communicative capitalism." Contrast this with Barbara Epstein (2001), who recognizes that Marxism has been eclipsed within contemporary social moments, which are largely inspired by anarchist principles of voluntary association, egalitarianism, direct action, and radical democracy.

Harvey and Dean tread a very slippery slope, one that—as I will argue—lacks *traction.* Hierarchy of course lays bare a sense of pecking order and is thus synonymous with authority. The etymology of the word *hierarchy* is revealing; the word originates from the Greek *hierarkhēs,* meaning "sacred ruler," where the earliest sense was the "system of orders of angels and heavenly beings."[1] Such a renewed call for political authority on the left, which is really a reiteration of Marxism that dates right back to the man that gave the theory a name, is not without consequence. As Anselme Bellegarrigue ([1850] 2005, 59) argued, "who says affirmation of political authority, says individual dependency; who says individual dependency, says class supremacy; who says class supremacy, says inequality." How is this a solution rather than a perpetuation of the problems that we face in the current moment where democracy has been reduced to a cipher for authoritarianism behind the illusions of participation and consent (Giroux 2004)? This can only be considered a recipe for ostensibly "rebel" cities in the most uninspired sense. To rebel is to rise up and oppose authority, not stand alongside it and promote reasons for its perpetuation. Since when are the politics of rebellion defined by abiding by the decisions that are handed down from above? Springer et al. (2012b, 1593) have attempted to tap the vein of rebellion by reanimating anarchist geographies, arguing that "much of the socialist left appears bereft of ideas beyond a state-regulated capitalism," and indeed the reconstitution of hierarchy represents a step backward, not "a new burst of colour" that sings for the possibilities of tomorrow.

In Harvey's (2012b) view, it is precisely scale itself that necessitates hierarchy. Though hierarchy is not tantamount to scale, there is a critical degree of coalescence between the two concepts that we cannot afford to ignore. Consequently, Harvey is not entirely incorrect in his assertion, yet the ontological understanding of such congruency is misaligned, where he makes a case for a politics of authority rather than appreciating this coalescence as the basis for a new politics of possibilities. One key difference that I attempt to convey in this chapter is that whereas scale is anchored in abstraction, hierarchy—and its refusal—begins at the level of the everyday. This aligns with David Graeber's (2007, 13) interpretation, where he understands hierarchy in its most elementary forms: "the way people avert their eyes or stand at attention, the sort of topics they avoid in formal conversation, what it means to treat another person as somehow abstract, sacred, transcendent, set apart from the endless entanglements and sheer physical messiness of ordinary existence." In other words, hierarchy is made flesh through its evasion of the intertwined materiality of our existence and our complicity in such processes. But embedded within this reading, we can also find the seed of scale, which grows arborescently out of the everyday into abstraction.[2] Scale sets things apart. Its vertical ontology attempts transcendence by standing above materiality, meaning that scale is literally a *dis*-traction. In this movement, scale has taken on a sacred quality within human geography because of the seemingly omniscient optic it provides to those who employ it. Although I concede that categorization and ranking are features of language as a system of representation (Foucault [1970] 2002), there is no reason to assume that a hierarchical "order of things" must define our forms of social organization. This is why a human geography without hierarchy is of critical importance. Only by interrogating the limits of particular concepts, like neoliberalism (Harvey 2005), like scale (Marston, Jones, and Woodward 2005), like hierarchy, can we begin to think in terms of rhizomatic alternatives to life beyond an allegedly inevitable centralized authority.

Flirtation with authority has always been a central problem with Marxism, hence its enduring predilection toward authoritarian arrangements. Under Marxism, the oppressed rise up and seize state power, where a selected few caretakers—the vanguard—make promises to destroy it after a period of transition. But the supposed withering away of the state never comes, and the proletarian dictatorship slowly starts to ossify, becoming as twisted, mangled, and barbarous as any other Leviathan. The proof is in the pudding of history, or rather in Stalin's gulags and Pol Pot's Tuol Sleng, as it were. There are, however, other possibilities within the political economic matrix, and in the face of greater autonomy, we need

FIGURE 1. The political economic matrix. Adapted from "The Anarchist Economical-Political Map," http://www.anarchy.no/a_e_p_m.html.

not recoil in horror and allow spent ideas to stifle our imagination for the "diverse economies" of other possible worlds (Gibson-Graham 1996; 2008; Pickerill and Chatterton 2006). Two domains of political thought are all but ignored by contemporary human geographers. We can have increased centralization coupled with capitalism, a positionality otherwise known as fascism and one that has thankfully seen little interest in the discipline outside of critically interrogating Nazi geographies (Barnes and Minca 2013; Flint 2001), or we can explore the most emancipatory coordinates of all, where decentralization is coupled with an anticapitalist sensibility, which is the rhizomatic domain of anarchism (Clough and Blumberg 2012; Springer et al. 2012b) (see Figure 1). It is, of course, the latter that is my focus here, as the uppermost quadrant is where a human geography without hierarchy can find the most *traction*.

THE FUTURE IS NOW

Decentralization has been at the heart of radical geographical ideas for a very long time, which makes it all the more peculiar that David Harvey has yet to come to grips with its possibilities, remaining committed to a geography of centralization premised upon the state (see also Smith 2010). This is perhaps unsurprising, given that "Harvey is a distinguished representative of [classical Marxism], his work marked by 'a degree of fidelity to the original spirit and letter of Marx that is quite remarkable: ... [his oeuvre is] not an epiphany that rewrites the word according to Saul along the road to a New Church, but a judicious rendering and extension of Marx's unfinished project'" (Castree 2006, 50, citing Walker 2004, 434). In contrast, some Marxist geographers, particularly those writing from an autonomist perspective, have looked beyond the state as the locus of politics, where the works of Hardt and Negri (2004), John Holloway (2002), and Silvia Federici (2004) have been particularly influential in articulating agency, uprisings, assemblages, and resistance (Chatterton 2005; Cumbers, Helms, and Swanson 2010; Marks 2012; Russell, Pusey, and Chatterton 2011). Feminist geographers have also fared well in advancing a new locus for politics, where Cindi Katz's (2001) work on countertopographies and Sara Koopman's (2011) project on altergeopolitics stand out as progressive reassessments of what kind of politics might be possible beyond the state. Earlier still, Richard Peet (1975; 1978) was intrepid in his exploration of anarchist geographer Peter Kropotkin's ideas, recognizing the sociospatiality of decentralization as imperative to the geography of human liberation. It was Kropotkin's time in Siberia that allowed him to think beyond the industrial frame of Europe that Marx universalized as the essential condition of human experience. As a result of Kropotkin's insights, anarchists developed a very different geographical imagination than that of the Marxists, envisioning a place for self-sufficiency that challenged the ostensible need for centralized government. Emphasis was placed not on the supposed centrality of the industrial worker but on the local production and decentralized organization of rural life (Galois 1976).

"Now we anarchists are not Marxists," Colin Ward (1990b, 131) once proclaimed. "We belong to a different tradition from the one which saw the steam-engine and the consequent concentration of industrial production as the ultimate factor in human history.... It is our tradition which corresponds more closely to the actual experience, both of our grandparents and of our grandchildren." What Ward is suggesting here is that there is a particular spatiotemporal myopia to Marxian thought that treats industrialization as an ever-present and worldwide experience rather than acknowledging it as various scattered moments in human history that arose within a series of contextually specific geographies. Industrialism can increasingly be seen as an anomaly precisely because it was preceded by thousands of years of nonindustrialized organization, and although it may currently be intensifying in some locations, particularly within the Global South (Kohli 2004), it is also presently being undone in those "traditional" industrial zones, such as the Rust Belt of America, where mechanization, automation, offshoring, and the rise of the service sector have all become increasingly common (Wilson and Wouters 2003). The idea of decentralization does not necessarily imply a return to rural life, wherein Kropotkin located his vision, but nor does it need to for this emancipatory idea to be considered meaningful. Murray Bookchin (Bookchin 1990b; 1992; see also Biehl and Bookchin 1997) made a proposal for a confederal network of municipal assemblies, wherein villages, towns, and neighborhoods willingly linked together via networks and power would flow through the practice of direct democracy and open assemblies. Harvey (2012b, 85) admits that the libertarian municipalism that Bookchin proposed would be "well worth elaborating as part of a radical anti-capitalist agenda," yet instead of actually doing so, he instead reverts to his centralization argument.

One of the crucial questions to arise from this centralizing rhetoric is to ask, as Ward ([1973] 2001) did, "Who is to plan?" Harvey (2012b, 83) addresses this issue when he suggests that "relations between independent and autonomously functioning communities have to be established and regulated somehow.... But we are left in the dark as to how such rules might be constituted, by whom, and how they might be open to democratic control." This is all well and good, and I don't dispute that these are issues that should form the domain of contestation within an agonistic public space. Yet the problem with centralization—which is the preferred alternative of most Marxists—is that such an organization of human landscapes actually licenses the privation of the majority by unfairly giving some form of advantage to a privileged minority who takes it upon themselves to plan for others (Breitbart 1975). If planning is the sublimation of politics, as Saul Newman (2011) contends is the case, then it becomes absolutely central to the questions that surround the nature of our collective organization. Although Harvey asks worthwhile questions about the structure of autonomous, horizontal, and anarchistic sensibilities, he shockingly declares that "rules must not only be established and asserted. They must also be enforced and actively policed" (83), a suggestion that lets slip a perhaps unconsidered degree of authoritarianism. Thus what we are effectively being asked to do by Harvey is what Marxism has been requesting of us all along:

> We are asked to establish political parties, centralized organizations, "revolutionary" hierarchies and elites, and a new state at a time when political institutions as such are decaying and when centralizing, elitism and the state are being brought into question on a scale that has never occurred before in the history of hierarchical society. We are asked, in short, to return to the past, to diminish instead of grow, to force the throbbing reality of our times, with its hopes and promises, into the deadening preconceptions of an outlived age. (Bookchin [1971] 2004, 201–2)

While Harvey stops short of outright calling for a proletarian dictatorship to be established in any postrevolutionary conjuncture, his centralizing logic conjures the spirit of cadres, vanguards, and leaders. Such an approach is very much at odds with the contemporary zeitgeist, which is characterized by a diffuse and nonhierarchical series of "convergence spaces" (Routledge 2003b) and "global justice networks" (Cumbers, Routledge, and Nativel 2008) that were organized on the ground through networks of affinity and maintained via the rhizome of processual direct action (Day 2005).

Harvey attempts to rescue his centralizing project—or at least encase it in a more accommodating and progressive veneer—by indicating, "I am not saying horizontality is bad—indeed, I think it is an excellent objective but that we should acknowledge its limits as a hegemonic organization principle and be prepared to go far beyond it when necessary." Without being aware of it, and without offering any suitable answers, Harvey turns his own line of questioning around on himself. How exactly can something that is "enforced" and "policed" be (mis)construed as democratic, especially in a radical sense? Who decides when it is necessary to go beyond autonomy and impose authority? How is such an imposition of rule meted out? What kind of enforcement is advisable, and what of the question of violence? Is it to be monopolized? If so, what are the implications? No answers are offered to these questions, and instead Harvey (2006, 411) falls back on what he once seemingly admitted is his own "vulgar" Marxism. Moreover, we should interrogate the notion of horizontality being an objective for the future, for it reveals the politics of waiting that is so deeply and problematically entrenched in Marxian thought. This suggestion is little more than a repackaging of the old "withering away of the state" line that Marxists have been feeding us for a very long time, without a shred of empirical verification. Worse still, such a notion sidesteps the insurrectionary possibilities of the present by delaying the revolutionary imperative to a future moment that is forever drifting toward infinity. "If we remember those times and places—and there are so many—where people have behaved magnificently, it energizes us to act," Howard Zinn (2007, 270) argues. "And if we do act, in however small a way, we don't have to wait for some grand utopian future. The future is an infinite succession of the present, and to live now as we think human beings should live, in defiance of all that is bad around us, is itself a marvelous victory."

Instead of actively attempting to construct autonomous relations through a revolution of the everyday (Vaneigem [1967] 2012) and the rematerialization of space through our living embodiment of egalitarian and nonhierarchical affinities, processes about us that can be felt as immediately emancipatory, the tomorrow of Marxism never comes. The reason for this is because of a fear that "decentralization and autonomy are the primary vehicles for producing greater inequality through neoliberalization" (Harvey 2012b, 83), which incorrectly assigns a capitalist logic to all libertarian ideas by painting with the same broad strokes of caricature that the oxymoronic anarchocapitalists use in misappropriating the term *anarchism* by severing it from its philosophical origins in socialist thought and its central tenet of anticapitalism. Certainly some danger comes with decentralization, given the predominance of neoliberal ideas in our current moment and their ability to infect a wide variety of political movements and ideas, but such an association is no more necessary than it is desirable by anarchists, who are starkly opposed to capitalism. Any potential risk is mitigated further when we recall that anarchist praxis is about embracing prefigurative politics, which means that anarchism lives through modes of organization and social relationships that strive to reflect the future society being sought. It is the recognition that to plan without practice is akin to theory without empirics, history without voices, and geography without context. In other words, prefiguration actively creates a new society in the shell of the old (Ince 2012). As Rudolf Rocker ([1956] 2005, 111) once declared, "I am an anarchist not because I believe anarchism is the final goal, but because there is no such thing as a final goal." So a prefigurative politics does not hoist the future up on a mantel to become a mere conversation piece; rather, it actively subverts the politics of waiting by embracing the immediate possibilities of the *here* and *now*.

FLATTENING THE WORLD

In the same way that a Marxian dismissal of horizontal organization rests on a particular temporal diffusion that overlooks *process* itself as the lifeblood of rebellion, there are problematic spatial implications to be found in Harvey's argument. Most pointedly, Harvey (2012b, 69–70) contends that

> there is, clearly, an analytically difficult "scale problem" at work here that needs (but does not receive) careful evaluation. . . . What looks like a good way to resolve problems at one scale does not hold at another scale. Even worse, patently good solutions at one scale (the "local" say) do not necessarily aggregate up (or cascade down) to make for good solutions at another scale (the global, for example).

Although I would agree that abstractions of the global do not necessarily flow to the local, and vice versa (but for very different reasons than Harvey), there is also no reason to assume that if we act in ethically and ecologically responsible ways within the immediate sites of our everyday lives, these actions won't *drift* outward across the networks within which we are all entwined (Ferrell 2012). A prefigurative politics is a politics that embraces the Gandhian notion of "be the change you wish to see in the world,"[3] where the underlying message is that our actions, however seemingly insignificant, have resonant geographies that travel far beyond the immediacy of place. The entire language Harvey deploys here is intensely problematic and has come under fire in the recent geographical literature, represented by the scale debate that was initiated by Marston, Jones, and Woodward (2005; see also Jones, Woodward, and Marston 2007), who sought to advance a flat or site ontology by expunging scale from the geographical vocabulary.[4] The delusion of scale is that it represents a theoretical distraction, a drawing away from the grounded particularities of the everyday. When we "jump scales," we engage in such *dis*-traction precisely because we lose our footing and relinquish our grip on our surroundings to soar off into an abstract sky, only to touch down on the immediate materiality of everyday life when and where it becomes convenient to our argument.

Marston, Jones, and Woodward (2005, 422) proposal for a human geography without scale has many resonances with anarchism, not least of which is its ability to embrace the rhizomatic notion of a processual politics that is conceived through its actual practice: "flat ontologies consist of self-organizing systems, or 'onto-genesis'...where the dynamic properties of matter produce a multiplicity of complex relations and singularities." This mirrors an anarchist politics of direct action insofar as its energies emerge not out of service to an end-state theory of predetermined results, which is the shared philosophical domain of Marxism and neoliberalism, but are instead embraced because of a desire for openness, disordering, and process itself, out of which future possibilities may emerge (Ferrell 2001). Metaphors such as "jumping scale" rub Marston, Jones, and Woodward (2005) the wrong way precisely because they impart a sense that politics should operate through vertical hierarchies rather than around multiple sites of horizontal activity and autonomous resistance. Such an orientation forestalls the potential that exists within a flat ontology of immediacy wherein social structures, power relations, and hierarchies become identifiable, accessible, and ultimately transformable. Any politics of waiting is erased as rebellion is brought to bear on one's own subjectivity through a prefigurative (as opposed to predetermined) politics, which in turn becomes the direct locus of "resubjectivation" as a means to disrupt neoliberal discourse (Gibson-Graham 1996). Woodward,

Jones, and Marston (2012) contend that subjectivity actually becomes suspended though the unanticipated connections and interactions that emerge from a site ontology, allowing for autonomous spaces to open up both organizationally and politically, as the material immanence—the *here* and *now* of prefiguration—makes the site the legislator of its own assembly, wherein subjectivity no longer conditions the political schemata. Such a reading notably does not negate subjectivity but instead seeks "to explain the situated, material suspension of their effects so that we might better understand the complexity of political unfoldings" (217).

The consequence of this ontological shift is that there is no need to wait for a class consciousness to emerge out of assigning significance to a "greater" cause, as one can immediately disengage from the circuits of capitalism and reorient the economic landscapes they inhabit in ways that enable alternative possibilities of organization, which is precisely what direct action is all about. This is why Marston, Jones, and Woodward (2005) emphasize the politically transformative potential of social reproductive practices that emerge through rejecting the scalar axiomatic. Such reproduction is, as Richard J. White and Collin C. Williams (2012) observe, actually already pervasive, as noncommodified practices such as mutual aid, inclusion, and reciprocity have long been advanced and are actively embedded in the present, which brings empirical charge to the idea that decentralized organization and representation are able to be organized through autonomous modes that defy hierarchy and authority. A flat ontology does not mean that flows of affinity are severed and networks of cooperation are not established. Geography still functions through space as the simultaneity of stories-so-far, and through place as collections of these stories (Massey 2005), so that Andrew Jonas's (2006, 405) charge that a flat ontology produces "a world without spatial difference or connection . . . in short, a world without human geography" rings hollow. What is new and different here is a dismissal of the hierarchy that human geographers continue to assume is embedded within notions of territory, a spatial assumption that perpetuates the dominance of capitalism and authority in society. In contrast, Anthony Ince (2012) links an alternative spatiality to prefiguration, wherein territory can instead become viewed as a processual and contested product of social relations. A flat ontology, then, simply means that we don't need to wait for some ostensible "higher-order importance" and "broader forces" to lend legitimacy to the idea that we can resist the alienation, domination, and boredom that neoliberalism attempts to impose on our everyday lives. It is precisely the revolution of the everyday that empowers us to transcend capitalist subjectivation through the social practices and territorialization we choose to engage (Vaneigem [1967] 2012).

Jonas (2006, 403) claims that to "equate scalar hierarchies with a vertical (and by implication state- or capital-centric) view of political action and change is misleading." But this is precisely what Harvey is proposing when he relies on scale as a device to lend credence to his centralizing project. To other Marxist geographers, such as Erik Swyngedouw (1997), though, scale is not a fixed geographical structure wherein identities are rendered static but rather a dynamic idea that is constituted through strategic actions and struggle. Castree, Featherstone, and Herod (2008) have argued that scale is a way to negotiate spatial difference through which different sites may be brought together or rendered apart for different strategic organizing purposes. Similarly, instead of focusing on scale as the prime object of political contestation, Danny MacKinnon (2011) emphasizes a "scalar politics" that focuses attention on the strategic deployment of scale by various actors, movements, and organizations to meet specific purposes. I can appreciate these more nuanced readings of scale, and to be clear, in line with these understandings, and in opposition to Harvey, my contention is that despite overlapping tendencies, scale is not synonymous with hierarchy. Nonetheless, the burden remains on geographers to demonstrate with conviction and clarity how scalar ontologies can productively shed themselves of their implicit and explicit hierarchies.[5] So while Jonas (2006, 403–4) may be correct that "empowerment is more than simply a question of jumping 'up' (or 'down') scales ... rather different site-scalar configurations and territorial structures create opportunities for a variety of different site-scalar strategic actions," I think he misses Marston, Jones, and Woodward's (2005) primary point, which is that the way the discourse of scale has been deployed evokes a particular presupposition that restricts the openness of a rhizomatic, horizontal politics by predetermining the political as an arborescent register. While Bookchin's (1990b; 1992) proposal for a confederation of libertarian municipalities can be said to invoke some sense of scale, it does so without the

Archimedean crutch of a hierarchical ontology, and indeed Bookchin would reject the idea that the "commune of communes" would be anything that even remotely resembles verticality. Likewise, and in productively demonstrating the potential alliances between autonomous Marxists and anarchists that Mark Purcell (2012) calls for, Cumbers, Routledge, and Nativel (2008) and Routledge, Cumbers, and Nativel (2007) reveal how global justice networks offer alternatives to neoliberalism by navigating scale in nonhierarchical ways through a relational politics that draws in a wide range of actors operating along horizontal lines. David Featherstone (2008) similarly advances a relational politics by situating resistances as dynamic subaltern spaces that are always already the product of different trajectories, wherein continuously exchanging properties construct and extend counterglobal networks. So although I would hesitate to discard scale altogether because of the alternative possibilities that may yet remain hidden within its theorization, ultimately, Marston, Jones, and Woodward (2005) are correct: there is a need for a flattening of the spatial register, a destruction of the assumed hierarchies, and a tearing down of the scaffold imaginary so that another, more autonomous politics becomes possible.

In contrast to the *dis*-traction of scale, a call for flattening is precisely about the materiality of the site: it offers a means of sticking our wheels in the dirt and rocks of immanence, and it is accordingly all about *traction*. This aligns to Anna Tsing's (2005, 1) ethnographic interpretation of universality as only being tenable outside of the abstract and through the *friction* that is "charged and enacted in the sticky materiality of practical encounters." Where there is friction, there exists a latent potential to spark a fire, and so a flattening of the world may enable us to raze the present order by making space for autonomous politics (Pickerill and Chatterton 2006), by demanding the impossible (Marshall 1992), and by inventing and organizing anarchist communities through the very process of destroying their opposite (Ferrell 2001). "The passion for destruction is a creative passion," Mikhail Bakunin once remarked, which is not an invocation for the creative destruction of capitalism but for the destructive creation of anarchism. In other words, this is not a flattening of the sort that Friedman (2005) proposes, wherein *The World Is Flat* serves as a metaphor for viewing competitors as having an equal opportunity and level playing field in terms of commerce. Rather, this is a flattening of the political imagination into more horizontal arrangements, where we no longer maintain our dependency on the structures of hierarchy and support the idea of sovereign rule. "Why do people consent to be ruled?" Ward ([1973] 2001, 19) rhetorically asked, answering, "It isn't only fear; what have millions of people to fear from a small group of professional politicians and their strong-arm men? It is because they subscribe to the same values as their governors. Rulers and ruled alike believe in the principle of authority, of hierarchy, of power." And so the embrace of an ontological flattening, and a commitment to treading its possibilities, reduces *dis*-traction and replaces it with clarity and focus:

> As a single footstep will not make a path on the earth, so a single thought will not make a pathway in the mind. To make a deep physical path, we walk again and again. To make a deep mental path, we must think over and over the kind of thoughts we wish to dominate our lives. (Thoreau 2006, 27)

The repeated footsteps, the deep physical path, the *traction* of doing in the *here* and *now* what a scalar ontology denies and what Marxism would have us wait for, flattens the structures of hierarchy and undoes the modes of governance and obedience that neoliberalism maintains through self-reflexive, situated, and autonomous action. Changing the world, as Karl Marx ([1888] 1994) compelled us to do, means first changing the citational chains that signify its representation (Heidegger 1971).

HERE BE DRAGONS

Scale is what Jacques Lacan ([1977] 2001) would refer to as a "master-signifier," through which the subject maintains the artifice of being identical with its own signifier. A master-signifier is devoid of value but provides a *point de capiton,* or anchoring point, around which other signifiers can stabilize. The *point de capiton* is thus the point in the signifying chain—in the case of scale, the Archimedean point—at which "the signifier stops the otherwise endless movement [*glissement*] of the signification" (231) and generates the essential(ist) illusion of a fixed meaning. There is only one exit. To envision a human geography without hierarchy, we must ultimately reject the Archimedean point by leaping out of the Cartesian map and into the world:

the map is an abstraction it cannot cover Earth with 1:1 accuracy. Within the fractal complexities of actual geography the map can see only dimensional grids. Hidden enfolded immensities escape the measuring rod. The map is not accurate; the map *cannot* be accurate. (Bey 1991b, 101)

The map is scale, and scale the map,[6] sustained on the exclusion of unconsciousness—the knowledge that is *not known* (here be dragons!)—and a failure to see the immensities that are enfolded within space through things like "hidden transcripts" (Scott 1990), which empower us in the everyday through their quiet declaration of alternative counterdiscourses that challenge, disrupt, and flatten the assumed "mastery" of those who govern, that is, those who control the map (Anderson 1991; Winichakul 1994).[7]

Newman (2011, 349) recognizes the potential of radical politics within spaces that are liberated from the discourse of the master and the particular relation of authority to knowledge that it erects in seeking to exclude the knowledge of the unconscious:

> The Master's position of authority over knowledge also instantiates a position of political authority: political discourses are, for instance, based on the idea of being able to grasp the totality of society, something that is, from a Lacanian point of view, impossible. Implicated in this discourse, then, is the attempt to use knowledge to gain mastery over the whole social field; it is a discourse of *governing*.

The *terra incognita* that scale, hierarchy, and governance inevitably produce becomes a powerful weapon in the hands of the oppressed, which is why the anarchist tactic of direct action—in contrast to civil disobedience—often proceeds outside of the view of authority (Graeber 2009b). Direct action is not fundamentally about a grand gesture of defiance but is instead the active prefiguration of alternative worlds, played out through the eternal process of becoming and a politics of infinitely demanding possibilities (Critchley 2007). As a decentralized practice, direct action does not appeal to authority in the hope that it can be reasoned with or temporarily bridled by a proletarian vanguard, for anarchism recognizes its corruption and conceit all too well and has nothing left to say. Instead, the geography of direct action is the spontaneous liberation of a particular area (of land, of time, of imagination) that produces a temporary autonomous zone (TAZ), which emerges outside of the gaze of authority, only to dissolve and reform elsewhere before capitalism and sovereignty can crush or co-opt it (Bey 1991b).[8] A TAZ is driven by the confluence of action, being, and rebellion, and its greatest strength is its invisibility. There is no separation of theory and practice here, and organizational choice is not subordinated to future events as in the Marxist frame of understanding; it is continually negotiated as an unfolding rhizome that arises though the actual course of *process.*

Such a rhizomatic sense of space must be confounding to traditional Marxism's totalizing view of capitalism and arborescent insistence on vertical structures. The predominance of Marxism within the discipline goes some way toward explaining why Hakim Bey's notion of TAZ has received such little attention among geographers. "How can radical decentralization...work without constituting some higher-order hierarchical authority?" Harvey (2012b, 84) characteristically asks. "It is simply naïve to believe that polycentrism or any form of decentralization can work without strong hierarchical constraints and active enforcement. Much of the radical left—particularly of an anarchist and autonomist persuasion—has no answer to this problem." The idea that alternatives might be immanent to social relations, if we were actually to summon the courage to let them blossom, has never been a suitable solution for Marxists. There must be a blueprint, a map, a *master* plan: "The crucial problem here is to figure out how a polycentric governance system (or something analogous, such as Bookchin's confederation of libertarian municipalities) might actually work, and to make sure that it doesn't mask something very different" (81). Aside from revealing what appears to be a deep-seated anxiety that something dangerous lurks within autonomous and anarchist politics, what Harvey fails to understand is the possibility of *process,* which is all the more baffling given that it is the sine qua non of space-time. His urge to plan sees him stuck in the "stages of history" thinking that is the hallmark of traditional Marxism rather than embracing the temporal fluidity that is latent to space. A confederation of libertarian municipalities will work precisely as a prefiguration, which is to be "worked out" in its living, breathing process by its participants, not through the predeterminism of (hierarchical) planning. The real danger of autonomous politics, then, is to be found in its progressive "uses of disorder" (Sennett 1992) as an affront to the ordering of hierarchy, which can only be feared from the vantage point, the Archimedean point, the *point de capiton,* of authority.

Paul Routledge's (2003b) attempt to think beyond the apparent problem of effecting politics across scale through his concept of convergence space is similarly dismissed, as Harvey asserts that "there is the vague and naïve hope that social groups who have organized their relations to their local commons satisfactorily will do the right thing or converge upon some satisfactory inter-group practices through negotiation and interaction.... History provides us with very little evidence that such redistributions can work on anything other than an occasional one-off basis." Though perhaps the authoritative voice of *His*tory actively denies nonhierarchical redistribution and horizontal intergroup relations, the prehistory of humanity amply demonstrates a global commons, which existed and functioned for millennia through mutuality, agonism, and a notion of people belonging to the land rather than land belonging to the people (Barclay 1982; Kropotkin [1902] 2008). This is not to romanticize the past but to recognize that human organization need not be conceived as a binary between a decentralized, all-against-all, survival-of-the-fittest competition (capitalism), on one hand, and a supposedly benevolent hierarchical association of proletariat interest that requires centralization to achieve a classless society (Marxism), on the other. There is also a more contemporary, rhizomatic history that evolves as a forever protean *means without end* (Agamben 2000), one filled with possibility and not inexorably or fatalistically determined (Freire [1970] 2000), a history where "other worlds" are being constantly (re)made (Gibson-Graham 2008) through mutual aid, reciprocity, and cooperation, which are so often ignored (the exclusion of unconsciousness) as crucial components of production, consumption, and exchange (White and Williams 2012). The continually unfolding spatial patterns of autonomous organization are all about us as *terra incognita,* in intentional communities, black bloc tactics, credit and trade unions, peer-to-peer file sharing, DIY activities, housing squats, childcare co-ops, wikis, tenants' associations, migrant support networks, open source software, and every time you have ever invited friends over to dinner. These practices demonstrate a flat ontology where decentralized organization can be understood as grounded in the material practices of the present. We must look for the dragons!

WE ARE THE HORIZON

The central role of geography in the emergence of anarchism, and anarchism in the emergence of geography, should be clear by now. Indeed, as Tim Cresswell (2013, 52) argues, "anarchism may be the only major political movement that can claim to have geography and the ideas of geographers right at its center." So, in returning to the epigraph that opened this chapter, let me ask again, what happened to ethics along the way? What has become of radical geography when it seems to willingly shed its heterodox skin to embrace the orthodoxy of hierarchy despite a rich history of anarchist ideas and the potential for something vastly different? Marston, Jones, and Woodward's (2005) flat ontology is a bold envisioning that yearns to think beyond *dis*-traction, and yet as they stormed the citadel of entrenched geographical thought, tearing its vertical scaffolding to the ground, other geographers came out in legion to disavow their project (Leitner and Miller 2007; Jessop, Brenner, and Jones 2008; Collinge 2006). By marching to the drum of a horizontal politics, where all participants in the dance that we call "life" become agonistically defined as legitimate and welcome claimants to the global commons, we invoke a very different kind of geography, one that is thoroughly radical in its orientation because it recognizes, much like Élisée Reclus (1894) did many years ago, that the earth is an integral system. It is not geography itself that summons hierarchy and authority, as is the assumption of some Marxist geographers who posit scale as inextricable to geography, but rather the delusion of scale itself, a concept that peels off conceptual layers of an onion and assumes that the individual strata that it isolates can somehow represent the complexity of the whole. This is a theoretical movement that literally takes geography out of context and partitions our thinking about space in rigid Cartesian snapshots. Hierarchy and authority are invoked precisely because of the Archimedean ontology and supposed mastery that the concept of scale assumes and the resultant unconsciousness that it implies. So is it a case of hierarchy being necessary for politics to function, as is the contention of some Marxist geographers, or is this actually a *dysfunction* in the mode of thinking that underpins scale as a means to conceptualize and order our world? Politics doesn't require authority any more than we actually require the concept of scale in human geography. Scale is an abstraction of visioning, an ocular objectification of geography that encourages hierarchical thinking, even if unintentionally or, more accurately, unconsciously. As an ontological precept, the detached gaze of scale invokes Donna Haraway's (1991, 189) "god-trick," "and like the god-trick, this eye fucks the world" through its *point de capiton* and the unconsciousness it maintains with respect to situated knowledges and rhizomatic spaces. By jumping scale and moving away from the grounded particularities that are woven through multiple sites of activity and resistance, we problematically "delimit entry into politics—and the openness of the political—by pre-assigning it to a cordoned register for resistance" (Marston, Jones, and Woodward 2005, 427).

A human geography without hierarchy does not mean that we should ignore hierarchy and pretend it doesn't exist; rather, it is a contention that our ontological premise should be attuned to a horizontal politics. Similarly, we cannot ignore scale in the hope that it will simply disappear (Moore 2008). The performative epistemology of scale ensures its perpetuation beyond ontology (Herod 2011), so even if we desire to *aban*don it as part of the geographical lexicon, the relationship of the ban, which functions on an inclusive exclusion (Agamben 1998), ensures that it will continue to haunt the way we think about the world. What is needed, then, is a project that both is reflexive about the limitations of scale and employs a language that subverts and rescinds hierarchy at every possible opportunity so that a flat ontology becomes possible. A flattening of the spatial register is thus a commitment to offering a new discursive formation so that our scholarship becomes oriented toward the reinforcement of a rhizomatic politics rather than making excuses as to why we supposedly require hierarchy. It is thus a commitment to both anarchism and the "freedom of geography" I discuss in chapter 1, with "its latent capacity to shatter its own disciplinary circumscriptions." Once we start to accept hierarchy as a worthwhile or unavoidable component of our political thought and practice—through particular scalar precepts or otherwise—this licenses other forms of hierarchy. Should we now expect a radical geography to start understanding hierarchies in other incarnations as acceptable means to an end? Why are hierarchies as a function of scale considered acceptable but hierarchies as a function of class and capital accumulation rejected? On what basis can we say that certain hierarchies are appropriate, whereas others are not? We can either indicate that all hierarchy is wrong and let that guide a new rhizomatic ethics, or we can build cathedrals of knowledge that proclaim a sense of mastery, a fabrication that is always a mere facade because it ignores the "hidden enfolded immensities," the "sheer physical messiness," the "sticky materiality of practical encounters," that can never be captured, pinned down, or fully understood.

More to the point, how can the idea of class be productively contested when we accept hierarchy as part of our political matrix? Is class simply about economic position, or does it not encompass stratification along social, political, and cultural lines as well? What exactly are we talking about when we conceptualize "class" as a form of hierarchy? In contrast to the Marxist project, anarchism intuitively brings together the ingredients for a deeper insight:

> by looking beyond the factory and even the marketplace into hierarchical relations that prevail in the family, the educational system, the community, and the relationship of humanity to the natural world, not to speak of the state, the bureaucracy, and the party. Accordingly, issues of ecological dislocation, sexism, ethnic oppression, and community breakdown are indigenous concerns of anarchism, issues that it has often raised even before they acquired social immediacy—not problems that must be tacked on to its theoretical corpus and altered to accommodate an economistic, class-oriented viewpoint. (Bookchin 1996, 28)

All of this leads us back to the fork in the road between decentralization and centralization, autonomous politics and authoritarian politics, horizontal geographies and hierarchical geographies. To this end, Harvey's (2012b) latest work demonstrates the classic divide between Marxists and anarchists. Marxists want a proletariat-led state to arise out of a postrevolutionary conjuncture and envision its eventual withering away, but anarchists recognize this idea as chimera. History has taught us well that it doesn't happen, and what we are left with is a recapitulation of all the hierarchies and violence that were initially sought to be undone. Why doesn't it happen? Harvey serves as a case in point: because Marxists (with the exception of autonomist Marxists) have caged themselves in a mode of thought that implicitly accepts hierarchy even as it suggests that it rejects it. The reason for this is that Marxism as a method of political philosophy has a very narrow vision, a class-centric outlook, where it is too caught up in ideas of economic exploitation to recognize that multiple modes of domination coincide with and perpetuate capital accumulation. This is where recent developments in feminism surpass even the more progressive variants of neo- and post-Marxism, and it is why—as Emma Goldman ([1917] 1969) recognized—the projects of feminism, with its intersectionality (Valentine 2007), and anarchism, with its integrality, make such good bedfellows.

And what of ethics? Harvey (2006, 411) has stated, "I do not reject either ethics (social justice in particular) nor rights (the right to the city, for example) as fields of struggle, but what I do reject is a de-politicized geography that eviscerates any mention of class and class struggle." Anarchism by definition goes beyond class exploitation—whose significance it never denies—into an understanding of the historical importance of hierarchical domination as the source of all authority (Bookchin 1996). While Harvey laments a depoliticized geography, he actively contributes to a version that is politicized only in the narrowest sense, constrained by a limited, scalar vision that suggests that politics can only happen in one particular way: hierarchically. However, the arborescent notion that hierarchical forms of organization are necessary for or synonymous with organization itself is about as tenable as the idea that the state and society are synonymous, an idea that is so evidently wrong yet has metastasized within the academy through the cancer of state-centric thinking. Such active unconsciousness for the everyday spaces of decentralized and autonomous politics that hide in plain view is perhaps to be expected, as authority too is a master-signifier, a *point de capiton* that survives on the basis of dismissing "knowledge that is *not known*," thereby attempting to bound the political economic imagination to a centralizing logic of hierarchy. Yet there is, as should be clear by now, a world beyond neoliberalism and Marxism, an organization outside of the state, and a geography without hierarchy, and they all become possible once we recognize that "only the autonomous can *plan* autonomy, organize for it, create it" (Bey 1991b, 100).

In this realization, we cast our view toward the horizon, which is never a fixed limit, a static end point, or as Dean (2012a) contends, a fundamental division. The horizon always moves away from us as we move toward it, suggesting a direction and a future but never a restriction of our movement (Purcell 2013). In this way Dean is correct—the horizon conditions our experience; but in arguing for a return to vanguardism and party politics, she leans on an Archimedean crutch that breaks under the weight of her failure to appreciate the message that the horizon communicates as a politics of possibility. The horizon is not a scalar epistemology or a vertical structuring of reality; it is instead both the expression and experience of a fundamental relationality. As a metaphor for politics, we need to take heed of the horizon's ontological premise by folding its beauty into our ethics, by weaving its freedom into our geographies, and as a means of prefiguration, by living its immanence as a mode of being. For the promise of spatial emancipation to be fulfilled as the realization of an anarchist geography, we must become beautiful ourselves, we must become the horizon. Beauty sets fear in the heart of the beast, whereby if one courageous act can make the Colossus tremble, then together, united as a vista of hope, we might just bring the giant to its knees.

Acknowledgments

First and foremost, I thank my beautiful family. Marni has been by my side for nearly twenty years, and I couldn't ask for a more wonderful, patient, and loving partner in life. Thank you for all that you are and all that you give. There is so much light in my life because of the love we share. My children, Solina, Odin, and Tyr, are my greatest teachers, and I'm humbled by the profound wisdom they reveal to me every single day. To the question of the meaning of life, you've each offered the answer. I'm so very lucky to be your dad! My mom, my dad, and my brother Steve have watched me stumble, fall down, and get back up my entire life. Thanks for being a witness to who I am, for being there for me when I've needed you, and for celebrating those times when I do succeed. I love each one of you.

The following people have offered both inspiration and critique, and I am thankful to each of them for the insights that they gave to me: Maleea Acker, Clara Ang, Allan Antliff, Ian Baird, Karen Bakker, Adam J. Barker, Gerónimo Barrera de la Torre, Lawrence Berg, Patrick Bigger, Kean Birch, Comrade Black, Nick Blomley, Renata Blumberg, Seb Bonet, Arden Duncan Bonokoski, Katherine Brickell, Graeme Bristol, Gavin Brown, Ian Bruff, Tim Bunnell, Lindsay Chase, Heather Chi, Chengying Chua, Nathan Clough, Olivia Coelho, Jesse Cohn, Mat Coleman, Rosemary-Claire Collard, Francis Leo Collins, Adam Cooper, Nick Crane, Tim Cresswell, Julie Cupples, Sarah de Leeuw, Kevin DeJesus, Jess Dempsey, Chris Dixon, Mark Drifter, Jordan Engel, Salvatore Engel-DiMauro, Nezihe Başak Ergin, Fabrizio Eva, Julian Evans, Kathy Ferguson, Jeff Ferrell, Federico Ferretti, Guil Figgins, Chris Fortney, Taro Futamura, Levi Gahman, Janice Gan, Jamie Gillen, Alexandre Gillet, Jim Glassman, Anne Godlewska, Peter Goheen, Gaston Gordillo, Uri Gordon, Gill Green, Derek Gregory, Carl Grundy-Warr, Tess Guiney, Jutta Gutberlet, David Harvey, Steve Herbet, Nik Heynen, Doug Hill, Shana Hirsch, Elaine Ho, Peter Holland, Anthony Ince, Merv Jefferies,

Louise Johnson, Ali Jones, John Paul Jones III, Reece Jones, Nathan Jun, Mat Keel, Andrew Kent, Boon Kian, Nicholas Kiersey, Paul Kingsbury, Audrey Kobayashi, Sara Koopman, Perry Kwok, Wendy Larner, Evelyne Laurin, Ben Lawrence, Victoria Lawson, Philippe Le Billon, Tian Lee, Carmelita Leow, Anthony Levenda, Shaun Lin, Martin Locret-Collet, Shawna Low, Nicholas Lynch, Minelle Mahtani, Kelvin Mason, Margo Matwychuk, Emma Mawdsley, Tyler McCreary, Martha McMahon, Andy McQuade, Nick Megoran, Jayme Melrose, Vanessa Sloan Morgan, Pamela Moss, Adrian Nel, Etienne Nel, Catherine Nolin, Jo Norcup, Robert Oprisko, Cam Owens, Shiri Pasternak, Jamie Peck, Richard Peet, Philippe Pelletier, Jenny Pickerill, Mark Purcell, Barry Riddell, Toby Rollo, Heather Rosenfeld, Reuben Rose-Redwood, Duane Rousselle, James Rowe, Samuel Rufat, James C. Scott, Jo Sharp, David Shulman, James Sidaway, Antonio Sobreira, Maral Sotoudehnia, Marcelo Lopes de Souza, Matt Sparke, Chris Strother, Erik Taje, Serene Tham, Eliot Tretter, Michael Truscello, Ebru Ustundag, Ophélie Véron, Nave Wald, Donni Wang, Guoyuan Wee, Chris Wilbert, Colin Williams, Ian Williams, Abbey Willis, David Murakami Wood, Patricia Wood, Keith Woodward, Takashi Yamazaki, Lou Yanjie, Henry Yeung, and Ming Li Yong. To those I have forgotten, I'm sorry, but thanks to you too!

I offer a very special thanks to Richard J. White and Jim McLaughlin for providing such amazing, challenging, encouraging, and insightful comments on the draft of this manuscript. Thanks as well to Jason Weidemann for believing in this project and for guiding it through to fruition. Thanks to Holly Monteith for her sharp editorial eye, to David Fideler for his assistance with the proofs, and to Lisa Rivero for compiling the index. And last but not least, thanks to Jennifer Mateer for her gracious willingness to help work through all the little details that come with bringing a book up to speed. A SSHRC Insight Development Grant (Award Number 430-2014-00644) made this project possible.

Notes

1. A BRIEF GENEALOGY OF ANARCHIST GEOGRAPHIES

1   White and Cudworth (2014, 210) make an interesting point that problematizes whether Reclus practiced vegetarianism or veganism, arguing that "it is highly probable that Reclus did eat a vegan diet but referred to it as vegetarianism," given that historically the vegetarian movement in Europe eschewed the consumption of all animal products.

2. WHAT GEOGRAPHY STILL OUGHT TO BE

1   Others have explored broadly "anarchistic" spatialities through a poststructuralist lens (see Koopman 2011; Routledge 2003b), but without plugging such concerns into the emergent literature that explicitly develops a theory of postanarchism.

3. RETURNING TO GEOGRAPHY'S RADICAL ROOTS

1   For example, Harvey (1999, 117) asks if Reclus's notion of social ecology and his vision of decentralized municipal socialism potentially delivering environmental justice are "any less arrogant in principle than the World Bank, which believes the market can do it best?" Contrast this with a recent interview during which Harvey (2012a) claimed, "One of my favorite characters in geography's history was Elisée Reclus, who fought in the Paris Commune and was close with people like Bakunin and Kropotkin. So I'm very much associated with that tradition."

2   All of this is traced in significant detail in McKay (2011).

3   To be fair, Harvey's (2013) reading of Proudhon is generally quite positive in *Paris, Capital of Modernity*.

4   Prefigurative politics refers to the idea that anarchism is made flesh through effecting social relationships and organizing principles in the present that attempt to reflect the future society being sought. The idea of prefiguration is thus not to be confused with predetermination, as it is about the active and ongoing process of building a new society in the shell of the old (Ince 2012). Here again we see a close political resemblance between anarchism and autonomist Marxism, as prefiguration is nearly

synonymous with Antonio Negri's (1989) notion of self-valorization.

5   The Situationists were a radical international organization comprising political theorists, artists, and intellectuals who espoused an anti-authoritarian version of Marxism. They aimed to create alternative life experiences by bringing together play, critical thinking, and freedom through the construction of situations and unitary urbanism (Wark 2011).

6   The number of recent human geography articles that uncritically assume that anarchism is tantamount to violence, chaos, and disorder is disheartening. For a small sampling from the last decade, see Watts (2004, 209), Dahlman and Ó Tuathail (2005, 578), Herod and Aguiar (2006, 430), Johnston (2006, 287), Hooper (2008, 2563), Wilford (2008, 653), Byrne and Wolch (2009, 746), Hastings (2009, 214), Raeymaekers (2009, 57), ten Bos (2009, 85), Shirlow and Dowler (2010, 389), Mohaghegh and Golestaneh (2011, 490), Hagman and Korf (2012, 207), Lim (2012, 1352), and Malm and Esmailian (2013, 486).

4. EMANCIPATORY SPACE

1   The categories "from above" and "from below" signify that modern political power has been appropriated from the direct control of the people through systematized rule (hierarchy, patriarchy, etc.) that strips the majority of their basic freedom. "From above" speaks to rationalities, strategies, technologies, and techniques of power originating from the minority entrenched in positions of authority through social, economic, and political "archies." "From below" represents applications of power originating from locations within the prevailing system where social, economic, and political power has been reduced via the repressions of systematized rule.

2   Such is the position of Habermas (1989), which signals his liberalism and is why (as discussed later) his public sphere is necessarily deliberative rather than material, and thus inappropriate for conceptualizing radical democracy.

3   See Thomassen (2005) for a critique of Barnett.

4   Anarchism conceived as means without end is thus an important line of differentiation with Marxism and its end-state thinking (cf. Harvey 2000).

5   Massey (2005, 6) refuses the distinction between place as meaningful versus space as an abstract container, encouraging us to view space as the simultaneity of stories-so-far and place as collections of these stories. This reconceptualization affords greater understanding to neoliberalism's

relational geographies, where any seemingly "local" contestation in place is necessarily tied to the wider assemblage of space. The reverse implication is that any ostensibly "global" imperative like neoliberalism-in-general" always combines with place-based experiences in a myriad of hybrid ways (Peck, 2003).

6   Identity formation also occurs in semipublic spaces, private spaces, and subaltern counterpublics, where subordinate groups formulate oppositional interpretations of their identities (Fraser 1990).

7   All spaces are socially scripted, if not by explicit rules then by competitive regulation. Yet the ideal of unscripted space should nonetheless be aspired to (Harvey 2000), because although unscripted public space is fantasy, the openness, uncertainty, and anarchy embodied in space and place make them potentially democratic crucibles. The challenge is to treat them this way, as instituting democratic spaces requires the foregrounding of exclusions (Massey 2005).

8   This idealized view of public space is universal inasmuch as humans are social animals desiring embodied connections with others, hence the emergence of language. The ontological priority of life is embodiment, and without a public to share our ideas and a space in which to do this, there would be no need for language. In contextualizing this claim, what is at issue is not the universality of the ideal but rather what "embodied self-representation" might mean in different sociocultural and geohistorical settings.

9   The supposed "violence" against property that many subaltern, anarchist, and marginalized groups engage in offers a case in point. Given that property itself is an institution of violence, I don't consider "violence" against property to be violence at all. When property is destroyed, what is actually occurring is an undoing of violence. See Springer (2013) for a discussion of the violences of property and the distinction that must be made between possession, which is synonymous with actual use, and property, which is a means for exploitation.

6. THE ANARCHIST HORIZON

1   Martin Parker (2009) offers a fascinating history of the legitimation of hierarchy, drawing it back to the writings of Pseudo-Dionysius, about fifteen hundred years ago, where he was ordering angels. He argues that although hierarchy is central to most theories of organization, the ontological origin of hierarchy, specifically its connection to angels, leaves significant room for doubt, where "angelic obedience should be treated

with suspicion, and that other sorts of angels, particularly the fallen ones, might lead us away from the tyranny of hierarchy" (1281).

2 The word *abstract* is derived from the Latin verb *abstrahere,* meaning "to draw away."

3 Mahatma Gandhi adopted this idea from his pen pal Leo Tolstoy (1900), who, for his part, developed this idea from his interest in anarchism and sympathies for anarchists.

4 Using Deleuze's ([1968] 2005) thesis on the univocity of being as an always differentiating process of folding, unfolding, and refolding, Manuel DeLanda (2002) had previously proposed a flat ontology, in which hierarchy was rejected, as no entity can be considered ontologically more fundamental than anything else.

5 Adam Moore (2008) has at least partially begun such a project, emphasizing a distinction between scale as a category of analysis and scale as a category of practice. Similarly, Robert Kaiser and Elena Nikiforova (2008) have begun exploring the political genealogy of scale ontologies, using performativity to reveal the discursive devices and citational practices that socially produce scale.

6 Any cartographer worth her salt will tell you that a map without scale is merely a diagram.

7 To be clear, I am not arguing for a geography devoid of maps. Radical cartography (Bhagat and Mogel 2008; Rankin 2003) presents a critically important intervention that challenges dominant representations and encourages alternative readings, yet at the same time, it does not fundamentally transform the ontological hierarchy that remains embedded within the map as a symbolic depiction of space. Thus, when using maps, even for a critical purpose, we need to maintain a sense of reflexivity and skepticism for their innate distortions (Monmonier 1996). The same reservations apply to scale.

8 It is in the desire for such spaces that anarchist and autonomist geographers may find a point of similitude (Clough and Blumberg 2012).

Bibliography

Abbey, Edward. 1989. *A Voice Crying in the Wilderness (Vox Clamantis in Deserto): Notes from a Secret Journal.* New York: St. Martin's Press.

Agamben, Giorgio. 1998. *Homo Sacer: Sovereign Power and Bare Life.* Translated by Daniel Heller Roazen. Palo Alto, Calif.: Stanford University Press.

———. 2000. *Means without End: Notes on Politics.* Minneapolis: University of Minnesota Press.

Agnew, John. 1994. "The Territorial Trap: The Geographical Assumptions of International Relations Theory." *Review of International Political Economy* 1, no. 1: 53–80.

———. 2009. *Globalization and Sovereignty.* Lanham, Md.: Roman and Littlefield.

Amin, Ash. 2007. "Re-thinking the Urban Social." *City* 11, no 1: 100–114.

Amsden, Jon. 1978. "Industrial Collectivization under Workers' Control: Catalonia, 1936–1939." *Antipode* 10: 99–114.

Amster, Randall. 2008. *Lost in Space: The Criminalization, Globalization, and Urban Ecology of Homelessness.* El Paso, Tex.: LFB.

———. 2010. "Anarchism and Nonviolence: Time for a 'Complementary of Tactics.'" http://wagingnonviolence.org/feature/anarchism-and-non violence-time-for-a-complementarity-of-tactics/.

Amster, Randall, Abraham DeLeon, Luis Fernandez, Anthony J. Nocella, and Deric Shannon, eds. 2009. *Contemporary Anarchist Studies: An Introductory Anthology of Anarchy in the Academy.* New York: Routledge.

Anderson, Ben. 2006. "Becoming and Being Hopeful: Towards a Theory of Affect." *Environment and Planning D: Society and Space* 24: 733–52.

Anderson, Ben, and Colin McFarlane. 2011. "Assemblage and Geography." *Area* 43: 124–27.

Anderson, Benedict. 1991. *Imagined Communities: Reflections on the Origin and Spread of Nationalism.* London: Verso.

———. 2005. *Under Three Flags: Anarchism and the Anti-colonial Imagination.* London: Verso.

Anderson, Jon. 2004. "Spatial Politics in Practice: The Style and Substance of Environmental Direct Action." *Antipode* 36: 106–25.

Angus, Ian. 2008. "The Myth of the Tragedy of the Commons." *Monthly*

Review, August 28. http://mrzine.monthlyreview.org/2008/angus250808 .html.

Arat, Zehra F. 1991. *Democracy and Human Rights in Developing Countries.* Boulder: Lynne Rienner.

Arefi, Mahyar, and William R. Meyers. 2003. "What Is Public about Public Space: The Case of Visakhapatnam, India." *Cities* 20: 331–39.

Arendt, Hannah. (1958) 1998. *The Human Condition.* Chicago: University of Chicago Press.

———. 1963. *Eichmann in Jerusalem: A Report on the Banality of Evil.* New York: Viking.

———. 1970. *On Violence.* New York: Harcourt.

Archer, Julian P. W. 1997. *The First International in France, 1864–1872: Its Origins, Theories, and Impact.* Lanham, Md.: University Press of America.

Atkinson, Rowland. 2003. "Domestication by Cappuccino or a Revenge on Urban Space? Control and Empowerment in the Management of Public Spaces." *Urban Studies* 40, no. 9: 1829–43.

Autonomous Geographies Collective. 2010. "Beyond Scholar Activism: Making Strategic Interventions inside and outside the Neoliberal University." *ACME: An International E-Journal for Critical Geographies* 9: 245–75.

Bailie, William. 1906. *Josiah Warren, the First American Anarchist: A Sociological Study.* Boston: Small, Maynard.

Bakunin, Michael. (1872) 2002. "The International and Karl Marx." In *Bakunin on Anarchism,* edited by Sam Dolgoff, 286–320. Montreal: Black Rose.

———. (1873) 1953. "Criticism of Marxism." In *The Political Philosophy of Bakunin: Scientific Anarchism,* edited by Grigorij Petrovic Maximoff, 283–89. New York: Free Press.

———. (1873) 2002. *Statism and Anarchy.* Cambridge: Cambridge University Press.

———. (1882) 2010. *God and the State.* Whitefish, Mont.: Kessinger.

Baldelli, Giovanni. 1971. *Social Anarchism.* New Brunswick, N.J.: Transaction.

Baldwin, Roger. 2005. "Note for 'Anarchism: Its Philosophy and Ideal.'" In *Kropotkin's Revolutionary Pamphlets,* edited by Roger Baldwin, 114. Whitefish, Mont.: Kessinger.

Barclay, Harold. 1982. *People without Government: An Anthropology of Anarchy.* London: Kahn and Averill.

Barker, Adam J., and Jenny Pickerill. 2012. "Radicalizing Relationships to and through Shared Geographies: Why Anarchists Need to Understand Indigenous Connections to Land and Place." *Antipode* 44: 1705–25.

Barnes, Trevor. 2009. "Quantitative Revolution." In *International Encyclopedia of Human Geography*, edited by Rob Kitchin and Nigel Thrift, 33–38. Amsterdam: Elsevier.

Barnes, Trevor J., and Claudio Minca. 2013. "Nazi Spatial Theory: The Dark Geographies of Carl Schmitt and Walter Christaller." *Annals of the Association of American Geographers* 103, no. 3: 669–87.

Barnett, Clive. 2004a. "Deconstructing Radical Democracy: Articulation, Representation, and Being-with-Others." *Political Geography* 23, no. 5: 503–28.

———. 2004b. "Media, Democracy, and Representation: Disembodying the Public." In *Spaces of Democracy: Geographical Perspectives on Citizenship, Participation, and Representation,* edited by Clive Barnett and Murray Low, 185–206. London: Sage.

———. 2009. "Violence and Publicity: Constructions of Political Responsibility after 9/11." *Critical Review of Social and Political Philosophy* 12, no. 3: 353–75.

Barnett, Clive, and Murray Low, eds. 2004. *Spaces of Democracy: Geographical Perspectives on Citizenship, Participation, and Representation.* London: Sage.

Bar On, Bat-Ami. 2002. *The Subject of Violence: Arendtean Exercises in Understanding.* Lanham, Md.: Rowman and Littlefield.

Barry, Andre, Thomas Osborne, and Nikolas Rose, eds. 1996. *Foucault and Political Reason: Liberalism, Neoliberalism, and Rationalities of Government.* Chicago: University of Chicago Press.

Bellegarrigue, Anselme. 1848. *L'Anarchie, Journal de l'Ordre.* http://kropot .free.fr/ Bellegarrigue-A02.htm.

———. (1850) 2005. "Anarchy Is Order." In *From Anarchy to Anarchism (300 CE to 1939),* vol. 1 of *Anarchism: A Documentary History of Libertarian Ideas,* edited by Robert Graham, 58–60. Montreal: Black Rose.

Benjamin, Walter. (1921) 1986. "Critique of Violence." In *Walter Benjamin, Reflections: Essays, Aphorisms, Autobiographical Writings,* edited by Peter Demetz, 277–300. New York: Schocken.

Berlin, Isaiah. 1963. *Karl Marx.* Oxford: Oxford University Press.

Bey, Hakim. 1991a. *Immediatism.* Oakland, Calif.: AK Press.

———. 1991b. *TAZ: The Temporary Autonomous Zone, Ontological Anarchy, Poetic Terrorism.* New York: Autonomedia.

Bhagat, Alex, and Lize Mogel. 2008. *An Atlas of Radical Cartography.* New York: Journal of Aesthetics and Protest Press.

Biehl, Janet, and Murray Bookchin. 1997. *The Politics of Social Ecology: Libertarian Municipalism.* Montreal: Black Rose.

Bill, James A. 1973. "Political Violence and Political Change: A Conceptual Commentary." In *Violence as Politics: A Series of Original Essays,* edited by Herbert Hirsch and David C. Perry, 220–31. New York: Harper and Row.

Billig, Michael. 1995. *Banal Nationalism.* London: Sage.

Blake, William. (1803) 2008. "Auguries of Innocence." In *The Complete Poetry and Prose of William Blake,* edited by David V. Erdman, 490–93. Berkeley: University of California Press.

Blunt, Alison, and Jane Wills. 2000. *Dissident Geographies: An Introduction to Radical Ideas and Practice.* London: Pearson Education.

Boggs, Carl. 1977. "Marxism, Prefigurative Communism, and the Problem of Workers' Control." *Radical America* 11, no. 6: 12.

Bohm, David. 2003. "The Super Implicate Order." In *The Essential David Bohm,* edited by Lee Nichol, 139–57. London: Routledge.

Bonanno, Alfred M. 1996. *The Anarchist Tension.* London: Elephant Editions.

Bondi, Liz. 1996. "Gender, Class, and Urban Space: Public and Private Space in Contemporary Urban Landscapes." *Urban Geography* 19, no. 2: 160–85.

Bookchin, Murry. (1962) 1974. *Our Synthetic Environment.* New York: Harper and Row.

———. (1965) 1978. "Ecology and Revolutionary Thought." *Antipode* 10: 21–32.

———. (1971) 2004. *Post-scarcity Anarchism.* Oakland, Calif.: AK Press.

———. (1982) 2005. *The Ecology of Freedom: The Emergence and Dissolution of Hierarchy.* Oakland, Calif.: AK Press.

———. 1990a. *The Philosophy of Social Ecology: Essays on Dialectical Naturalism.* Montreal: Black Rose.

———. 1990b. *Remaking Society: Pathways to a Green Future.* London: South End Press.

———. 1992. *Urbanization without Cities: The Rise and Decline of Citizenship.* Montreal: Black Rose.

———. 1994. "A Meditation on Anarchist Ethics." *The Raven: Anarchist Quarterly* 7: 328–46.

———. 1996. "Anarchism: Past and Present." In *Reinventing Anarchy, Again,* edited by Howard J. Ehrlich, 19–30. Edinburgh: AK Press.

Bourdieu, Pierre. 2001. *Masculine Domination.* Stanford, Calif.: Stanford University Press.

Brand, Ulrich, and Markus Wissen. 2005. "Neoliberal Globalization and the Internationalization of Protest: A European Perspective." *Antipode* 37: 9–17.

Breitbart, Myrna Margulies. 1975. "Impressions of an Anarchist Landscape."
    Antipode 7: 44–49.

———. 1978a. "Anarchist Decentralism in Rural Spain, 1936–1939: The Integration of Community and Environment." *Antipode* 10: 83–98.

———. 1978b. "Introduction." *Antipode* 10: 1–5.

———. 1981. "Peter Kropotkin, the Anarchist Geographer." In *Geography,
    Ideology, and Social Concern,* edited by David R. Stoddart, 134–53. Oxford:
    Blackwell.

———. 1990. "Calling up the Community: Exploring the Subversive Terrain
    of Urban Environmental Education." *Contemporary Issues in Geography
    and Education* 3: 94–112.

———. 2009. "Anarchism/Anarchist Geography." In *International Encyclopedia of Human Geography,* edited by Rob Kitchin and Nigel Thrift,
    108–15. Amsterdam: Elsevier.

Brenner, Neil. 1999. "Beyond State-Centrism? Space, Territoriality, and Geographical Scale in Globalization Studies." *Theory and Society* 28: 39–78.

Brenner, Neil, and Nik Theodore. 2002. "Cities and the Geographies of 'Actually Existing Neoliberalism.'" *Antipode* 34: 349–79.

———, eds. 2003. *Spaces of Neoliberalism: Urban Restructuring in North America and Western Europe.* Oxford: Blackwell.

Brown, Gavin. 2007. "Mutinous Eruptions: Autonomous Spaces of Radical
    Queer Activism." *Environment and Planning A* 39, no. 11: 2685–98.

Brown, Susan. 1996. "Beyond Feminism: Anarchism and Human Freedom."
    In *Reinventing Anarchy, Again,* edited by Howard J. Ehrlich, 149–55.
    Edinburgh: AK Press.

Butler, Judith. 1997. *Excitable Speech: A Politics of the Performative.* London:
    Routledge.

———. 2001. "Bodies in Alliance and the Politics of the Street." European
    Institute for Progressive Cultural Policies. http://www.eipcp.net/trans
    versal/1011/butler/en.

———. 2004. *Precarious Life: The Powers of Mourning and Violence.* New
    York: Verso.

Butler, Ruth, and Sophia Bowlby. 1997. "Bodies and Spaces: An Exploration
    of Disabled People's Experiences of Public Space." *Environment and
    Planning D: Society and Space* 15: 411–33.

Byrne, Jason, and Jennifer Wolch. 2009. "Nature, Race, and Parks: Past Research and Future Directions for Geographic Research." *Progress in Human Geography* 33: 743–65.

Calhoun, Craig. 1997. "Nationalism and the Public Sphere." In *Public and*

Private in Thought and Practice: Perspectives on a Grand Dichotomy, edited by Jeff Weintraub and Kumar Krishan, 75–102. Chicago: University of Chicago Press.

———. 1998. "Community without Propinquity Revisited: Communication Technology and the Transformation of the Urban Public Sphere." *Social Inquiry* 68, no. 3: 373–97.

Call, Lewis. 2002. *Postmodern Anarchism*. Oxford: Lexington.

Carey, George W. 1978. "The Vessel, the Deed, and the Idea: Anarchists in Paterson, 1895–1908." *Antipode* 10: 46–58.

Carlsson, Chris. 2008. *Nowtopia: How Pirate Programmers, Outlaw Bicyclists, and Vacant-Lot Gardeners Are Inventing the Future Today!* Oakland, Calif.: AK Press.

Carlsson, Chris, and Francesca Manning. 2010. "Nowtopia: Strategic Exodus?" *Antipode* 42: 924–53.

Carr, Stephen, Mark Francis, Leanne G. Rivlin, and Andrew M. Stone. 1992. *Public Space*. Cambridge: Cambridge University Press.

Carson, Rachel. (1962) 2002. *Silent Spring*. New York: Houghton Mifflin.

Castells, Manuel. 2000. *The Rise of Network Society*. Malden, Mass.: Blackwell.

Castree, Noel. 2006. "David Harvey's Symptomatic Silence." *Historical Materialism* 14, no. 4: 35–57.

Castree, Noel, and Bruce Braun, eds. 2001. *Social Nature: Theory Practice and Politics*. Oxford: Blackwell.

Castree, Noel, David Featherstone, and Andrew Herod. 2008. "Contrapuntal Geographies: The Politics of Organizing across Sociospatial Difference." In *The Sage Handbook of Political Geography*, edited by Kevin R. Cox, Murray Low, and Jennifer Robinson, 305–21. London: Sage.

Cavanaugh, William T. 2009. *The Myth of Religious Violence: Secular Ideology and the Roots of Modern Conflicts*. Oxford: Oxford University Press.

Chatterton, Paul. 2002. "'Squatting Is Still Legal, Necessary and Free': A Brief Intervention in the Corporate City." *Antipode* 34: 1–7.

———. 2005. "Making Autonomous Geographies: Argentina's Popular Uprising and the 'Movimiento de Trabajadores Desocupados' (Unemployed Workers Movement)." *Geoforum* 36, no. 5: 545–61.

———. 2006. "'Give up Activism' and Change the World in Unknown Ways, or, Learning to Walk with Others on Uncommon Ground." *Antipode* 38: 259–81.

Chomsky, Noam. 2012. *Occupy*. Vol. 1. New York: Zuccotti Park.

Chouinard, Vera. 1994. "Reinventing Radical Geography: Is All That's Left Right?" *Environment and Planning D: Society and Space* 12: 2–6.

Clark, John P. 1984. *The Anarchist Moment: Reflections on Culture, Nature, and Power*. Montreal: Black Rose.

———. 1997. "The Dialectical Social Geography of Elisée Reclus." In *Philosophy and Geography 1: Space, Place, and Environmental Ethics*, edited by Andrew Light and Jonathan M. Smith, 117–42. Lanham, Md.: Rowman and Littlefield.

———. 2009. "Reclus, E." In *International Encyclopedia of Human Geography*, edited by Rob Kitchin and Nigel Thrift, 107–10. Amsterdam: Elsevier.

———. 2013. *The Impossible Community: Realizing Communitarian Anarchism*. New York: Bloomsbury.

Clark, John P., and Camille Martin, eds. 2004. *Anarchy, Geography, Modernity: The Radical Social Thought of Élisée Reclus*. Oxford: Lexington Books.

Clastres, Pierre. (1989) 2007. *Society against the State: Essays in Political Anthropology*. New York: Zone Books.

Cleaver, Harry. 1992. "Kropotkin, Self-Valorization, and the Crisis of Marxism." Paper presented at the Conference on Pyotr Alexeevich Kropotkin organized by the Russian Academy of Science. http://libcom.org/library/kropotkin-self-valorization-crisis-marxism.

Clough, Nathan L. 2012. "Emotion at the Center of Radical Politics: On the Affective Structures of Rebellion and Control." *Antipode* 44: 1667–86.

Clough, Nathan, and Renata Blumberg. 2012. "Toward Anarchist and Autonomist Marxist Geographies." *ACME: An International E-Journal for Critical Geographies* 11: 335–51.

Cockburn, Cynthia. 2004. "The Continuum of Violence: A Gender Perspective on War and Peace." In *Sites of Violence: Gender and Conflict Zones*, edited by Wenona Mary Giles and Jennifer Hyndman, 24–44. Berkeley: University of California Press.

Cohen, Stanley, and Laurie Taylor. 1992. *Escape Attempts: The Theory and Practice of Resistance to Everyday Life*. 2nd ed. London: Routledge.

Cohn, Jesse. 2010. "This Is No Social Crisis (Just Another Tricky Day for You): Anarchist Representations of Crisis." Paper presented at the seventeenth Charles F. Fraker Conference ("The Turning Point: Crisis and Disaster"), Ann Arbor, Mich.

Collective Autonomy Research Group. 2014. "The Anarchist Commons." *Ephemera: Theory and Politics in Organization* 14: 879–900.

Collinge, Chris. 2006. "Flat Ontology and the Deconstruction of Scale: A Response to Marston, Jones, and Woodward." *Transactions of the Institute of British Geographers* 31, no. 2: 244–51.

Colson, Daniel. 2001. *Petit Leisure Philosophique de l'Anarchisme de Proudhon a' Deleuze.* Paris: Librairie Générale Française.

Comte-Sponville, André. 2007. *The Little Book of Atheist Spirituality.* New York: Viking.

Cook, Ian. 1990. "Anarchist Alternatives: An Introduction." *Contemporary Issues in Geography and Education* 3: 9–21.

Cook, Ian, and David Pepper. 1990. "Editorial: Anarchism." *Contemporary Issues in Geography and Education* 3: 5–8.

Crampton, Jeremy W., and Stuart Elden, eds. 2007. *Space, Knowledge, and Power: Foucault and Geography.* Burlington, Vt.: Ashgate.

Crane, Nicholas J. 2012. "Are 'Other Spaces' Necessary? Associative Power at the Dumpster." *ACME: An International E-Journal for Critical Geographies* 11: 352–72.

Crang, Mike. 2000. "Public Space, Urban Space, and Electronic Space: Would the Real City Please Stand Up?" *Urban Studies* 37, no. 2: 307–17.

Cresswell, Tim. 2013. *Geographic Thought: A Critical Introduction.* Malden, Mass.: John Wiley.

CrimethInc. Ex-Workers' Collective. 2008. *Expect Resistance: A Field Manual.* Salem, Mass.: CrimethInc.

CrimethInc. Writers' Bloc. 2013. "Anarchism and the English Language." http://www.crimethinc.com/texts/recentfeatures/language.php.

Critchley, Simon. 2004. "True Democracy: Marx, Political Subjectivity, and Anarchic Meta-politics," In *Radical Democracy: Politics between Abundance and Lack*, edited by Lars Tønder and Lasse Thomassen: 219–35. Manchester: Manchester University Press.

———. 2007. *Infinitely Demanding: Ethics of Commitment, Politics of Resistance.* London: Verso.

Cumbers, Andrew, Gesa Helms, and Kate Swanson. 2010. "Class, Agency, and Resistance in the Old Industrial City." *Antipode* 42: 46–73.

Cumbers, Andrew, Paul Routledge, and Corinne Nativel. 2008. "The Entangled Geographies of Global Justice Networks." *Progress in Human Geography* 32, no. 2: 183–201.

Curran, Giorel, and Morgan Gibson. 2013. "WikiLeaks, Anarchism, and Technologies of Dissent." *Antipode* 45: 294–314.

Dabashi, Hamid. 2012. *The Arab Spring: The End of Postcolonialism.* London: Zed.

Dahl, Robert A. 1971. *Polyarchy: Participation and Opposition.* New Haven, Conn.: Yale University Press.

Dahlman, Carl, and Gearóid Ó Tuathail. 2005. "The Legacy of Ethnic

Cleansing: The International Community and the Returns Process in Post-Dayton Bosnia–Herzegovina." *Political Geography* 24, no. 5: 569–99.

Davidson, Joyce, Liz Bondi, and Mick Smith, eds. 2007. *Emotional Geographies.* Aldershot, U.K.: Ashgate.

Davies, Paul. 1993. *The Mind of God: The Scientific Basis for a Rational World.* New York: Simon and Schuster.

Day, Richard. 2005. *Gramsci Is Dead: Anarchist Currents in the Newest Social Movements.* Ann Arbor, Mich.: Pluto.

Dean, Jodi. 2003. "Why the Net Is Not a Public Sphere." *Constellations* 10: 95–112.

———. 2012a. *The Communist Horizon.* London: Verso.

———. 2012b. "Interview with Jodi Dean." Interviewed by Michael Schapira. http://www.full-stop.net/2012/11/14/interviews/michael-schapira/jodi-dean/.

———. 2013. "What Is to Be Done with the Actually Existing Marxist Left? An Interview with Jodi Dean." Interviewed by Ross Wolfe. http://platypus1917.org/2013/03/01/what-is-to-be-done-with-the-actually-existing-marxist-left-an-interview-with-jodi-dean/.

de Cleyre, Voltairine. 1901. *The First Mayday: The Haymarket Speeches 1895–1910.* Orkney, U.K.: Cienfuegos Press.

Debord, Guy. (1967) 1994. *Society of the Spectacle.* New York: Zone.

DeLanda, Manuel. 2002. *Intensive Science and Virtual Philosophy.* New York: Continuum.

Del Casino, Vincent J., and Christine L. Jocoy. 2008. "Neoliberal Subjectivities, the 'New' Homelessness, and Struggles over Spaces of/in the City." *Antipode* 40: 192–99.

Deleuze, Gilles. (1968) 2005. *Difference and Repetition.* New York: Continuum.

Deleuze, Gilles, and Félix Guattari. 1987. *A Thousand Plateaus.* Minneapolis: University of Minnesota Press.

Derrida, Jacques. (1967) 2001. *Writing and Difference.* 2nd ed. London: Routledge.

Diamond, Larry. 1993. "Introduction: Political Culture and Democracy." In *Political Culture and Democracy in Developing Countries,* edited by Larry Diamond, 1–33. Boulder, Colo.: Lynne Rienner.

Dollar, David, and Aart Kraay. 2002. "Growth Is Good for the Poor." *Journal of Economic Growth* 7, no. 3: 195–225.

Dominick, Brian A. 1995. *Animal Liberation and Social Revolution: A Vegan Perspective on Anarchism or an Anarchist Perspective on Veganism.* Syracuse, N.Y.: Critical Mess Media.

Driver, Felix. 2001. *Geography Militant: Cultures of Exploration and Empire.* Oxford: Blackwell.

Dryzek, John S. 2000. *Deliberative Democracy and Beyond: Liberals, Critics, Contestations.* Oxford: Oxford University Press.

Dugatkin, Lee Alan. 2011. *The Prince of Evolution: Peter Kropotkin's Adventures in Science and Politics.* Seattle, Wash.: CreateSpace.

Duménil, Gérard, and Dominique Lévy. 2011. *The Crisis of Neoliberalism.* Cambridge, Mass.: Harvard University Press.

Dunbar, Gary. 1978. "Élisée Reclus, Geographer and Anarchist." *Antipode* 10: 16–21.

Duncan, Nancy. 1996. "Renegotiating Gender and Sexuality in Public and Private Spaces." In *Bodyspace: Destabilizing Geographies of Gender and Sexuality,* edited by Nancy Duncan, 127–45. London: Routledge.

Durkheim, Emile. (1915) 2008. *The Elementary Forms of the Religious Life.* New York: Dover.

Ealham, Chris. 2010. *Anarchism and the City: The Revolution and Counterrevolution in Barcelona, 1898–1937.* Oakland, Calif.: AK Press.

Einstein, Albert. 2003. *Bite-Size Einstein: Quotations on Just about Everything from the Greatest Mind of the Twentieth Century.* 2nd ed. Edited by Jerry Mayer and John P. Holms. London: Gramercy.

Eley, Geoff. 1992. "Nations, Publics, and Political Cultures: Placing Habermas in the Nineteenth Century." In *Habermas and the Public Sphere,* edited by Craig Calhoun, 289–339. Cambridge, Mass.: MIT Press.

Engels, Fredrick. (1872) 1978. "On Authority." In *The Marx-Engels Reader,* edited by Robert C. Tucker, 730–33. New York: W. W. Norton.

England, Kim. 2003. "Towards a Feminist Political Geography." *Political Geography* 22, no. 6: 611–16.

England, Kim, and Kevin Ward, eds. 2007. *Neoliberalization: States, Networks, Peoples.* Oxford: Blackwell.

Enrenberg, John. 1996. *Proudhon and His Age.* Atlantic Highlands, N.J.: Humanities Press International.

Entrikin, J. Nicholas. 2002. "Perfectibility and Democratic Place-making." In *Progress: Geographical Essays,* edited by Robert D. Sack, 97–112. Baltimore: Johns Hopkins University Press.

Epstein, Barbara. 2001. "Anarchism and the Anti-Globalization Movement." *Monthly Review* 53. http://monthlyreview.org/2001/09/01/anarchism-and-the-anti-globalization-movement.

Escobar, Arturo. 2004. "Development, Violence, and the New Imperial Order." *Development* 47: 15–21.

Featherstone, David. 2008. *Resistance, Space, and Political Identities: The Making of Counter-global Networks.* Oxford: Blackwell.

Federici, Silvia. 2004. *Caliban and the Witch: Women, the Body, and Primitive Accumulation.* New York: Autonomedia.

Ferrell, Jeff. 2001. *Tearing down the Streets: Adventures in Urban Anarchy.* New York: Palgrave.

———. 2012. "Anarchy, Geography, and Drift." *Antipode* 44: 1687–704.

Ferretti, Federico. 2011. "The Correspondence between Élisée Reclus and Petör Kropotkin as a Source for the History of Geography." *Journal of Historical Geography* 37, no. 5: 216–22.

———. 2013. "'They Have the Right to Throw Us Out': Élisée Reclus' New Universal Geography." *Antipode* 45: 1337–55.

Feyerabend, Paul. 2010. *Against Method.* 4th ed. London: Verso.

Fleming, Marie. 1988. *The Geography of Freedom: The Odyssey of Elisée Reclus.* Montreal: Black Rose.

Flint, Colin. 2001. "A TimeSpace for Electoral Geography: Economic Restructuring, Political Agency, and the Rise of the Nazi Party." *Political Geography* 20, no. 3: 301–29.

Folke, Steen. 1972. "Why a Radical Geography Must Be Marxist." *Antipode* 4: 13–18.

Foucault, Michel. (1970) 2002. *The Order of Things: An Archeology of the Human Sciences.* New York: Routledge.

———. 1982. "The Subject and Power." *Critical Inquiry* 8: 777–95.

———. 1996. *Foucault Live (Interviews, 1961–1984).* Edited by Sylvère Lotringer, Lysa Hochroth, and John Johnston. New York: Semiotext(e).

Fraser, Nancy. 1990. "Rethinking the Public Sphere: A Contribution to the Critique of Actually Existing Democracy." *Social Text* 25: 56–80.

Freire, Paulo. (1970) 2000. *Pedagogy of the Oppressed.* New York: Continuum.

Freund, Peter. 2001. "Bodies, Disability, and Spaces: The Social Model and Disabling Spatial Organizations." *Disability and Society* 16: 689–706.

Friedman, Thomas L. 1999. *The Lexus and the Olive Tree: Understanding Globalization.* New York: Farrar, Strauss, and Giroux.

———. 2005. *The World Is Flat: A Brief History of the Twenty-First Century.* New York: Farrar, Strauss, and Giroux.

Fukuyama, Francis. 1992. *The End of History and the Last Man.* New York: Free Press.

Galois, Bob. 1976. "Ideology and the Idea of Nature: The Case of Peter Kropotkin." *Antipode* 8: 1–16.

Galtung, Johan. 1996. *Peace by Peaceful Means: Peace and Conflict, Development and Civilization.* London: Sage.

Garcia-Ramon, Maria Dolores. 1978. "The Shaping of a Rural Anarchist Landscape: Contributions from Spanish Anarchist Theory." *Antipode* 10: 71–82.

Gautney, Heather. 2009. "Between Anarchism and Autonomist Marxism." *Working USA* 12, no. 3: 467–87.

Gibson-Graham, Julie Katherine. 1996. *The End of Capitalism (as We Knew It): A Feminist Critique of Political Economy.* Cambridge: Blackwell.

———. 2008. "Diverse Economies: Performative Practices for 'Other Worlds.'" *Progress in Human Geography* 32: 613–32.

Giddens, Anthony. 1999. *The Third Way: The Renewal of Social Democracy.* Malden, Mass.: Polity.

Giroux, Henry A. 2004. *The Terror of Neoliberalism: Authoritarianism and the Eclipse of Democracy.* Boulder, Colo.: Paradigm.

Glassman, Jim. 1999. "State Power beyond the 'Territorial Trap': The Internationalization of the State." *Political Geography* 18: 669–96.

———. 2002. "From Seattle (and Ubon) to Bangkok: The Scales of Resistance to Corporate Globalization." *Environment and Planning D: Society and Space* 20, no. 5: 513–33.

———. 2006. "Primitive Accumulation, Accumulation by Dispossession, Accumulation by 'Extra-Economic' Means." *Progress in Human Geography* 30: 608–25.

Godlewska, Anne, and Neil Smith, eds. 1994. *Geography and Empire.* Oxford: Blackwell.

Godwin, William. (1793) 1976. *Enquiry Concerning Political Justice and Its Influence on Modern Morals and Happiness.* London: Penguin.

Goheen, Peter G. 1998. "Public Space and the Geography of the Modern City." *Progress in Human Geography* 22, no. 4: 479–96.

Goldberg, David T. 2009. *The Threat of Race: Reflections on Racial Neoliberalism.* Oxford: Blackwell.

Golden, Lester. 1978. "The Libertarian Movement in Contemporary Spanish Politics." *Antipode* 10: 114–18.

Goldman, Emma. 1916. "The Philosophy of Atheism." *Mother Earth.* http://dwardmac.pitzer.edu/anarchist_archives/goldman/philosophyatheism.html.

———. 1917. "Anarchism: What It Really Stands For." *Mother Earth.* http://dwardmac.pitzer.edu/Anarchist_Archives/goldman/aando/anarchism.html.

———. (1917) 1969. *Anarchism and Other Essays*. New York: Dover.

———. (1923) 1996. *Red Emma Speaks: An Emma Goldman Reader*. Edited by Alix Kates Shulman. New York: Humanity.

———. (1923) 2003. *My Disillusionment in Russia*. Mineola, N.Y.: Dover.

———. 2006. *Vision on Fire: Emma Goldman on the Spanish Revolution*. Edited by David Porter. Oakland, Calif.: AK Press.

Gordon, Uri. 2012. "Afterword: Anarchist Geographies and Revolutionary Strategies." *Antipode* 44: 1742–51.

Goss, Jon. 1996. "Disquiet on the Waterfront: Reflections on Nostalgia and Utopia in the Urban Archetypes of Festival Marketplaces." *Urban Geography* 17, no. 3: 221–47.

Gouldner, Alvin W. 1982. "Marx's Last Battle: Bakunin and the First International." *Theory and Society* 11, no. 6: 853–84.

Graeber, David. 2002. "The New Anarchists." *New Left Review* 13: 61–73.

———. 2004. *Fragments of an Anarchist Anthropology*. Chicago: Prickely Paradigm.

———. 2007. *Possibilities: Essays on Hierarchy, Rebellion, and Desire*. Oakland, Calif.: AK Press.

———. 2009a. "Anarchism, Academia, and the Avant-Garde." In *Contemporary Anarchist Studies: An Introductory Anthology of Anarchy in the Academy,* edited by Randall Amster, Abraham DeLeon, Luis Fernandez, Anthony J. Nocella, and Deric Shannon, 103–12. London: Routledge.

———. 2009b. *Direct Action: An Ethnography*. London: AK Press.

Graham, Robert, ed. 2005. *From Anarchy to Anarchism (300 CE to 1939)*. Vol. 1 of *Anarchism: A Documentary History of Libertarian Ideas*. Montreal: Black Rose.

Gregory, Derek. 2004. *The Colonial Present*. Malden, Mass.: Blackwell.

———. 2010. "War and Peace." *Transactions of the Institute of British Geographers* 35: 154–86.

Grillo, Trina. 1995. "Anti-Essentialism and Intersectionality: Tools to Dismantle the Master's House." *Berkeley Women's Law Journal* 10: 16–30.

Guérin, Daniel. 2005. *No Gods, No Masters: An Anthology of Anarchism*. Oakland, Calif.: AK Press.

Habermas, Jürgen. 1989. *The Structural Transformation of the Public Sphere*. Cambridge, Mass.: MIT Press.

Hagman, Tobias, and Benedikt Korf. 2012. "Agamben in the Ogaden: Violence and Sovereignty in the Ethiopian–Somali Frontier." *Political Geography* 31: 205–14.

Halfacree, Keith. 1999. "'Anarchy Doesn't Work Unless You Think about It':

Intellectual Interpretation and DIY Culture." *Area* 31, no. 3: 209–320.

———. 2004. "'I Could Only Do Wrong': Academic Research and DIY Culture." In *Radical Theory/Critical Praxis: Making a Difference beyond the Academy?*, edited by Duncan Fuller and Rob Kitchin, 68–78. Kelowna, B.C.: Praxis.

Haraway, Donna. 1988. "Situated Knowledges: The Science Question in Feminism and the Privilege of Partial Perspectives." *Feminist Studies* 14: 575–99.

———. 1991. *Simians, Cyborgs, and Women: The Reinvention of Nature.* New York: Routledge.

Hardin, Garrett. 1968. "The Tragedy of the Commons." *Science* 162: 1243–48.

Hardt, Michael, and Antonio Negri. 2000. *Empire.* Cambridge, Mass.: Harvard University Press.

———. 2004. *Multitude: War and Democracy in the Age of Empire.* London: Penguin.

Hardy, Dennis. 1990. "The Anarchist Alternative: A History of Community Experiments in Britain." *Contemporary Issues in Geography and Education* 3: 35–51.

Harris, Cole. 2004. "How Did Colonialism Dispossess? Comments from an Edge of Empire." *Annals of the Association of American Geographers* 94: 65–182.

Hart, Gillian. 2008. "The Provocations of Neoliberalism: Contesting the Nation and Liberation after Apartheid." *Antipode* 40: 678–705.

Harvey, David. 1972. "Revolutionary and Counter Revolutionary Theory in Geography and the Problem of Ghetto Formation." *Antipode* 4: 1–13.

———. 1973. *Social Justice and the City.* London: Edward Arnold.

———. 1982. *The Limits to Capital.* Oxford: Blackwell.

———. 1996. *Justice, Nature, and the Geography of Difference.* Cambridge: Blackwell.

———. 1999. "Considerations on the Environment of Justice." In *Global Ethics and Environment,* edited by Nicholas Low, 109–30. London: Routledge.

———. 2000. *Spaces of Hope.* Edinburgh: Edinburgh University Press.

———. 2003. *The New Imperialism.* Oxford: Oxford University Press.

———. 2005. *A Brief History of Neoliberalism.* Oxford: Oxford University Press.

———. 2006. "The Geographies of Critical Geography." *Transactions of the Institute of British Geographers* 31: 409–12.

———. 2009. *Cosmopolitanism and the Geographies of Freedom.* New York: Columbia University Press.

————. 2011. "The Future of the Commons." *Radical History Review* 109: 101–7.

————. 2012a. "Interview with David Harvey." Interviewed by Matt Mahon. http://www.thewhitereview.org/interviews/interview-with-david-harvey/.

————. 2012b. *Rebel Cities: From the Right to the City to the Urban Revolution.* London: Verso.

————. 2013. *Paris, Capital of Modernity.* London: Routledge.

Harvey, David, and Donna Haraway. 1995. "Nature, Politics, and Possibilities: A Debate and Discussion with David Harvey and Donna Haraway." *Environment and Planning D: Society and Space* 13: 507–27.

Hastings, Justin. 2009. "Geographies of State Failure and Sophistication in Maritime Piracy Hijackings." *Political Geography* 28: 213–23.

Hawking, Stephen, and Leonard Mlodinow. 2010. *The Grand Design.* New York: Bantam.

Haworth, Robert H., ed. 2012. *Anarchist Pedagogies: Collective Actions, Theories, and Critical Reflections on Education.* Oakland, Calif.: PM Press.

Hee, Limin, and Giok Ling Ooi. 2003. "The Politics of Public Space Planning in Singapore." *Planning Perspectives* 18: 79–103.

Heidegger, Martin. 1971. "Martin Heidegger: An Interview." *Listening* 6 (Winter): 35–38.

Hénaff, Marcel, and Tracy B. Strong. 2001. "Conclusion: Public Space, Virtual Space, and Democracy." In *Public Space and Democracy,* edited by Marcel Hénaff and Tracy B. Strong, 221–31. Minneapolis: University of Minnesota Press.

Herod, Andrew. 2011. *Scale.* New York: Routledge.

Herod, Andrew, and Luis Aguiar. 2006. "Introduction: Cleaners and the Dirty Work of Neoliberalism." *Antipode* 38: 425–34.

Hewitt, Kenneth. 2001. "Between Pinochet and Kropotkin: State Terror, Human Rights, and the Geographers." *Canadian Geographer* 45, no. 3: 338–55.

Heynen, Nik. 2010. "Cooking up Non-violent Civil-Disobedient Direct Action for the Hungry: 'Food Not Bombs' and the Resurgence of Radical Democracy in the US." *Urban Studies* 47: 1225–40.

Heynen, Nik, and Jason Rhodes. 2012. "Organizing for Survival: From the Civil Rights Movement to Black Anarchism through the Life of Lorenzo Kom'boa Ervin." *ACME: An International E-Journal for Critical Geographies* 11: 393–412.

Hodkinson, Stuart, and Paul Chatterton. 2006. "Autonomy in the City?

Reflections on the Social Centres Movement in the UK." *City* 10, no. 3: 305–15.

Hoffmann, Banesh, and Helen Dukas. 1972. *Albert Einstein: Creator and Rebel.* London: Plume.

Holland, Edward. 2011. "Barack Obama's Foreign Policy, Just War, and the Irony of Political Geography." *Political Geography* 30, no. 2: 59–60.

Holloway, John. 2002. *Change the World without Taking Power: The Meaning of Revolution Today.* London: Pluto.

Hooper, Barbara. 2008. "Dialegesthai: Towards a Posttranscendent Politics— or, Let's Talk about Bodies." *Environment and Plannning, Series A* 40: 2562–77.

Horner, G. M. 1978. "Kropotkin and the City: The Socialist Ideal in Urbanism." *Antipode* 10: 33–45.

Howell, Philip. 1993. "Public Space and the Public Sphere: Political Theory and the Historical Geography of Modernity." *Environment and Planning D: Society and Space* 11: 303–22.

Hubbard, Phil. 2001. "Sex Zones: Intimacy, Citizenship, and Public Space." *Sexualities* 4: 51–72.

Huston, Shaun. 1997. "Kropotkin and Spatial Social Theory: Unfolding an Anarchist Contribution." *Anarchist Studies* 5: 109–30.

Huxley, Thomas H. 1888. "The Struggle for Existence: A Programme." *The Nineteenth Century* 23 (February): 161–80.

Hyams, Edward. 1979. *Pierre-Joseph Proudhon: His Revolutionary Life, Mind, and Works.* London: J. Murray.

Iadicola, Peter, and Anson Shupe. 2003. *Violence, Inequality, and Human Freedom.* Lanham, Md.: Rowman and Littlefield.

Ince, Anthony. 2010a. "Organizing Anarchy: Spatial Strategy, Prefiguration, and the Politics of Everyday Life." PhD diss., Department of Geography, Queen Mary, University of London.

———. 2010b. "Whither Anarchist Geography?" In *New Perspectives on Anarchism,* edited by Nathan Jun and Shane Wahl, 281–302. Lanham, Md.: Lexington.

———. 2012. "In the Shell of the Old: Anarchist Geographies of Territorialisation." *Antipode* 44: 1645–66.

Invisible Committee. 2009. *The Coming Insurrection.* Los Angeles, Calif.: Semiotext(e).

Iveson, Kurt. 2003. "Justifying Exclusion: The Politics of Public Space and the Dispute over Access to McIvers Ladies' Baths, Sydney." *Gender, Place, and Culture* 10, no. 3: 215–28.

Jensen, Derrick. 2006. *Endgame*, vol. 1 of *The Problem of Civilization*. New York: Seven Stories.

Jessop, Bob. 2007. *State Power: A Strategic-Relational Approach*. Cambridge: Polity.

Jessop, Bob, Neil Brenner, and Martin Jones. 2008. "Theorizing Sociospatial Relations." *Environment and Planning D: Society and Space* 26, no. 3: 389–401.

Jiwani, Yasmin. 2011. "Pedagogies of Hope: Counter Narratives and Anti-disciplinary Tactics." *Review of Education, Pedagogy, and Cultural Studies* 33, no. 4: 333–53.

Johnson, Blair T., and Marcella H. Boynton. 2010. "Putting Attitudes in Their Place: Behavioral Prediction in the Face of Competing Variables." In *The Psychology of Attitudes and Attitude Change*, edited by Joseph P. Forgas, Joel Cooper, and William D. Crano, 19–38. New York: Psychology Press.

Johnston, Ron. 2001. "Out of the 'Moribund Backwater': Territory and Territoriality in Political Geography." *Political Geography* 20, no. 6: 677–93.

———. 2006. "The Politics of Changing Human Geography's Agenda: Textbooks and the Representation of Increasing Diversity." *Progress in Human Geography* 31: 286–303.

Jonas, Andrew E. G. 2006. "Pro Scale: Further Reflections on the 'Scale Debate' in Human Geography." *Transactions of the Institute of British Geographers* 31, no. 3: 399–406.

Jones, John Paul, Keith Woodward, and Sallie A. Marston. 2007. "Situating Flatness." *Transactions of the Institute of British Geographers* 32, no. 2: 264–76.

Jones, Martin. 2009. "Phase Space: Geography, Relational Thinking, and Beyond." *Progress in Human Geography* 33, no. 4: 487–506.

Kaiser, Robert, and Elena Nikiforova. 2008. "The Performativity of Scale: The Social Construction of Scale Effects in Narva, Estonia." *Environment and Planning D: Society and Space* 26: 537–62.

Kalyvas, Andreas. 2010. "An Anomaly? Some Reflections on the Greek December 2008." *Constellations* 17, no. 2: 351–65.

Katsiaficas, George. 2006. *The Subversion of Politics: European Autonomous Social Movements and the Decolonization of Everyday Life*. Oakland, Calif.: AK Press.

Katz, Cindi. 2001. "On the Grounds of Globalization: A Topography for Feminist Political Engagement." *Signs* 26: 1213–34.

Keane, John. 2004. *Violence and Democracy*. Cambridge: Cambridge University Press.

Kearns, Gerry. 2004. "The Political Pivot of Geography." *The Geographical Journal* 170, no. 4: 337–46.

———. 2009a. *Geopolitics and Empire: The Legacy of Halford Mackinder.* Oxford: Oxford University Press.

———. 2009b. "Kropotkin." In *International Encyclopedia of Human Geography,* edited by Rob Kitchin and Nigel Thrift, 56–58. Amsterdam: Elsevier.

Keighren, Innes M. 2010. *Bringing Geography to Book: Ellen Semple and the Reception of Geographical Knowledge.* London: Tauris.

Keith, Michael. 1997. "Street Sensibility? Negotiating the Political by Articulating the Spatial." In *The Urbanization of Injustice,* edited by Andy Merrifield and Erik Swyngedouw, 137–60. New York: New York University Press.

Kindon, Sara, Rachel Pain, and Mike Kesby, eds. 2007. *Participatory Action Research Approaches and Methods: Connecting People, Participation, and Place.* London: Routledge.

Kingfisher, Catherine. 2007. "Spatializing Neoliberalism: Articulations, Recapitulations (a Very Few) Alternatives." In *Neoliberalization: States, Networks, Peoples,* edited by Kim England and Kevin Ward, 195–222. Malden, Mass.: Blackwell.

Kinna, Ruth. 1992. "Kropotkin and Huxley." *Politics* 12, no. 2: 41–47.

Kobayashi, Audrey. 2009. "Geographies of Peace and Armed Conflict: Introduction." *Annals of the Association of American Geographers* 99: 819–26.

Kohl, Benjamin. 2006. "Challenges to Neoliberal Hegemony in Bolivia." *Antipode* 38: 304–26.

Kohli, Atul. 2004. *State-Directed Development: Political Power and Industrialization in the Global Periphery.* Cambridge: Cambridge University Press.

Koopman, Sara. 2011. "Alter-Geopolitics: Other Securities Are Happening." *Geoforum* 42, no. 3: 274–84.

Kothari, Rajni. 2005. *Rethinking Democracy.* New Delhi: Orient Longman.

Kropotkin, Peter. (1880) 2005. "The Spirit of Revolt." In *Kropotkin's Revolutionary Pamphlets,* edited by Roger N. Baldwin, 34–44. Whitefish, Mont.: Kessinger.

———. 1885. "What Geography Ought to Be." *The Nineteenth Century* 18 (December): 940–56.

———. (1885) 1992. *Words of a Rebel.* Montreal: Black Rose.

———. 1887. "The Coming Anarchy." *The Nineteenth Century* CXXVI (August), 149–64.

———. (1887) 2002. "Anarchist Communism: Its Basis and Principles." In *Peter Kropotkin, Anarchism: A Collection of Revolutionary Writings,* edited by Roger N. Baldwin, 44–78. New York: Dover.

———. (1892) 2011. *The Conquest of Bread.* New York: Dover.

———. 1897. "The State: Its Historic Role." http://dwardmac.pitzer.edu /Anarchist_Archives/kropotkin/state/state_toc.html.

———. 1898. "Anarchist Morality." http://dwardmac.pitzer.edu/Anarchist _Archives/kropotkin/AM/anarchist_morality.html.

———. (1898) 2002. "Anarchism: Its Philosophy and Ideal." In *Peter Kropotkin, Anarchism: A Collection of Revolutionary Writings,* edited by Roger N. Baldwin, 114–45. New York: Dover.

———. (1902) 2008. *Mutual Aid: A Factor in Evolution.* Charleston, S.C.: Forgotten.

———. (1908) 1995. "Modern Science and Anarchism." In *Peter Kropotkin, Evolution and Environment,* edited by George Woodcock, 15–110. Montreal: Black Rose.

———. 1910. "Anarchism." *Encyclopedia Britannica.* http://dwardmac.pitzer .edu/anarchist_archives/kropotkin/britanniaanarchy.html.

———. (1912) 1994. *Fields, Factories, and Workshops.* Montreal: Black Rose.

Lacan, Jacques. (1977) 2001. *Écrits: A Selection Life.* New York: Routledge.

Laclau, Ernesto, and Chantal Mouffe. 2001. *Hegemony and Socialist Strategy: Towards a Radical Democratic Politics.* 2nd ed. New York: Verso.

Lacoste, Yves. 1976. *La Geographie, ça Sert d'Abord, à Faire la Guerre* [Geography is primarily for making war]. Paris: Francois Maspero.

Landauer, Gustav. (1910) 2005. "Destroying the State by Creating Socialism." In *From Anarchy to Anarchism (300 CE to 1939),* vol. 1 of *Anarchism: A Documentary History of Libertarian Ideas,* edited by Robert Graham, 164–66. Montreal: Black Rose.

Larner, Wendy. 2000. "Neo-Liberalism: Policy, Ideology, Governmentality." *Studies in Political Economy* 63: 5–25.

Lauria, Mickey. 1978. "The Anarchist Seminar? USG Newsletter." *Union of Socialist Geographers* 3, no. 3: 2–6.

Lawson, Victoria. 2009. "Instead of Radical Geography, How about Caring Geography?" *Antipode* 41: 210–13.

Le Billon, Philippe. 2008. "Corrupting Peace? Peacebuilding and Post-conflict Corruption." *International Peacekeeping* 15, no. 3: 344–61.

Lees, Lynn Hollen. 1994. "Urban Public Space and Imagined Communities in the 1980s and 1990s." *Journal of Urban History* 20, no. 4: 443–65.

Lefebvre, Henri. (1958) 2008. *Critique of Everyday Life.* 3 vols. London: Verso.

———. 1984. *Everyday Life in the Modern World.* New Brunswick, N.J.: Transaction.

———. 1991. *The Production of Space.* Oxford: Blackwell.

Leier, Mark. 2006. *Bakunin: The Creative Passion.* New York: Thomas Dune.

Leitner, Helga, and Byron Miller. 2007. "Scale and the Limitations of Ontological Debate: A Commentary on Marston, Jones and Woodward." *Transactions of the Institute of British Geographers* 32: 116–25.

Leitner, Helga, Jamie Peck, and Eric S. Sheppard, eds. 2007. *Contesting Neoliberalism Urban Frontiers.* New York: Guilford Press.

Lemke, Thomas. 2001. "'The Birth of Bio-Politics': Michel Foucault's Lecture at the Collège de France on Neo-liberal Governmentality." *Economy and Society* 30, no. 2: 190–207.

Levinas, Emmanuel. 1979. *Totality and Infinity: An Essay on Exteriority.* Vol. 1. New York: Springer Science and Business Media.

Lewis, Tom. 2000. "Marxism and Nationalism." *International Socialist Review* 13. http://www.isreview.org/issues/13/marxism_nationalism_part1.shtml.

Lim, Kean Fan. 2012. "What You See Is (Not) What You Get? The Taiwan Question, Geo-economic Realities, and the 'China Threat' Imaginary." *Antipode* 44: 1348–73.

Lummis, C. Douglas. 1996. *Radical Democracy.* Ithaca, N.Y.: Cornell University Press.

MacKinnon, Danny. 2011. "Reconstructing Scale: Towards a New Scalar Politics." *Progress in Human Geography* 35: 21–36.

MacLaughlin, Jim Mac. 1986. "State-Centered Social Science and the Anarchist Critique: Ideology in Political Geography." *Antipode* 18: 11–38.

Malatesta, Errico. (1897) 1977. *Errico Malatesta: His Life and Ideas.* Edited by Vernon Richards. London: Freedom Press.

———. 1924. *Democracy and Anarchy.* http://theanarchistlibrary.org/library/errico-malatesta-democracy-and-anarchy.

Malm, Andreas, and Shora Esmailian. 2013. "Ways in and out of Vulnerability to Climate Change: Abandoning the Mubarak Project in the Northern Nile Delta, Egypt." *Antipode* 45: 474–92.

Mamadouh, Virginie. 2011. "Forum on the 2011 'Arab Spring'—Introduction." *The Arab World Geographer* 14, no. 2: 111–15.

Mann, Michael. 2005. *The Dark Side of Democracy: Explaining Ethnic Cleansing.* Cambridge: Cambridge University Press.

Mannin, Ethel. (1944) 2009. "The Will to Dream." In *The Emergence of the New Anarchism (1939–1977),* vol. 2 of *Anarchism: A Documentary History of Libertarian Ideas,* edited by Robert Graham, 72–75. Montreal: Black Rose.

Marks, Brian. 2012. "Autonomist Marxist Theory and Practice in the Current Crisis." *ACME: An International E-Journal for Critical Geographies* 11: 467–91.

Marshall, Peter. 1992. *Demanding the Impossible: A History of Anarchism.* London: HarperCollins.

Marston, Sallie A., John Paul Jones, and Keith Woodward. 2005. "Human Geography without Scale." *Transactions of the Institute of British Geographers* 30, no. 4: 416–32.

Marx, Karl. (1847) 2013. *The Poverty of Philosophy.* Charleston: Forgotten Books.

———. (1867) 1976. *A Critique of Political Economy,* vol. 1 of *Capital V.* New York: Vintage.

———. (1888) 1994. "Theses on Feuerbach." In *Selected Writings: Karl Marx,* edited by Lawrence H. Simon, 98–101. Indianapolis, Ind.: Hackett.

Marx, Karl, and Friedrich Engels. (1848) 2002. *The Communist Manifesto.* London: Penguin.

Massey, Doreen. 1994. *Space, Place, and Gender.* Minneapolis: University of Minnesota Press.

———. 2004. "The Political Challenge of Relational Space: Introduction to the Vega Symposium." *Geografiska Annaler: Series B, Human Geography* 86, no. 3.

———. 2005. *For Space.* London: Sage.

Maxwell, Barry, and Raymond Craib, eds. 2015. *No Gods, No Masters, No Peripheries: Global Anarchisms.* Oakland, Ca.: PM Press.

May, Todd. 1994. *The Political Philosophy of Poststructuralist Anarchism.* University Park: Penn State University Press.

———. 2008. *The Political Thought of Jacques Rancière: Creating Equality.* University Park: Penn State University Press.

———. 2009a. "Anarchism from Foucault to Rancière." In *Contemporary Anarchist Studies: An Introductory Anthology of Anarchy in the Academy,* edited by Randall Amster, Abraham DeLeon, Luis Fernandez, Anthony J. Nocella, and Deric Shannon, 11–17. London: Routledge.

———. 2009b. "Democracy Is Where We Make It: The Relevance of Jacques Rancière." *Symposium (Canadian Journal of Continental Philosophy)* 13: 3–21.

McCann, Eugene. 1999. "Race, Protest, and Public Space: Contextualizing Lefebvre in the U.S. City." *Antipode* 31: 163–84.

McCormack, Derek P. 2003. "An Event of Geographical Ethics in Spaces of Affect." *Transactions of the Institute of British Geographers* 28, no. 4: 488–507.

McKay, Iain. 2008. *An Anarchist FAQ.* Vol. 1. Oakland, Calif.: AK Press.

———. 2011. "Proudhon and Marx." In *Property Is Theft! A Pierre-Joseph Proudhon Anthology,* edited by Iain McKay, 67–78. Oakland, Calif.: AK Press.

Megoran, Nick. 2007. *The War on Terror: How Should Christians Respond?* Nottingham, U.K.: Inter-Varsity Press.

————. 2008. "Militarism, Realism, Just War, or Nonviolence? Critical Geo-politics and the Problem of Normativity." *Geopolitics* 13, no. 3: 473–97.

————. 2010. "Towards a Geography of Peace: Pacific Geopolitics and Evan-gelical Christian Crusade Apologies." *Transactions of the Institute of British Geographers* 35: 382–98.

————. 2011. "War and Peace? An Agenda for Peace Research and Practice in Geography." *Political Geography* 30: 178–89.

————. 2013. "On (Christian) Anarchism and (Non)Violence: A Response to Simon Springer." *Space and Polity* 18: 97–105.

Miles, Malcolm. 2002. "After the Public Realm: Spaces of Representation, Transition and Plurality." *International Journal of Art Design Education* 19, no. 3: 253–61.

Milstein, Cindy. 2000. "Reclaim the Cities: From Protest to Popular Pow-er." https://archive.org/details/al_Cindy_Milstein_Reclaim_the_Cities _From_Protest_to_Popular_Power_a4.

Mitchell, Don. 1996. "Political Violence, Order, and the Legal Construction of Public Space: Power and the Public Forum Doctrine." *Urban Geog-raphy* 17, no. 2: 152–78.

————. 2003a. "The Liberalization of Free Speech: Or, How Protest in Public Space Is Silenced." *Stanford Agora* 4: 1–45.

————. 2003b. *The Right to the City: Social Justice and the Fight for Public Space.* New York: Guilford.

Mitchell, Don, and Lynn A. Staeheli. 2006. "Clean and Safe? Property Rede-velopment, Public Space, and Homelessness in Downtown San Diego." In *The Politics of Public Space,* edited by Setha Low and Neil Smith, 143–75. London: Routledge.

Mitchell, Timothy. 2002. *Rule of Experts: Egypt, Techno-politics, Modernity.* Berkeley: University of California Press.

Mohaghegh, Jason B., and Seema Golestaneh. 2011. "Haunted Sound: Noth-ingness, Movement, and the Minimalist Imagination." *Environment and Planning D: Society and Space* 29, no. 3: 485–98.

Monmonier, Mark. 1996. *How to Lie with Maps.* Chicago: University of Chicago Press.

Moore, Adam. 2008. "Rethinking Scale as a Geographical Category: From Analysis to Practice." *Progress in Human Geography* 32: 203–25.

Morris, Brian. 2003. *Kropotkin: The Politics of Community.* Amherst, N.Y.: Humanity.

Mouffe, Chantal. 2000. *The Democratic Paradox.* New York: Verso.

————. 2004. "For an Agonistic Public Sphere." In *Radical Democracy: Politics between Abundance and Lack,* edited by Lars Tønder and Lasse Thomassen, 123–32. Manchester, U.K.: Manchester University Press.

———. 2006. *The Return of the Political.* New York: Verso.

Mudu, Pierpaolo. 2012. "At the Intersection of Anarchists and Autonomists: Autogestioni and Centri Sociali." *ACME: An International E-Journal for Critical Geographies* 11: 413–38.

Mueller, Tadzio. 2003. "Empowering Anarchy: Power, Hegemony, and Anarchist Strategy." *Anarchist Studies* 11, no. 2: 122–49.

Nadler, Steven. 2011. *A Book Forged in Hell: Spinoza's Scandalous Treatise and the Birth of the Secular Age.* Princeton, N.J.: Princeton University Press.

Negri, Antonio. 1989. *The Politics of Subversion: A Manifesto for the Twenty-First Century.* Cambridge: Polity.

Newman, Janis. 1990. "Emma Goldman: Anarcho-feminist." *Contemporary Issues in Geography and Education* 3: 27–30.

Newman, Saul. 2001. *From Bakunin to Lacan: Anti-authoritarianism and the Dislocation of Power.* Oxford: Lexington.

———. 2007. "Anarchism, Poststructuralism, and the Future of Radical Politics." *SubStance* 36: 3–19.

———. 2010. *The Politics of Postanarchism.* Edinburgh: Edinburgh University Press.

———. 2011. "Postanarchism and Space: Revolutionary Fantasies and Autonomous Zones." *Planning Theory* 10: 344–65.

Nolin, Catherine. 2010. "'Geography That Breaks Your Heart': Feminist Geography from/to the Peripheries." Suzanne Mackenzie Memorial Lecture presented to the Canadian Association of Geographers Annual Conference, Regina, Canada.

Notes from Nowhere. 2003. *We Are Everywhere: The Irresistible Rise of Global Anticapitalism.* London: Verso.

O'Brien, Richard. 1992. *Global Financial Integration: The End of Geography.* New York: Council on Foreign Relations.

Olstad, Tyra A. 2010. "Here There Be Dragons: Experiencing Terrae Incognitae." *Focus on Geography* 53, no. 2: 59–64.

O'Neil, Mary Lou. 2002. "Youth Curfews in the United States: The Creation of Public Spheres for Some Young People." *Journal of Youth Studies* 5: 49–68.

Ong, Aihwa. 2007. "Neoliberalism as a Mobile Technology." *Transactions of the Institute of British Geographers* 32: 3–8.

Orwell, George. 1993. *A Collection of Essays.* San Diego, Calif.: Harcourt.

Ostrom, Elinor. 1990. *Governing the Commons: The Evolution of Institutions for Collective Action.* Cambridge: Cambridge University Press.

Parker, Martin. 2009. "Angelic Organization: Hierarchy and the Tyranny of Heaven." *Organization Studies* 30, no. 11: 1281–99.

Parekh, Bhikhu C. 1981. *Hannah Arendt and the Search for a New Political Philosophy*. London: Macmillan.

Peck, Jamie. 2001. "Neoliberalizing States: Thin Policies/Hard Outcomes." *Progress in Human Geography* 25: 445–55.

———. 2003. "Geography and Public Policy: Mapping the Penal State." *Progress in Human Geography* 27: 222–32.

———. 2010. *Constructions of Neoliberal Reason*. Oxford: Oxford University Press.

Peck, Jamie, and Adam Tickell. 2002. "Neoliberalizing Space." *Antipode* 34: 380–404.

Peet, Richard. 1975. "For Kropotkin." *Antipode* 7: 42–43.

———. 1977. "The Development of Radical Geography in the United States." *Progress in Human Geography* 1: 240–63.

———. 1978. "The Geography of Human Liberation." *Antipode* 10: 119–34.

Pepper, David. 1990. "Geography and the Landscapes of Anarchistic Visions of Britain: The Example of Morris and Kropotkin." *Contemporary Issues in Geography and Education* 3: 63–79.

Peters, Michael A. 2001. *Poststructuralism, Marxism, and Neoliberalism: Between Theory and Politics*. New York: Roman and Littlefield.

Pickerill, Jenny, and Paul Chatterton. 2006. "Notes towards Autonomous Geographies: Creation, Resistance and Self Management as Survival Tactics." *Progress in Human Geography* 30: 1–17.

Pile, Steve. 2009. "Emotions and Affect in Recent Human Geography." *Transactions of the Institute of British Geographers* 35: 5–20.

Pissaria, Bill. 1978. "Why Study Anarchism? USG Newsletter." *Union of Socialist Geographers* 3, no. 3: 6–10.

Plath, Sylvia. 1998. *The Colossus and Other Poems*. New York: Vintage.

Pleyers, Geoffrey. 2011. *Alter-globalization: Becoming Actors in a Global Age*. Cambridge: Polity.

Popke, Jeff. 2009. "Geography and Ethics: Non-representational Encounters, Collective Responsibility and Economic Difference." *Progress in Human Geography* 33: 81–90.

Porter, Philip W. 1978. "Anarchytecture for Our Time: USG Newsletter." *Union of Socialist Geographers* 3, no. 3: 10–14.

Proctor, James D. 2005. "Ethics in Geography: Giving Moral Form to the Geographical Imagination." *Area* 30: 8–18.

Proudhon, Pierre-Joseph. (1840) 2008. *What Is Property? or, An Inquiry into the Right and Principle of Government*. Charleston, S.C.: Forgotten.

———. 1846. "Proudhon to Marx. Lyon, 17 May." http://www.marxists.org /reference/subject/economics/proudhon/letters/46_05_17.htm.

———. (1851) 2007. *General Idea of the Revolution in the Nineteenth Century.* New York: Cosimo.

———. (1864) 2005. "Manifesto of Sixty Workers from the Seine Department (17 February 1864)." In *No Gods, No Masters: An Anthology of Anarchism,* edited by Daniel Guérin, 103–10. Oakland, Calif.: AK Press.

———. (1865) 2011. "Appendix: The Theory of Property." In *Property Is Theft: A Pierre-Joseph Proudhon Anthology,* edited by Iain McKay, 775–84. Oakland, Calif.: AK Press.

Purcell, Mark. 2008. *Recapturing Democracy: Neoliberalization and the Struggle for Alternative Urban Futures.* London: Routledge.

———. 2012. "Gramsci Is Not Dead: For a 'both/and' Approach to Radical Geography." *ACME: An International E-Journal for Critical Geographies* 11: 512–24.

———. 2013. *The Down-Deep Delight of Democracy.* Malden, Mass.: Wiley-Blackwell.

Rancière, Jacques. 1999. *Disagreement: Politics and Philosophy.* Minneapolis: University of Minnesota Press.

———. 2001. "Ten Theses on Politics." *Theory and Event* 5.

———. 2006. *The Politics of Aesthetics.* London: Continuum.

Rankin, Bill. 2003. "Radical Cartography." http://www.radicalcartography.net/.

Rapley, John. 2004. *Globalization and Inequality: Neoliberalism's Downward Spiral.* Boulder, Colo.: Lynne Rienner.

Rapoport, David C., and Leonard Weinberg. 2001. Introduction to *The Democratic Experience and Political Violence,* edited by David C. Rapoport and Leonard Weinberg. Portland, Oreg.: Frank Cass.

Rapp, John A. 2012. *Daoism and Anarchism: Critiques of State Autonomy in Ancient and Modern China.* London: Continuum.

Reclus, Élisée. 1884. "An Anarchist on Anarchy." *Contemporary Review* 45: 627–41.

———. 1894. *The Earth and Its Inhabitants: The Universal Geography.* Vol. 1. London: J. S. Virtue.

———. 1901. "On Vegetarianism." *Humane Review.* http://dwardmac.pitzer .edu/Anarchist_Archives/bright/reclus/onvegetarianism.html.

———. 1905. *L'Homme et la Terre.* Vol. 1. Paris: Librairie Universelle.

———. n.d. "Why Anarchists Don't Vote." *Mother Earth.* http://dwardmac .pitzer.edu/Anarchist_Archives/bright/reclus/dontvote.html.

Richards, Vernon. 1995. *Lessons of the Spanish Revolution, 1936–1939.* 3rd ed. London: Freedom.

Rigby, Andrew. 1990. "Lessons from Anarchistic Communes." *Contemporary Issues in Geography and Education* 3, no. 3: 52–62.

Robinson, Jennifer. 2006. *Ordinary Cities: Between Modernity and Development.* London: Routledge.

Rocker, Rudolf. (1956) 2005. *The London Years.* Nottingham, U.K.: Five Leaves.

——. 1981. "Marx and Anarchism." In *The Poverty of Statism: Anarchism vs. Marxism: A Debate (Bukharin, Fabbri, Rocker),* edited by Albert Meltzer, translated by Paul Sharkey, 75–93. Orkney, U.K.: Cienfuegos Press.

Rouhani, Farhang. 2012a. "Anarchism, Geography, and Queen Space-Making: Building Bridges over Chasms We Create." *ACME: An International E-Journal for Critical Geographies* 11: 373–92.

——. 2012b. "Practice What You Teach: Placing Anarchism in and out of the Classroom." *Antipode* 44: 1726–41.

Rousselle, Duane, and Süreyya Evren. 2011. *Post-anarchism: A Reader.* New York: Pluto.

Routledge, Paul. 1998. "Anti-Geopolitics: Introduction." In *The Geopolitics Reader,* edited by Gearóid Ó Tuathail, Simon Dalby, and Paul Routledge, 245–55. London: Routledge.

——. 2003a. "Anti-geopolitics." In *A Companion to Political Geography,* edited by John A. Agnew, Katharyne Mitchell, and Gerard Toal, 236–48. Oxford: Blackwell.

——. 2003b. "Convergence Space: Process Geographies of Grassroots Globalization Networks." *Transactions of the Institute of British Geographers* 28: 333–49.

——. 2009a. "Relational Ethics of Struggle." In *Radical Theory/Critical Praxis: Making a Difference beyond the Academy?,* edited by Duncan Fuller and Rob Kitchin, 79–91. Kelowna, B.C.: Praxis.

——. 2009b. "Towards a Relational Ethics of Struggle: Embodiment, Affinity, and Affect." In *Contemporary Anarchist Studies: An Introductory Anthology to Anarchy in the Academy,* edited by Randall Amster, Abraham DeLeon, Luis Fernandez, Anthony J. Nocella, and Deric Shannon, 82–92. New York: Routledge.

Routledge, Paul, Andrew Cumbers, and Corinne Nativel. 2007. "Grassrooting Network Imaginaries: Relationality, Power, and Mutual Solidarity in Global Justice Networks." *Environment and Planning A* 39: 2575–92.

Ruddick, Susan. 1996. "Constructing Difference in Public Spaces: Race, Class, and Gender as Interlocking Systems." *Urban Geography* 17, no. 2: 132–51.

Russell, Bertie, Andre Pusey, and Paul Chatterton. 2011. "What Can an Assemblage Do? Seven Propositions for a More Strategic and Politicized Assemblage Thinking." *City* 15, no. 5: 577–83.

Ryan, Michael. 1989. *Politics and Culture: Working Hypothesis for a Post-revolutionary Society.* Baltimore: Johns Hopkins University Press.

Said, Edward. 1993. *Culture and Imperialism.* New York: Knopf.

———. 2003. *Orientalism.* 25th anniversary ed. New York: Vintage.

Sayer, Andrew. 2003. "(De)commodification, Consumer Culture, and Moral Economy." *Environment and Planning D: Society and Space* 21: 341–57.

Scheper-Hughes, Nancy, and Philippe Bourgois. 2004. "Introduction: Making Sense of Violence." In *Violence in War and Peace,* edited by Nancy Scheper-Hughes and Philippe Bourgois, 1–31. Malden, Mass.: Blackwell.

Schmitter, Philippe C., and Terry Lynn Karl. 1993. "What Democracy Is … and Is Not." In *The Global Resurgence of Democracy,* edited by Larry Jay Diamond and Marc F. Plattner, 39–52. Baltimore: Johns Hopkins University Press.

Scott, James C. 1990. *Domination and the Arts of Resistance: Hidden Transcripts.* New Haven, Conn.: Yale University Press.

———. 2009. *The Art of Not Being Governed: An Anarchist History of Upland Southeast Asia.* New Haven, Conn.: Yale University Press.

———. 2012. *Two Cheers for Anarchism: Six Easy Pieces on Autonomy, Dignity, and Meaningful Work and Play.* Princeton, N.J.: Princeton University Press.

Sennett, Richard. 1992. *The Uses of Disorder: Personal Identity and City Life.* New York: W. W. Norton.

Seoane, José. 2004. "Rebellion, Dignity, Autonomy and Democracy: Shared Voices from the South." *Antipode* 36: 383–91.

Sharp, Joanne. 2007. "Geography and Gender: Finding Feminist Political Geographies." *Progress in Human Geography* 31, no. 3: 381–87.

Sharp, Joanne, Paul Routledge, Chris Philo, and Ronan Paddison. 2000. "Entanglements of Power: Geographies of Domination/Resistance." In *Entanglements of Power: Geographies of Domination/Resistance,* edited by Joanne Sharp, Paul Routledge, Chris Philo, and Ronan Paddison, 1–42. London: Routledge.

Shirlow, Peter, and Lorraine Dowler. 2010. "'Wee Women No More': Female Partners of Republican Political Prisoners in Belfast." *Environment and Planning A* 42, no. 2: 384–99.

Sidaway, James D. 2000. "Postcolonial Geographies: An Exploratory Essay." *Progress in Human Geography* 24, no. 4: 591–612.

Slater, David. 2004. *Geopolitics and the Post-colonial: Rethinking North–South Relations.* Malden, Mass.: Blackwell.

Smith, Adrian, Alison Stenning, and Katie Willis, eds. 2009. *Social Justice and Neoliberalism: Global Perspectives.* London: Zed.

Smith, Michael P. 2001. *Transnational Urbanism.* Oxford: Blackwell.

Smith, Neil. 2005. *The Endgame of Globalization.* New York: Routledge.

———. 2010. "The Revolutionary Imperative." *Antipode* 41: 50–65.

Smith, Neil, and Setha Low. 2006. "Introduction: The Imperative of Public Space." In *The Politics of Public Space,* edited by Setha Low and Neil Smith, 1–16. London: Routledge.

Smith, Woodruff D. 1986. *The Ideological Origins of Nazi Imperialism.* Oxford: Oxford University Press.

Soja, Edward W. 1996. *Thirdspace: Journeys to Los Angeles and Other Real-and-Imagined Places.* Oxford: Blackwell.

Sorkin, Michael. 1992. "Introduction: Variations on a Theme Park." In *Variations on a Theme Park: The New American City and the End of Public Space,* edited by Michael Sorkin, xi–xv. New York: Hill and Wang.

Sparke, Mathew. 2013. "From Global Dispossession to Local Repossession: Towards a Worldly Cultural Geography of Occupy Activism." In *The New Companion to Cultural Geography,* edited by Jamie Winders and Richard Schein, 387–408. Oxford: Blackwell.

Spinoza, Benedictus de. (1677) 2001. *Ethics.* Hertfordshire, U.K.: Wordsworth.

Springer, Simon. 2008. "The Nonillusory Effects of Neoliberalisation: Linking Geographies of Poverty, Inequality, and Violence." *Geoforum* 39: 1520–25.

———. 2009. "Culture of Violence or Violent Orientalism? Neoliberalisation and Imagining the 'Savage Other' in Post-transitional Cambodia." *Transactions of the Institute of British Geographers* 34: 305–19.

———. 2010a. *Cambodia's Neoliberal Order: Violence, Authoritarianism, and the Contestation of Public Space.* London: Routledge.

———. 2010b. "Neoliberal Discursive Formations: On the Contours of Subjectivation, Good Governance, and Symbolic Violence in Post-transitional Cambodia." *Environment and Planning D: Society and Space* 28: 931–50.

———. 2010c. "Neoliberalism and Geography: Expansions, Variegations, Formations." *Geography Compass* 4: 1025–38.

———. 2011. "Violence Sits in Places? Cultural Practice, Neoliberal Rationalism, and Virulent Imaginative Geographies." *Political Geography* 30: 90–98.

———. 2012a. "Neoliberalising Violence: Of the Exceptional and the Exemplary in Coalescing Moments." *Area* 44: 136–43.

———. 2012b. "Neoliberalism as Discourse: Between Foucauldian Political Economy and Marxian Poststructuralism." *Critical Discourse Studies* 9: 133–47.

———. 2013. "Illegal Evictions? Overwriting Possession and Orality with Law's Violence in Cambodia." *Journal of Agrarian Change* 13: 520–46.

———. 2015. *Violent Neoliberalism: Development, Discourse, and Dispossession in Cambodia.* New York: Palgrave Macmillan.

Springer, Simon, Heather Chi, Jeremy Crampton, Fiona McConnell, Julie Cupples, Kevin Glynn, Barney Warf, and Wes Attewell. 2012a. "Leaky Geopolitics: The Ruptures and Transgressions of WikiLeaks." *Geopolitics* 17: 681–711.

Springer, Simon, Anthony Ince, Jenny Pickerill, Gavin Brown, and Adam J. Barker. 2012b. "Reanimating Anarchist Geographies: A New Burst of Color." *Antipode* 44: 1591–604.

Staeheli, Lynne A., and Albert Thompson. 1997. "Citizenship, Community, and Struggles for Public Space." *Professional Geographer* 49: 28–38.

Stirner, Max. (1845) 1993. *The Ego and Its Own: The Case of the Individual against Authority.* London: Rebel.

Sundberg, Juanita. 2007. "Reconfiguring North–South Solidarity: Critical Reflections on Experiences of Transnational Resistance." *Antipode* 39: 144–66.

Sussia, Judith. 2010. *Anarchism and Education: A Philosophical Perspective.* Oakland, Calif.: PM Press.

Swyngedouw, Erik. 1997. "Neither Global nor Local: 'Glocalisation' and the Politics of Scale." In *Spaces of Globalisation: Reasserting the Power of the Local,* edited by Kevin Cox, 137–66. New York: Guilford.

———. 2011. "Interrogating Post-democratization: Reclaiming Egalitarian Political Spaces." *Political Geography* 30, no. 7: 370–80.

Taylor, Peter J. 1991a. "The Crisis of the Movements: The Enabling State as Quisling." *Antipode* 23: 214–28.

———. 1991b. "The Geography of Freedom: The Odyssey of Élisée Reclus." Book review. *Urban Studies* 28: 658–60.

———. 1994. "The State as Container: Territoriality in the Modern World-System." *Progress in Human Geography* 18: 151–62.

———. 1996. "Embedded Statism and the Social Sciences: Opening up to New Spaces." *Environment and Planning A* 28: 1917–27.

ten Bos, Rene. 2009. "Towards an Amphibious Anthropology: Water and Peter Sloterdijk." *Environment and Planning D: Society and Space* 27: 73–86.

Thien, Deborah. 2005. "After or beyond Feeling? A Consideration of Affect and Emotion in Geography." *Area* 37, no. 4: 450–54.

Thomas, Paul. 1980. *Karl Marx and the Anarchists*. London: Routledge.

Thomassen, Lasse. 2005. "Reading Radical Democracy: A Commentary on Clive Barnett." *Political Geography* 24, no. 5: 631–39.

Thoreau, Henry David. (1854) 2004. *Walden*. New Haven, Conn.: Yale University Press.

———. 2006. *Thoreau and the Art of Life*. Edited by Roderick MacIver. North Ferrisburg, Vt.: Heron Dance.

Thrift, Nigel. 2007. *Non-representational Theory: Space, Politics, Affect*. London: Routledge.

Tilly, Charles. 2003. *Politics of Collective Violence*. Cambridge: Cambridge University Press.

Tolstoy, Leo. (1869) 2006. *War and Peace*. Translated by Anthony Briggs. London: Penguin.

———. (1894) 2004. *The Kingdom of God Is within You*. Whitefish, Mont.: Kessinger.

———. 1900. "On Anarchy." http://tolstoyandpeace.wordpress.com/tolstoy-on-non-violence/on-anarchy-1900/.

———. (1900) 2004. *The Slavery of Our Times*. Whitefish, Mont.: Kessinger.

Trapese Collective. 2007. *Do It Yourself: A Handbook for Changing the World*. London: Pluto.

Tsing, Anna Lowenhaupt. 2005. *Friction: An Ethnography of Global Connection*. Princeton, N.J.: Princeton University Press.

Tucker, Benjamin Ricketson. 1883. "Karl Marx as Friend and Foe." *Liberty* 2: 9–35. http://libertarian-labyrinth.org/liberty/02–09.pdf 17.

———. (1897) 2005. *Instead of a Book by a Man Too Busy to Write One: A Fragmentary Exposition of Philosophical Anarchism*. Colorado Springs, Colo.: Ralph Myles.

———. 1926. "Passive Resistance." In *Individual Liberty*, edited by Clarence Lee Swartz, 69–73. New York: Vanguard.

Turpin, Jennifer E., and Lester R. Kurtz, eds. 1996. *The Web of Violence: From Interpersonal to Global*. Urbana: University of Illinois Press.

UNDP. 2002. *Human Development Report: Deepening Democracy in a Fragmented World*. New York: Oxford University Press.

Valentine, Gill. 1996. "Children Should Be Seen and Not Heard: The Production and Transgression of Adults' Public Space." *Urban Geography* 17, no. 3: 205–20.

———. 2007. "Theorizing and Researching Intersectionality: A Challenge for Feminist Geography." *The Professional Geographer* 59: 10–21.

Vaneigem, Raoul. (1967) 2012. *The Revolution of Everyday Life*. Oakland, Calif.: PM Press.

Verter, Mitchell. 2010. "The Anarchism of the Other Person." In *New Perspectives on Anarchism*, edited by Nathan J. Jun and Shane Wahl, 67–83. Lanham, Md.: Lexington.

Vieta, Marcelo. 2010. "The New Cooperativism." *Affinities* 4: 1–11.

Vincent, K. Steven. 1984. *Pierre-Joseph Proudhon and the Rise of French Republican Socialism*. Oxford: Oxford University Press.

Wade, Robert Hunter. 2003. "Is Globalization Reducing Poverty and Inequality?" *International Journal of Health Services* 34, no. 4: 381–414.

Wainwright, Joel, and Sook-Jim Kim. 2008. "Battles in Seattle Redux: Transnational Resistance to a Neoliberal Trade Agreement." *Antipode* 40: 513–34.

Walker, Richard. 2004. "The Spectre of Marxism: The Return of *The Limits to Capital*." *Antipode* 36: 434–43.

Ward, Colin. (1973) 2001. *Anarchy in Action*. London: Freedom.

———. 1976. *Housing: An Anarchist Approach*. London: Freedom Press.

———. (1978) 1990. *Child in the City*. London: Bedford Square.

———. 1990a. "An Anarchist Looks at Urban Life." *Contemporary Issues in Geography and Education* 3: 80–93.

———. 1990b. *Talking Houses: Ten Lectures by Colin Ward*. London: Freedom.

———. 2004. *Anarchism: A Very Short Introduction*. Oxford: Oxford University Press.

Ward, Dana. 2010. "Alchemy in Clarens: Kropotkin and Reclus, 1977–1881." In *New Perspectives on Anarchism*, edited by Nathan Jun and Shane Wahl, 209–26. Lanham, Md.: Lexington.

Wark, McKenzie. 2011. *The Beach beneath the Street: The Everyday Life and Glorious Times of the Situationist International*. London: Verso.

Warren, Bill. 1980. *Imperialism: Pioneer of Capitalism*. London: Verso.

Watson, Sophie. 2006. *City Publics: The (Dis)enchantments of Urban Encounters*. London: Routledge.

Watts, Alan. 1960. "The Nature of Consciousness." http://www.erowid.org /culture/characters/watts_alan/watts_alan_article1.shtml.

———. 2006. *Eastern Wisdom, Modern Life: Collected Talks, 1960–1969*. Novato, Calif.: New World Library.

Watts, Michael J. 2004. "Antinomies of Community: Some Thoughts on Geography, Resources, and Empire." *Transactions of the Institute of British Geographers* 29: 195–216.

Whatmore, Sarah. 2002. *Hybrid Geographies: Natures, Cultures, Spaces*. London: Sage.

White, Damian F., and Chris Wilbert, eds. 2011. *Autonomy, Solidarity, Possibility: The Colin Ward Reader*. Oakland, Calif.: AK Press.

White, Richard J., and Erika Cudworth. 2014. "Taking It to the Streets: Challenging Systems of Domination from Below." In *Defining Critical Animal Studies: An Intersectional Social Justice Approach for Liberation*, edited by Anthony J. Nocella II, John Sorenson, Kim Socha, and Atsuko Matsuoka, 202–20. New York: Peter Lang.

White, Richard J., and Colin C. Williams. 2012. "The Pervasive Nature of Heterodox Economic Spaces at a Time of Neo-liberal Crisis: Towards a 'Post-neoliberal' Anarchist Future." *Antipode* 44: 1625–44.

Wiles, Janine, and Audrey Kobayashi. 2009. "Equity." In *International Encyclopedia of Human Geography*, edited by Rob Kitchin and Nigel Thrift, 580–85. Amsterdam: Elsevier.

Wilford, Justin. 2008. "Out of Rubble: Natural Disaster and the Materiality of the House." *Environment and Planning D: Society and Space* 26, no. 4: 647–62.

Williams, Philippa, and Fiona McConnell. 2011. "Critical Geographies of Peace." *Antipode* 43: 927–31.

Wilson, David, and Jared Wouters. 2003. "Spatiality and Growth Discourse: The Restructuring of America's Rust Belt Cities." *Journal of Urban Affairs* 25, no. 2: 123–38.

Winichakul, Thongchai. 1994. *Siam Mapped: A History of the Geo-body of a Nation*. Honolulu: University of Hawai'i Press.

Wong, Yuk-Lin Renita, and Jana Vinsky. 2009. "Speaking from the Margins: A Critical Reflection on the 'Spiritual-but-Not-Religious' Discourse in Social Work." *British Journal of Social Work* 39, no. 7: 1343–59.

Wood, David Murakami. 2013. "What Is Global Surveillance? Towards a Relational Political Economy of the Global Surveillant Assemblage." *Geopolitics* 49: 317–26.

Woodward, Keith, John Paul Jones, and Sallie A. Marston. 2012. "The Politics of Autonomous Space." *Progress in Human Geography* 36, no. 2: 204–24.

Wright, Melissa. 2006. "Differences That Matter." In *David Harvey: A Critical Reader*, edited by Noel Castree and Derek Gregory, 80–110. Oxford: Blackwell.

Yashar, Deborah. 2005. *Contesting Citizenship in Latin America: The Rise of Indigenous Movements and the Postliberal Challenge*. Cambridge: Cambridge University Press.

Young, Iris Marion. 1990. *Justice and the Politics of Difference*. Princeton, N.J.: Princeton University Press.

———. 2000. *Inclusion and Democracy*. New York: Oxford University Press.

————. 2007. *Global Challenges: War, Self-Determination, and Responsibility for Justice.* Malden, Mass.: Polity.

Zerzan, John. 2002. *Running on Emptiness: The Pathology of Civilization.* Los Angeles, Calif.: Feral House.

Zinn, Howard. 2007. *A Power Governments Cannot Suppress.* San Francisco: City Lights Books.

Žižek, Slavoj. 1999. *The Ticklish Subject: The Absent Centre of Political Ontology.* London: Verso.

————. 2008. *Violence.* New York: Picador.

Index

Abbey, Edward, 95

abstraction, 13, 48; derivation of *abstract,* 184n2; and public space, 108–9, 182–83n5; and scale, 158, 164–65, 168, 170, 174

ACME: An International E-Journal for Critical Geographies, 38, 41, 68

affinity, 13, 15–16, 31, 37, 149; and affective structures of radical politics, 39, 59; affinity groups and networks, 7–8, 62–63, 81, 83, 90, 162, 166; and anarchism, 86, 95, 133; and decentralization of power, 152

Agamben, Giorgio, 50, 97, 104–5, 134, 150, 172, 174

Agnew, John, 48–49

agonism: agonistic pluralism, 102, 146; defined, 102; and nonviolence, 128–29; and prehistory, 172; and public space, 18, 97–108, 113, 118, 120–29; and radical democracy, 97–108, 114–15, 118, 120–29, 134, 146–47, 172–73

Amin, Ash, 5

Amsden, Jon, 34

Amster, Randal, 14, 38, 132

anarchism: and affinity, 86, 95, 133; and alternatives to the state, 55–60; and *archy* (systems of rule), 43, 55, 102, 104, 114, 116, 126–28, 132, 147; and capitalism, 26, 28, 30, 38–39, 46–50, 61, 63, 66–67, 118; defined, 25, 43; and direct action, 27, 37–39, 90, 92–94, 106, 148, 157, 165–66, 170; and geography, 25–27; and means without end, 90, 92, 104, 114, 121, 124–29, 153, 172, 182n4; misuse of the term, 83; and mutual aid, 39, 58–59, 64, 70, 72–73, 79, 85, 88, 90, 92, 94, 104, 139, 145, 152, 166, 172; and neoliberalism, 59–61; postanarchism, 39–40, 42, 49–50, 55, 61, 151, 181n1; and prefiguration, 13, 16, 20, 89, 92, 164, 166, 170–71, 177, 181–82n4; and property, 38, 41, 43, 67, 70, 75–76; and radicalizing democracy, 101–6; seen as synonym for violence, 18, 44, 92, 131, 182n6; theory and practice as complementary, 1, 4, 12, 15–16, 26–27, 37, 43, 49, 95, 153, 164, 171

anarchist geographies: and alternatives to Marxist geographies, 90–95; defined, 3, 46, 148; and freedom of geography, 40–42; and identities, 17, 54, 61, 63; and Marxism, 65–95; new anarchist geographies, 36–40; origins of, 28–30; and revolution,

84–90; rise of, 30–33; role of anarchism in radical geography, 33–36; and sovereign violence, 17, 46, 51–54, 57–58. *See also* anarchism; direct action; mutual aid; solidarity

anarchocapitalism, 30, 67, 70, 85, 163

anarchofeminism, 45. *See also* feminism

Anderson, Benedict, 4, 6, 54–55, 62, 146, 170

Anderson, Jon, 37

Angus, Ian, 8

antigeopolitics, 36, 41

Antipode: A Radical Journal of Geography, 33–35, 38–41, 66, 68, 79

Arab Spring, 26, 41, 116–17, 156

Arat, Zehra F., 101

Archer, Julian P. W., 29, 75

Arefi, Mahyar, 108

Arendt, Hannah, 107, 124–25, 147, 151; *On Violence,* 124

Atkinson, Rowland, 113–14, 122

Bailie, William, 44

Bakunin, Mikhail, 8, 29–30, 50–51, 70, 142–43, 151, 153, 168, 181n1; *God and the State,* 138–39; and Marx, 67, 69, 74, 78, 80, 89

Baldelli, Giovanni, 45, 73

Barclay, Harold, 28, 172

Barker, Adam J., 39

Barnes, Trevor, 42, 159

Barnett, Clive, 105–6, 109–11, 124–25

Bar On, Bat-Ami, 124

Barry, Andre, 54

Bellegarrigue, Anselme, 58, 81, 157

Benjamin, Walter, 50, 125

Berkman, Alexander, 44

Berlin, Isaiah, 86

Bey, Hakim, 37, 49, 89, 169–71, 176

Bhagat, Alex, 184n7

Biehl, Janet, 161

Bill, James A., 123

Billig, Michael, 54

binary thinking, 19, 98, 155, 172

bin Laden, Osama, 109

Black Anarchism, 39

Blumberg, Renata, 38, 41, 68, 71, 83, 159, 184n8

Blunt, Alison, 27, 46

Boggs, Carl, 7

Bohm, David, 137

Bonanno, Alfred M., 95

Bondi, Liz, 112, 133

Bookchin, Murray, 33–36, 48–49, 71, 82, 93, 155, 161–62, 167–68, 171, 175–76; "Ecology and Revolutionary Thought," 34; *The Ecology of Freedom,* 35–36; *Post-scarcity Anarchism,* 33

Bourdieu, Pierre, 125

Bourgois, Philippe, 121, 125, 134

Bowlby, Sophia, 189

Bowman, Halford, 36

Brand, Ulrich, 116

Braun, Bruce, 136

Breitbart, Myrna Margulies, 34, 36, 46–47, 66, 162

Brenner, Neil, 48, 116, 128, 156, 173

Brousse, Paul, 44

Brown, Gavin, 49

Brown, Susan, 55

Butler, Judith, 91, 149–51

Butler, Ruth, 112

Calhoun, Craig, 109, 113

Call, Lewis, 49, 111

Cambodia, 38
Canadian Association of
     Geographers, 40
capitalism: anarchism as alternative
     to, 26, 28, 30, 38–39, 46–50, 61, 63,
     66–67, 118; anticapitalism, 19, 63,
     66–67, 74, 93, 159, 163; and binary
     thinking, 172; and the commons,
     7–9; communicative capitalism,
     109, 157; and decentralization,
     159, 161, 163; and emancipation,
     97; and flat ontologies, 166–68;
     language of, 12–14; and Marxism,
     19–20, 51–58, 73–77, 81–83, 91,
     171; and neoliberalism, 18–19, 46,
     57, 116, 118, 127–28; and public
     space, 97–101, 104, 109, 111,
     114–18, 126–28; and revolution,
     85–86, 89; and social Darwinism,
     31. *See also* anarchocapitalism
Carey, George W., 34
caring geography, 31, 137
Carlsson, Chris, 38
Carr, Stephen, 14
Carson, Rachel, 33
cartography, 62, 184nn6–7
Castells, Manuel, 109
Castree, Noel, 136, 160, 167
Cavanaugh, William, 140
Chatterton, Paul, 37, 49, 63, 83, 86,
     159, 160, 168
Chomsky, Noam, 156
Chouinard, Vera, 26
Clark, John, 2, 7, 30–31, 40, 48, 67,
     69
Clastres, Pierre, 49
Cleaver, Harry, 83
Clough, Nathan, 38–39, 41, 68, 71,
     83, 159, 184n8
Cockburn, Cynthia, 125

Cohen, Stanley, 116
Cohn, Jesse, 57, 191
Collective Autonomy Research
     Group, 11
Collinge, Chris, 173
colonialism, 2, 6, 18, 38, 40, 44–45,
     47–58, 61, 63, 114, 117, 129, 135–
     38, 152. *See also* postcolonialism
commons, 4, 28, 172–73; defined,
     7, 10; and mutual aid, 7–12; and
     relationality, 11; tragedy of the
     commons, 8–9
communism, 34, 51–52, 55, 67,
     85–86, 149, 157. *See also* Marxism;
     socialism
*Contemporary Issues in Geography and
     Education*, 36, 66
Cook, Ian, 36, 66
Crane, Nicholas J., 39
Cresswell, Tim, 14, 173
crime, 41, 114
CrimethInc. Ex-Workers' Collective,
     1
CrimethInc. Writers' Bloc, 13
criminalization, 38, 57
Critchley, Simon, 60, 90, 104–6, 146,
     153, 170
Critical Mass cycling events, 41
Cudworth, Erika, 181n1
Cumbers, Andrew, 160, 162, 168
Curran, Giorel, 156

Dabashi, Hamid, 156
Dahl, Robert, 102, 128
Darwinism. *See* social Darwinism
Davies, Paul, 137
Day, Richard, 39, 59, 62, 152, 162
Dean, Jodi, 74, 85–86, 109, 156–57,
     176–77
Debord, Guy, 86

decentralization, 6, 19, 32, 34, 70–71, 94, 152, 155–56, 159–61, 163, 166, 170
de Cleyre, Voltairine, 20
DeLanda, Manuel, 184n4
Del Casino, Vincent J., 112
Deleuze, Gilles, 39, 53, 155, 184n4
democracy: deliberative democracy, 99–100, 102–3, 108, 113, 122–23; etymology, 102; and polyarchy, 102; representative democracy, 102, 146. *See also* radical democracy
Derrida, Jacques, 149, 151
Diamond, Larry, 101–2
direct action, 15, 17–18, 64, 73; and affinity groups, 11; and anarchism, 27, 37–39, 90, 92–94, 106, 148, 157, 165–66, 170; and DIY culture, 58, 71, 86; and mutual aid, 3; and public space, 38, 111, 128; and revolution, 85–86, 90
DIY culture, 17, 27, 37, 58, 71, 86, 172
Dollar, David, 123
Driver, Felix, 135
Dryzek, John S., 103
Dugatkin, Lee Alan, 6, 8
Duménil, Gérard, 155
dumpster diving, 39, 41, 73
Dunbar, Gary, 30, 34, 46–47, 66
Duncan, Nancy, 112, 115
Durkheim, Émile, 140

Ealham, Chris, 32
Einstein, Albert, 137, 143
Eley, Geoff, 113
Engels, Friedrich, 51, 58, 74–76, 79, 86–88
England, Kim, 53, 57, 155
Entrikin, J. Nicholas, 107–8, 114
environmental determinism, 2–3

Epstein, Barbara, 93, 157
Escobar, Arturo, 118, 122
ethics, 30, 34, 37, 59, 62–63, 106, 133, 143–45, 148, 152, 164, 173–77
Evren, Süreyya, 42, 49

fascism, 159
Featherstone, David, 167, 168
Federici, Silvia, 160
feminism, 26, 32, 34–35, 42, 45, 53, 59, 61, 66, 69, 73, 112, 137, 148–49, 152, 160, 176
Ferrell, Jeff, 38–39, 106, 108, 126, 132, 164–65, 168
Ferretti, Federico, 6, 40–42
First International (1864), 29, 51, 79
flat ontologies, 20, 165–74, 184n4
Fleming, Marie, 2, 7, 25, 31, 42, 64, 70
Flint, Colin, 159
Foucault, Michel, 39, 53, 61, 125, 158
Fraser, Nancy, 112, 183n6
freedom of geography, 17, 40–42, 174
free market anarchism, 30, 67. *See also* anarchocapitalism
Freire, Paulo, 172
Freund, Peter, 112
Friedman, Thomas L., 155; *The World Is Flat*, 168
"from above" and "from below," 98, 100, 120–22, 128, 182
Fukuyama, Francis, 49, 105, 146

Gaia, 14, 22, 63
Galois, Bob, 32–34, 66, 160
Galtung, Johan, 123, 125
Gandhi, Mahatma, 164, 184n3
Garcia-Ramon, Maria Dolores, 34
Gautney, Heather, 83
geography, 1–3, 17–20; and

anarchism, 25–27; caring geography, 31, 137; defined, 25; and education, 13–14; freedom of geography, 17, 40–42, 174; radical geography, 1, 17–18, 26, 34–35, 39, 44–50, 54–55, 60–68, 77, 92–95, 160, 173–74; and relational space, 4–5, 12; and theory, 16; universal geography, 4–7, 11, 48, 136. *See also* anarchist geographies
Gibson, Morgan, 156
Gibson-Graham, J. K., 53, 58, 89, 155, 159, 165, 172
Giddens, Anthony, 102, 146
Giroux, Henry A., 128–29, 157
Glassman, Jim, 51, 120, 156
globalization, 36, 48–49, 63; alterglobalization movement, 86; antiglobalization movement, 17, 118. *See also* neoliberalism
Global South, 98, 117–18, 128, 161
Godlewska, Anne, 47, 135
Godwin, William, 28, 44
Goheen, Peter G., 107, 110, 115
Goldberg, David T., 59, 122
Golden, Lester, 34
Goldman, Emma, 32–33, 36, 45, 53, 70, 73, 140, 143, 176
Gordon, Uri, 39, 42
Goss, Jon, 115
Gouldner, Alvin W., 74
Graeber, David, 37, 58, 70–72, 78, 85, 89–90, 93, 102, 118, 132, 140, 146, 152, 158, 170
Graham, Robert, 25, 28
Great Man theory, 78
Gregory, Derek, 117, 134
Grillo, Trina, 152
Guattari, Félix, 39, 155
Guérin, Daniel, 29

Habermas, Jürgen, 108–11, 113, 182n2
Halfacree, Keith, 37, 49, 58
Haraway, Donna, 56, 135, 138, 174
Hardin, Garrett, 9
Hardy, Dennis, 36
Harris, Cole, 54
Hardt, Michael, 84, 104–5, 155, 160
Hart, Gillian, 54, 99–100, 128
Harvey, David, 9, 49, 52–56, 65–66, 74, 77, 86, 94, 105, 115, 123, 156–58, 160–67, 171; *New Imperialism,* 52; *Paris, Capital of Modernity,* 181n3; *Rebel Cities,* 156
Hawking, Stephen, 137
Haworth, Robert H., 13
Hee, Limin, 114
Heidegger, Martin, 169
Helms, Gesa, 160
Hénaff, Marcel, 111–12
Herod, Andrew, 167, 174
Heynen, Nik, 37, 39, 49
Hodkinson, Stuart, 86
Holdich, Thomas, 36
Holland, Edward, 137–38
Holloway, John, 60, 88, 160
homelessness, 38, 41, 112, 122
Homer: *Iliad,* 28
Horner, G. M., 34, 47
Howell, Philip, 108, 110–11
Hubbard, Phil, 112
Huntington, Ellsworth, 36
Huston, Shaun, 40
Huxley, Thomas Henry, 47
Hyams, Edward, 77–78

Iadicola, Peter, 121, 125
identity formation, 107, 132, 183n6
identity politics, 41, 93, 105, 149
imperialism, 3, 17, 40–41, 47, 51, 61, 69, 73, 117; new imperialism, 52

Ince, Anthony, 7, 27, 39, 49, 70, 164, 166, 181n4
Industrial Revolution, 28, 51, 78
International Encyclopedia of Human Geography, 40
Iveson, Kurt, 112–13

James, William, 91
Jensen, Derrick, 151
Jessop, Bob, 173
Jiwani, Yasmin, 15
Jocoy, Christine L., 112
Johnston, Ron, 53
Jonas, Andrew, 166–67
Jones, John Paul, 158, 165–68, 173–74

Kaiser, Robert, 184n5
Karl, Terry Lynn, 101
Katsiaficas, George, 83
Katz, Cindi, 160
Keane, John, 121, 123–24, 126
Kearns, Gerry, 1–2, 35, 40, 47
Keith, Michael, 111
Kim, Sook-Jim, 101
Kingfisher, Catherine, 150
Kinna, Ruth, 47
Kobayashi, Audrey, 148–49
Kohl, Benjamin, 99
Kohli, Atul, 161
Koopman, Sara, 58, 133, 160
Kothari, Rajni, 97, 129
Kraay, Aart, 123
Kropotkin, Peter, 4, 6, 8, 16–17, 21–22, 78, 82, 85, 131, 138, 160–61, 172; on anarchist communism, 67–68; on capitalism, 75; *The Conquest of Bread,* 31; contributions to anarchist geographies, 25–28, 30–36, 40–41, 46–48, 60, 62, 64–68, 70, 72; on education, 13; and emancipation, 55; *Fields,*

Factories, and Workshops, 31; on forms of anarchism, 73; on mutual aid, 4, 6, 22, 31, 40, 47–48, 139–40, 145; *Mutual Aid,* 6, 8, 31, 47; and naturalism, 146, 151; on Paris Commune, 79–80; professional and political background, 1–2; on religion, 135–36; on violence, 44; "What Geography Ought to Be," 34

Lacan, Jacques, 53, 169–70
Laclau, Ernesto, 105, 116
Lacoste, Yves, 134
Landauer, Gustav, 85
language, 12–16
Larner, Wendy, 54, 155
Lauria, Mickey, 35, 66
Lawson, Vicky, 31, 59, 137
Lees, Lynn Hollen, 107, 115
Lefebvre, Henri, 90–91, 94–95, 108, 111, 114; *The Critique of Everyday Life,* 9, 116
Leitner, Helga, 100, 173
Lemke, Thomas, 155
Lenin, Vladimir, 88
Leroux, Pierre, 75
Levinas, Emmanuel, 104
Lévy, Dominique, 155
Lewis, Tom, 54
libertarianism, 29–30, 33–34, 51, 75, 82–83, 86, 161, 163, 167, 171
Livingstone, David, 47, 135
Low, Murray, 111
Low, Setha, 116
Lummis, C. Douglas, 106, 129

Mackinder, Halford, 2, 36, 40, 47, 135
MacKinnon, Danny, 167
MacLaughlin, Jim, 36

Malatesta, Errico, 44, 70, 101
Mamadouh, Virginie, 156
Mann, Michael, 126
Mannin, Ethel, 87
Manning, Francesca, 38
Marks, Brian, 83, 160
Marshall, Peter, 28, 29, 87–88, 131–32, 136, 168
Martin, Camille, 2, 7, 31, 48, 69
Martson, Sallie A., 158, 165–68, 173–74
Marx, Karl, 7, 64, 160, 169; and Bakunin, 29, 67, 69; and capitalism, 51–52, 54, 58, 82; *The Communist Manifesto,* (with Engels), 51; *Das Kapital,* 76–77; *The Poverty of Philosophy,* 77–78; and Proudhon, 29, 75–79, 87
Marxism: 18–20; autonomists, 38–39, 82–84, 89–94, 160, 171, 175, 181–82n4, 184n8; and capitalism, 19–20, 51–58, 73–77, 81–83, 91, 171; Marxist turn, 1; and monopolies, 75–82; and neoliberalism, 52–53, 56, 67, 74, 85–86, 90, 92; and revolution, 84–90; Situationists, 86, 90, 182n5; and state-centricity, 69–75; and vanguardism, 18, 54–55, 68, 80–82, 85, 89, 91, 93, 95, 157, 158, 162, 170, 177
Massey, Doreen, 5, 14, 63, 94, 99, 106–7, 112, 118, 125, 166, 182–83n5, 183n7; *For Space,* 4
May, Todd, 42, 49, 53, 81, 97, 146, 151
McCann, Eugene, 108, 112, 120
McCormack, Derek P., 133
McKay, Iain, 9, 74, 76–78
means without end, 90, 92, 104, 114, 121, 124–29, 153, 172, 182n4

Megoran, Nick, 133–37, 139, 142–43
Meyers, William R., 108
Miles, Malcolm, 113
Miller, Byron, 173
Milstein, Cindy, 115
Minca, Trevor, 159
Mitchell, Don, 106–10, 112, 114–15, 118, 122, 124, 128
Mitchell, Timothy, 56
Mlodinow, Leonard, 137
Mogel, Lize, 184n7
Monmonier, Mark, 184n7
monopolies, 62, 68, 75–83, 119. *See also* violence: monopolization of
Moore, Adam, 174, 184n5
Most, Johann, 44
Mouffe, Chantal, 102–6, 115–16, 120, 122–23, 126, 146–47
Mudu, Pierpaolo, 38–39, 83
Mueller, Tadzio, 152
mutual aid, 17–18, 27; and anarchism, 39, 58–59, 64, 70, 72–73, 79, 85, 88, 90, 92, 94, 104, 139, 145, 152, 166, 172; and the commons, 7–12, 14; and direct action, 3; examples of, 27, 41, 73, 172; and Kropotkin, 4, 6, 22, 31, 40, 47–48, 139–40, 145
mutualism, 29

Nativel, Corinne, 162, 168
Negri, Antonio, 84, 104–5, 155, 160, 181–82n4
neoliberalism, 17–19, 26, 35, 38–39, 49, 137, 158, 163–69, 176; and anarchism, 59–61; and binary thought, 19, 155–56; and drift, 39; and language, 12; and Marxism, 52–53, 56, 67, 74, 85–86, 90, 92; and new imperialism, 52; and new world order, 145; and public space,

97, 99–101, 105, 116–18, 121–23, 127–29, 182–83n5; and role of government, 45–46, 56–61; and tragedy of the commons, 8; and war on terror, 150
neosocial Darwinism, 30. *See also* social Darwinism
New Left, 26, 35
Newman, Janis, 36
Newman, Saul, 42, 49, 53–54, 59, 63, 88, 93, 151, 162, 170
Nikiforova, Elena, 184n5
noble savage, 19, 134, 151
Nolin, Catherine, 59, 137
nonviolence, 10, 17, 19, 38, 44–46, 58, 88, 97–100, 103–4, 121–24, 131–39, 142–43, 153. *See also* peace; violence
normativity, 14, 61, 113, 116, 149–50; ordinary normativity, 150

O'Brien, Richard, 49
Occupy Movement, 26, 41, 156
Olstad, Tyra A., 155
O'Neil, Mary Lou, 112
Ong, Aihwa, 156
Ooi, Giok Ling, 114
Orientalism, 117, 152
Orwell, George, 101
Osborne, Thomas, 54
Ostrom, Elinor, 9
Owen, Robert, 75

Parekh, Bhikhu C., 119
Paris Commune of 1871, 2, 29, 75, 78–80, 181n1
Parker, Martin, 183–84n1
peace, 10–11, 19, 43–44, 87–88, 117, 121–22, 131–35, 145–53. *See also* nonviolence

Peaceful Revolutionist, 44
Peck, Jamie, 49, 53, 57, 100, 123, 155, 182–83n5
Peet, Richard, 25, 26, 34, 47, 66, 160
Pepper, David, 36, 66
Peters, Michael A., 53
Pickerill, Jenny, 37, 39, 63, 83, 159, 168
Pissaria, Bill, 35
Pleyers, Geoffrey, 86
Porter, Philip, 35
postcolonialism, 5, 38, 41, 44–45, 54, 59, 99, 114, 135. *See also* colonialism
postmodernity, 12, 111
praxis, 1, 12, 15–16, 19, 27, 45, 47, 49, 68, 98, 106, 133, 152, 164
prefiguration: and anarchism, 13, 16, 20, 89, 92, 164, 166, 170–71, 177, 181–82n4; defined, 7; prefigurative politics, 7, 11, 18–19, 39, 68, 85, 90, 92, 94, 164
Project for the New American Century, 145
property, 136, 140; and anarchism, 38, 41, 43, 67, 70, 75–76; and commons, 7–10, 28–29; and crime, 114; and mutualism, 29; and public space, 114–15, 129; and violence, 10, 183n9
Proudhon, Pierre-Joseph, 21, 58, 132, 151, 181n3; contributions to anarchist geographies, 28–30, 33, 44, 70; and Marx, 29, 75–79, 87; and mutualism, 29; on property, 9–10, 28, 38, 70; *What Is Property?,* 28–29, 70, 76
public space, 18–19, 183n8; and agonism, 18, 97–108, 113, 118, 120–29, 161; and capitalism,

97–101, 104, 109, 111, 114–18, 126–28; and cultural value, 112; and direction action, 38, 111, 128; "Disneyfication" of, 115–16; and emancipation, 97, 100–101, 104, 121, 127–29; and radical democracy, 18–19, 97–107, 111, 114–18, 124–29; and self-representation, 119–20, 183n8; and space of appearance, 106–13; and theatricality, 108; unscripted, 91, 98, 104, 108, 114, 183n7; and violence, 119–25

Purcell, Mark, 39, 99, 168, 176–77

Pusey, Andre, 160

radical democracy, 6, 37, 71, 90, 93, 134, 145–46, 157, 182n2; and agonism, 97–108, 114–15, 118, 120–29, 134, 146–47, 172–73; and public space, 18–19, 97–107, 111, 114–18, 124–29

Ranciére, Jacques, 104–5, 146–48, 151

Rankin, Bill, 184n7

Rapley, John, 123

Rapoport, David C., 121

Rapp, John A., 136

Ratzel, Friedrich, 47, 135; *Lebensraum,* 2

Reaganomics, 35

Reclaim the Streets, 41

Reclus, Élisée, 4–7, 17, 20, 25–27; *The Earth and Its Inhabitants,* 5–6, 30; professional and political background, 1–2; and universal geography, 4–7, 11, 48, 136

relationality, 4–6, 16, 149, 177; and the commons, 11; defined, 5; relational geography, 5, 28;

relational space, 4–5, 12

religion, 19, 65, 133, 146, 149–50, 152; and bondage, 139–45; Christianity, 135–36, 138–44; and democracy, 126; fundamentalism, 150; and identity formation, 132; and insurrection, 84; and neoliberalism, 116, 150; and nonviolence, 133–39, 150; and public space, 126

resistance, 19, 41, 54, 73, 81, 98, 101, 104–5, 118, 124, 127, 160, 165, 168, 174

revolutionary imperative, 18, 45, 57–58, 68, 84, 89–90, 92, 163

Reybaud, Louis, 75

rhizomatic politics, 3, 16, 20, 158–59, 165, 167, 171–72, 174–75

Rigby, Andrew, 36

Robinson, Jennifer, 98

Roch, Marie, 75

Rocker, Rudolf, 76, 164

Rose, Nikolas, 54

Rouhani, Farhang, 39

Rousselle, Duane, 42, 49

Routledge, Paul, 4, 36–37, 63, 162, 168, 172

Ruddick, Susan, 107, 112

Russell, Bertie, 160

scale, 176, 178, 184n5–7; and abstraction, 158, 164–65, 168, 170, 174; and flat ontologies, 165–74; and hierarchy, 157–58; jumping scales, 156, 164–65, 167, 174; as master-signifier, 169–70

Said, Edward, 61, 117

Sayer, Andrew, 150

Scheper-Hughes, Nancy, 121, 125, 134

Schmitter, Philippe C., 101
Scott, James C., 16, 60, 118, 170
self-representation, 119–20, 183n8
Semple, Ellen Churchill, 2–3, 36
Sennett, Richard, 171
Seoane, Jóse, 101
Sharp, Joanne, 53, 61
Sheppard, Eric S., 100
Shupe, Anson, 121, 125
Sidaway, James, 135–36
Slater, David, 98, 117
Smith, Adam, 51
Smith, Adrian, 155
Smith, Michael, 99
Smith, Neil, 47, 57–58, 68, 88–89,
   116, 133, 135, 156, 160
Smith, Woodruff, 3
social Darwinism, 2, 8, 31, 47. *See also*
   neosocial Darwinism
socialism, 29–30, 35, 50–51,
   66–69, 73–87, 92–93, 155, 157,
   163, 181n1. *See also* anarchism;
   Marxism
social justice, 15, 26, 35, 41, 68, 100,
   107, 127, 129, 176. *See also* ethics
Soja, Edward W., 90–91
Sorkin, Michael, 115–16
Sparke, Mathew, 156
Spinoza, Benedictus de: *Ethics*,
   143–44
Springer, Simon, 10–11, 38, 42, 49,
   56, 68, 117, 121, 125–28, 134
Staeheli, Lynn A., 107, 112
state centricity, 35–36, 48–50, 53, 69,
   86, 176
statism, 3–4, 18, 48, 51, 53–56, 60, 82,
   84, 136
Stenning, Alison, 155
Stirner, Max, 84, 86, 91
Strong, Tracy B., 111–12

suicidal impulse, 14
Sundberg, Juanita, 101
Sussia, Judith, 13
Swanson, Kate, 160
Swyngedouw, Erik, 146, 167

Taylor, Laurie, 116
Taylor, Peter, 53, 67–70
temporary autonomous zone (TAZ),
   170–71
tenants' associations, 27, 73, 172
Thatcherism, 35
Theodore, Nik, 116, 128, 156
theory and practice, 1, 4, 12, 15–16,
   26–27, 37, 43, 49, 95, 153, 164,
   171. *See also* praxis
Thien, Deborah, 59, 137
Thompson, Albert, 107
Thoreau, Henry David, 44, 90, 169
Tiananmen Square, 115
Tickell, Adam, 123
Tilly, Charles, 123–25
Tolstoy, Leo, 8, 44, 141, 184n3; *The
   Kingdom of God Is within You*, 136;
   War and Peace, 131–32
tragedy of the commons, 8–9. *See also*
   commons
Trapese Collective, 37, 58
Tsing, Anna, 168
Tucker, Benjamin Ricketson, 76–77,
   87

United Nations Security Council,
   117

Valentine, Gill, 108, 112, 152, 176
Vaneigem, Raoul, 58, 86, 163, 167
vanguardism, 18, 54–55, 68, 80–82,
   85, 89, 91, 93, 95, 157, 158, 162,
   170, 177

Verter, Mitchell, 28
Vieta, Marcelo, 86
Vincent, K. Steven, 77
Vinksy, Jana, 141
violence, 10–11, 43–46, 91–92, 94, 175; anarchism as nonviolence practice, 131–53; anarchism viewed as synonym for, 18, 44, 92, 131, 182n6; and colonialism, 51–54; monopolization of, 8, 45, 50, 54, 57, 62, 80, 122, 131; and property, 10, 183n9; and public space, 97–106, 114, 117, 119–29; and revolution, 87–89; and self-defense, 10; sovereign/ state violence, 3, 17, 29, 38, 40, 46, 51–54, 57–58, 120, 148. *See also* nonviolence

Wade, Robert Hunter, 123
Wainwright, Joel, 101
Walker, Richard, 160
Ward, Colin, 14, 16, 31, 33, 35–36, 55, 65, 72, 82, 86, 160–61, 169; *Anarchy in Action,* 33; *Child in the City,* 33; *Housing: An Anarchist Approach,* 33
Wark, McKenzie, 182n2
war on terror, 109, 139, 150
Warren, Bill, 51–52
Warren, Josiah, 44

Watson, Sophie, 113
Watts, Alan, 144, 150–51
Weinberg, Leonard, 121
Westphalian system, 48
White, Damian F., 33
White, Richard, 39, 89, 166, 172, 181n1
WikiLeaks, 156
Wilbert, Chris, 33
Wiles, Janine, 148–49
Williams, Colin, 36, 39, 89, 166, 172
Willis, Katie, 155
Wills, Jane, 27, 46
Wilson, David, 161
Winichakul, Thongchai, 170
Wissen, Markus, 116
Wong, Yuk-Lin Renita, 141
Woodward, Keith, 158, 165–68, 173–74
World Bank, 181n1
Wouters, Jared, 161
Wright, Melissa, 52–53

Yashar, Deborah, 86
Young, Iris Marion, 102, 113, 124

Zapatista movement, 118
Zerzan, John, 151
Zinn, Howard, 163
Žižek, Slavoj, 125, 146, 151

Simon Springer is associate professor of geography at the University of Victoria, Canada. He is the author of *Violent Neoliberalism: Development, Discourse, and Dispossession in Cambodia* and *Cambodia's Neoliberal Order: Violence, Authoritarianism, and the Contestation of Public Space* and the coeditor of *The Handbook of Neoliberalism*, *The Handbook of Contemporary Cambodia*, and *The Radicalization of Pedagogy: Anarchism, Geography, and the Spirit of Revolt*.